First Reviewers:

It was a great pleasure to read this book that Ruth has written about Kundalini. Though she speaks about her own experiences, she also weaves in others' experiences and references that give so much depth.

I had to keep reading; it was as if the book kept unfolding bits and pieces of information that had been omitted from so many other books written on this subject. It fills in missing links and connections that make it coherent and flowing.

She makes Kundalini come alive and transmits a feeling of familiarity with this rare spiritual experience, but, at the same time, we feel it is very sacred.

There is something in this book for everyone to relate to whether they are ready or not for this spiritual journey.

The story is personal, yet, at the same time, it is holistic and encompassing; it moves with a rhythm that is like the Kundalini force, taking the reader out beyond the mundane into the complex spiritual realms then bringing us back into the known. Ruth shares her knowledge in a way that is compassionate, grounding and deeply informative.

I am very happy to know that this sacred journey will be given to the public, and that Ruth has so bravely opened her heart to share this with us.

Diane Stacey, Encinitas, CA

Last night I read chapter 16,...This chapter to me is one example of seeing the world not through the trained eyes but through the energy's eyes. It seems when we shift our focus inward, a new experience of understanding emerges. As you wonderfully describe as the 'overlay of visions', and seeing both the beauty and the horror simultaneously, inner pain/traumas take on forms of entities that are a part of us. The heart begins to have fingers of energy that can wrap around things too. The knowledge of multiple levels existing simultaneously are intensified and one begins to understand that everything is not as it seems. To begin to experience the world in this way is the formation of the roots of compassion for ourselves and our environment. I am really enjoying your book. I find a lot of strength in it. Thank you for writing it.

Cary W., M.F.A., Artist, Sculptor. Jacksonville, OR

The Guru's Gift:

A Kundalini Awakening

by
Ruth Angela

Lotus-Blessings
Mill Valley, CA

ISBN for SMASHWORDS Digital
978 0 9846604-2-1

ISBN for CREATESPACE - PRINT Version
978 0 9846604-1-4

ISBN for KINDLE (AMAZON)
978 0 9846604-0-7

Printed in the United States.
Lotus-Blessings Publishing
PO Box 1438
Mill Valley, CA 94942

Acknowledgements

*All comes from these great beings of divine awareness,
and all ultimately returns to THAT source that is
the very essence of beingness.*

To my esteemed guru and teacher, I offer this as a small token of my gratitude. The gift you gave me has lifted my life to a quantum level. How to possibly repay you and the lineage of saints before you who all conspired to lift me up! Namaste to Bade Baba who has guided this book from birth to publication. To Dee W. for putting up with so much. To the authors who have helped shape my understanding and acceptance of this great gift, I am most grateful. I especially want to recognize my teacher's books, Dr. Stan Grof and his wife, Christina Grof, Eckhart Tolle, Elizabeth Gilbert, Max Freedom Long, Swami Vishnu Tirtha, Gangaji and her guru, Poonjaji, Shri Ramana Maharshi, Dennis (David) Gersten M.D., Bruce Lipton, M.D. and Itzhak Bentov. I also want to recognize Dr. Susan A. Carlson, Bhavin Desai, and Robin Rustad of the Kundalini Support Network for their devotion to Kundalini.

Cover: For the inspired painting of this experience by my talented sculptor/artist friend, CW, MFA Univ. of Hawaii, of Jacksonville, OR, I thank you sincerely. Your mystic talent is a light to everyone.

Design: To Patricia Rasch, Graphic Designer of www.patriciarasch.com www. bookandcoverdesign.com for formatting the cover and interior design; I am most grateful for your attention to detail and quality, for being so flexible and for your invaluable support.

Editing: *For my editor and gentle supporter, Nicole Elbert, thank you; your help came in good time.*

Permissions: *To those who have given special permissions: Jade Wahoo Grigori, Dr. Emma Bragdon, Dr. Stanislav Grof. I thank you for your kindness and inspiration.*

My gratitude for permission to reprint from *Trials of the Visionary Mind: Spiritual Emergency and the Renewal Process,* by John Weir Perry, the State University of New York Press © 1999, State University of New York. All rights reserved.

Disclaimer:

The author of this book does not dispense medical advice nor prescribe the use of any method, technique, supplement or food as a form of treatment for physical, emotional or medical problems without the advice of a physician, either directly or indirectly. The information in this book should not be used as a substitute for professional medical, therapeutic, spiritual, or psychological advice. Consult competent professionals to answer specific questions. It is recommended that transpersonal therapists or the Spiritual Emergency Network resources be consulted to determine if the symptoms are in fact true awakening symptoms. At no time does the author or her agents advocate raising *Kundalini* deliberately, and they caution that there are real and often irreversible negative mental, emotional and physical consequences to such practices. This book does not explain the technical process of ascending *Kundalini*. Any advice is based on the authors' and others' experiences, but makes no claims about their efficacy. The material is based upon the author's experiences as they have been recalled from 1979, and research conducted over 30 years. The sequence of events may or may not be accurate and should not be relied upon as indications of progress. Anyone using this information does so at his or her own risk.

Invocation

I bow to That Shiva who is the supreme principle and cause of all worlds manifest and unmanifest. I bow to my guru and beloved teacher, and to his guru, Bade Baba, for the gifts of shaktipat and their watchful care of my life and heart. I surrender my acts before their feet and cast before the reader the jewels of light that have been bestowed upon me, so that the reader may see beyond the obscuring veils of human limitation.

It is these enormous beings that speak through me, a fortunate recipient of their wisdom who has been given the fulfillment of writing this testimony to their wonder.

Dedication

To my **Grandchildren,**
brilliant souls full of love and light,
I offer this gift of my wisdom and pain.

To my **Daughter,**
gentle goddess, I offer my apologies for
disrupting your childhood and ask you accept this as a token.

To **Krista Masher Henley,**
an extraordinary friend and bright star in
Silicon Valley who sadly passed on the
full moon, October 11, 2011,
I offer this opus of my heart.

Table of Contents

Invocation.. ix

Dedication.. xi

Introduction.. xvii

Prologue to The Guru's Gift:
A Kundalini Awakening.. xix

CHAPTER 1
The Opportunity 3
The Sages: 5
Meditation: 6
The Ego: 7
The Struggle for Control: 9

CHAPTER 2
What is Kundalini? 12
The Heroic Journey: 17
Advaita: 18
The Goddess: 19

CHAPTER 3
The Time is Now: Earth Changes 22
Signs of Change: 25

CHAPTER 4
The Gift 27
Adolescence: 29
The Vision: 30
Leaving England: 31
The Tiger Dream: 32

CHAPTER 5
Preparation 35
Pools of Tears: 36

Wings of Flight: 39
Aloha of Hawaii: 40
Temptation: 42

CHAPTER 6
Mercurius: The Genie in the Bottle 44
Past Life Recall: 44
Rising Tension: 46

CHAPTER 7
Shaktipat Initiation 51
The Genie Escapes: 53

CHAPTER 8
The Kundalini Awakens 56
Caduceus: 57
Serpents and Snakes: 61
The Third Eye: 63

CHAPTER 9
The Journey Begins 65
Shaktipat: 66
Chakras: 67
Subconscious: 69
Complications: 72

CHAPTER 10
The Ascending Goddess: A Rebirth 76
Signs of Awakened Kundalini: 77
Rebirth: 78
Involution vs. Evolution: 80

CHAPTER 11
The Kundalini at Play 83
Visit to Texas: 83
Visit to England: 85
Return to Hawaii: 89
Spinning Episodes: 91
Intellectual Gifts: 91
Resisting Temptation: 92
Smell of Death: 95

CHAPTER 12
No Boundaries 97
Left/Right Brain: 98
No Boundaries: 99

Beloved Companion: 101
Changing Frequencies: 103
Inner Visions: 104
Time Reverses: 106
Time Stretches: 107
Meta Processing: 108
The Heart: 110
Poetic union: 110
Instant Knowledge: 111
Kriya Moves: 112
Tongue Moves: 112
Kumbhak Breath: 113
Noises and Voices: 113
Spontaneous Yoga: 114
Xray/Double vision: 115
Flying Siddhi: 117
Parallel Universe: 121
Blisses: 123

CHAPTER 13
Dying While Living 124
Experiment: 124
My Magic Wand: 126
Karmic debts: 127
The Bardos: 130
Christian Missionary: 131
Luminosity: 132
Samsara: 134
Pandora's Box: 135
Devilish Darshan: 139
The Grim Reaper: 140
Possession: 140

CHAPTER 14
The Rising Kundalini: Rapture. 144
Sexual Desire: 145
Inner Bliss: 148

CHAPTER 15
The Crucible 151
Ego Disintegration: 151
Surrender: 154
Resistance: 156
Foreign Resisters: 157

The Matrix: 159
"Glowing Coat": 160
The Rulers: 160
The Root of Truth: 161
The Mind Exits: 163
The Subconscious: 166
The Kundalini Code: 167

CHAPTER 16
The Abyss 169
Turiya State: 169
Pineal Gland: 172
The Abyss: 174
The Primitive Will: 176
Disaster Visions: 176
The Ayatolla: 178
Nuclear Disaster: 178
Ego Death Struggle: 179
Trauma Emerges: 181
The Guru's Mercy: 184
The Doctor: 185
The Guru Gita: 187
Gangaji: 188
Return to Self: 189

CHAPTER 17
Integration and Balance 191
Grounding: 193
Guru Visit: 193
Releasing the Vows: 194
The Ashram: 195
Seva Lessons: 196
The Song of my Soul: 197
Grounding Practice: 198
Meeting my Guru: 199
My Guru's Farewell: 201
Heart Opening: 201
1982 – 1991: 203
The Direct Method: 203
The Final Gift: 206
The Jewel Inside: 208
The Goddess Shakti Kundalini: 209

CHAPTER 18
Epilogue: On Becoming Human 210

Notes 216

Helpful Books 220

Bibliography 222

Index 231

Introduction

This is a memoir of my experience of Shaktipat or Kundalini awakening through the grace of a great guru in 1979. I did not understand what was happening at the time, but I endeavored to research it and share my findings. I write this with the loving guidance of my guru, and his esteemed guru, Bade Baba, without whom not only would I have no power to write, and no power to comprehend my experience, but most certainly no power at all to have had this experience in the first place. My homage and reverence go to their successor who has for over thirty years sustained the teachings.

When I received this gift of awakened *Kundalini* from my guru in 1979, I had no idea of its value. Over the years of reading, researching and watching the changes in my life, I gradually came to realize the immense significance of it. I wondered how I had earned such a gift. I wondered how it could be that no one in my culture, none of my readings and education had prepared me for this gift of spirit.

I wanted to share the good news, but no one could hear my words, for they knew nothing at all about such an awakening. Here was one of the most important events in all my lifetimes, yet I had to hide it and even feel ashamed of being so different to others. For me, in 1979, only my teacher understood what I was going through; everyone else misjudged me. This is why I wrote this book, for being seen as "crazy" when one is going "sane" is very lonely, disheartening and tragic. I want others who may be going through this to know that awakening to one's spiritual power and truth is a great event that should be heralded as we salute saints and Olympic heroes.

I trust that, as the years of our evolution continue blossoming and more and more human beings emerge from the nightmare of our confinement in ignorance and misery, such transcendent experiences will not be hidden shamefully behind locked doors. They will not be medicated and obscured, stifled and suppressed, but brought out into the light of day to be celebrated and honored. I trust that human beings who awaken to their full humanity as the most rare of the creatures God has created, be brought before the congress of universes to receive due respect and acknowledgement for their courage.

We are the sovereign, transcendent survivors of millions of years of cellular development. We are the ones that we have been seeking. We are the butterflies that have emerged from the chrysalis. It is to us newly born humans that the galaxies sing their lullabies. It is our destiny to BE God on Earth, to BE God as matter, to be our own complete, sovereign selves as we have been formed. This is the destiny that we are heir to. Our rare birth gives us an even rarer gift of knowing God within ourselves.

This book has been twenty years in the making, a love affair with my heart. Some will be able to receive its wisdom, some not yet. But now it is published it will find its own audience and its seeds will fall where they will. My symptoms may not be the same symptoms as the reader's. But in describing this process, I hope to show the paradox and wonder of being human and to bring hope for those who are struggling with depression or *Kundalini* symptoms. My struggles to know the truth were like a valiant, heroic battle, yet when I got to that state I sought, I found it was as easy as going 'home,' as simple as breathing.

To that soul who can open to a glimpse of the true wonder of who human beings are and the beauty and nobility of the human heart from reading this, I salute you, and thank you.

Hari Om Tat Sat.
San Francisco, California
Ruth Angela © 2013

ॐ

Prologue to
The Guru's Gift:
A Kundalini Awakening

By Ruth Angela © 2013

I was spinning delightfully. The joy was so full I could barely breathe. I looked down to see Wendy, my German shepherd dog, standing in the middle of the living room and staring up at me with a question in her eyes. Next to her, my cat, Tiddles, quietly stared with her chin raised, head to one side, watching these ceiling spins. They both sat together beneath me, seeming unconcerned yet curious.

The bliss of spinning, lifting off the ground and flying in the air was more exquisite than anything I had ever known in my life. But even more than this, I was not alone. I was accompanied by an invisible beloved companion who showered love and blessings upon me as we joined in this aeronautical dance, twirling dervish-like off the ground into the air. Together, we violated the laws of Newtonian physics. But it felt natural, real, delightful fun like a child's game, spinning around and around. We were galaxies twirling in space. We were dancers, Nataraj, thrilling each other in unified joy, spinning like binary stars. Through it all, there was bliss so ineffably delicious—a familiar ecstasy like a long forgotten warm, totally satisfying, wholly joyful pleasure.

Twenty five years later I watched a Chinese movie by Ang Lee,

"Crouching Tiger, Hidden Dragon," where the Chinese warrior adepts flew through trees without gravity pulling them down, and I witnessed on the screen then what I too had experienced in 1979 in the ceiling of my Hawaii home. For years I had said nothing of these incredible spinning adventures because— who would believe it? But watching this movie, even though I knew it was photography, wires and animation that showed this skill, I, none-the-less, instantly understood that in ancient times these adepts had had the power and ability to fly; it confirmed for me that my ceiling spins were not entirely impossible if Chinese adepts could do this. Like them, I was able to fly, to reverse gravity and spin into the air effortlessly and without fear.

This spinning was a daily event in my life in the months after I received Shaktipat or Kundalini awakening from my spiritual teacher in 1979. This event was so life-altering in the scheme of life events, that it has taken me many years of pondering, integration and research to put it together into some kind of framework that I can understand and explain. This book is the result of my research and contemplation; it tells of my dramatic spiritual awakening, the strange and mysterious things that happened to me through an alchemical process that was triggered by my soul's magnetizing a great saint's energy. This sparked a process of evolution and return to my true nature.

This account of my experiences and insights may offer a modicum of comfort to others going through their own awakening, those whose numbers are increasing with every year as we approach a spiritual doorway for our species. Perhaps from these pages they can integrate the wild thrusts of energy that pulse through them, in order to become healers, artists and leaders in the world today.

ॐ

The Guru's Gift:

A Kundalini Awakening

by Ruth Angela
2013

CHAPTER 1

The Opportunity

The human rebirth is said to be extremely rare. The Majjhima Nikaya compares it to a wooden cattle-yoke floating on the waves of the sea, tossed this way and that by the winds and currents. The likelihood of a blind turtle, rising from the depths of the ocean to the surface once in a hundred years, putting its head through the hole in the yoke is considered greater than... rebirth as a human.

"Human Beings in Buddhism." [1]

Few passages can explain so clearly the wonder and privilege of birth as a human being. I often heard my spiritual teacher say to be born a human is extremely rare and auspicious. It is a paradox for these saints to tell us how rare this life is when we live in pain, and many people seem by their addictions and use of mind-altering substances to be trying to find an escape from this life. Who is truly happy here? We might ask: Why on Earth would souls clamor to be born here?

Yet, as human beings, we seem to have an instinct or a built in magnetic compass to seek happiness. The saints tell us that happiness is the real purpose of man's life. So we know it is there—elusively—somewhere. Yet where is it? How many human beings die disappointed, regretful, not satiated, having not found this elusive thing called 'happiness'? This is the truth for so many humans. We are slaves to a job, to a society, to a lifestyle, but how much of this endeavor brings us lasting joy? Don't Americans have the rights to "life, liberty and the pursuit of happiness"? Yet what do Americans pursue in this effort to find bliss? It could more accurately be said they pursue *relief from misery*.

It is estimated that, "Each year in the United States, depression affects an estimated 17 million people at an approximate annual direct and indirect cost of $53 billion...."[2] This is 17% of all the people living in the United States of America, and these are only the "identified" depressed people. Norman Shealy, M.D. Ph.D., writing in *Audacious Aging*, has estimated that only "20 per cent of people are really happy, 40 percent are clinically depressed (half of those, or 20 percent of all Americans, are on antidepressant drugs), and 40 percent suffer from what I call subclinical depression—they feel dull and are not happy."[3] These numbers are staggering.

If Shealy is correct, then there is plenty of numbing through drugs and other medications going on in America, but does it cure the lack of happiness? Even for those not on medications for depression, there are plenty of ways to be distracted from misery in America: sports, shopping, sex, food—both eating and preparing, intellectual pursuits, research, inventions, marriages, children and child-rearing, travel, books, art, design, science, technological gadgets such as computers and phones, multiple TV channels with movies, and on it goes. These interests help time pass and maybe some of these distractions can be managed to last a lifetime since the mind is constantly moving. The distractions allow inner misery to be pushed away from conscious awareness for a while. When one distraction no longer keeps misery at bay, then there are others like new spouses, new houses, decorating, bigger toys, travel, upward social mobility, social media, affairs, new possessions and the acquisition of money to keep back the tide of unhappiness. Since these are on the level of interests or distractions, they are of the mind, so the happiness quotients are as temporary as the mind is fleeting. Truly, not one of these brings a lasting happiness for the soul.

The Sages:

H.L. Poonja says: "The mind has been cheating you for thirty-five million years, my dear children. You have been cheated."[4] The mind is the thought energy with the awareness, "I am my thoughts; I am this physical body." Most people believe this to be who they are, for no one informs them otherwise. For too long we have been seeking lasting joy from the mind, the body, and the world around us where many are newly discovering, it *cannot* be found.

So we feel cheated of this happiness, yet still Poonjaji, the disciple of the great Ramana Maharshi, says, "Take very good care of the body because this is the rarest gift that nature can give you—a human birth."[5] How can we truly believe this? The message from the sages contradicts our experience, as from these statistics, being human seems to provide us a permanent state of depression. Why could it be such a great privilege to be born here? Is this just a cruel joke? Like an impossible riddle, the wise and knowing sages of antiquity have only enigmas and paradoxes to offer our minds on this mystery. The famous ancient aphorisms of Patanjali, revered author of sacred wisdom, tell us to seek happiness within ourselves.

> Verse 36. *Concentration may also be attained by fixing the mind upon the Inner Light, which is beyond sorrow....* The ancient yogis believed that there was an actual center of spiritual consciousness, called "the lotus of the heart," situated between the abdomen and the thorax, which could be revealed in deep meditation... it was said to be beyond sorrow, since those who saw it were filled with an extraordinary sense of peace and joy.[6]

Thus, the sages tell us the answers—the lasting joys we seek— lie within us in our hearts, a location not outside ourselves and certainly not found in any artificial drugs.

If a person is lucky, after a while, when these distractions of the mind have been exhausted, a space opens within the soul; a yearning arises for something more meaningful, more deeply significant than the mind's distractions. This turning point is called "the dark night of the soul." Rather than believe that a deeper depression has come, this should be understood to be the call of the spirit and a trumpet call to a new act, a new dawn to the real happiness.

Those who have made it through the "dark night" may then delight that they have the answer at last. The hopeful ones with enthusiastic interest in finding the source of joy might sign up for the meditation or yoga class, hoping for the cure of their dearth of happiness. They will look hopefully towards the goal of "bliss" that the scriptures promise. They will get up at the crack of dawn and sit expectantly in their new silk shirts, on woolen mats, cross-legged, on the sitz bones with incense and icons ready; as they turn their eyes to the tip of the nose, they await this taste of happiness.

Fortunately, for most people, respite in meditation does come; there is relief from the mind's activities; depression and stress can be allayed by regular practice. Jack Kornfield, the Buddhist author, says that "we must learn to step back from all the stories of the mind,... we can release ourselves from its [the mind's] iron grip of separatism and come to rest in the body and heart."[7] The seekers are relieved to find that turning within to the root of the mind and heart in meditation is the beginning of the true journey to peace.

Meditation:

The quiet of their inner world brings all they had been yearning for. For these souls now on an inward seeking path, sufficient peace is at last attained; they are content. Something profound has been found within. Yoga and quiet living without extremes, keep the peace going and promote a lifestyle that is healing, calming and rewarding. They meet themselves inside, learn to identify and name their misery like watching a movie of their inner domain and achieving distance from the chattering mind. Joy and happiness appear. Moments of happiness spring up without any particular cause. They begin to feel some mastery of their feelings, and control over their reactions. They have solved the issue of depression. They have removed themselves from an insane world of *do* and *go* and *show*. They have muted the voices of inner discontent. They wonder how this world within could have been there all along yet not known. It is a wonderful gift.

The Ego:

What most people do not know is that hidden behind the daily activities of life, behind the censorship of mentation, lurks a subconscious, childlike, powerful "me" that is replete with anger, possessiveness, jealousy, revenge, greed, hatred, injuries, obsessions, rage, fear, control issues and so forth. Eckhart Tolle calls it the "pain body." He states, "because of the human tendency to perpetuate old emotion, almost everyone carries in his or her energy field an accumulation of old emotional pain, which I call "the pain-body."[8] It is the suppressed feelings that everyone has while growing up that are unresolved and thus festering in the hidden embers of one's inner world, the subconscious. In meditation the "pain body" can sometimes be activated by intense yogic practices, causing discomfort and unpleasant feelings; the meditator may decide against further meditation and stop the practice. She might understandably return to external distractions and give up the search for enduring happiness in meditation, saying, "It is not for me."

Inner voices of the threatened ego justify this retreat and defeat. The chattering mind is inactive during long periods of silence in meditation. It has no function unless there is an ego following its directives. Some part of the mind is like a restless animal that is constantly alert and stimulated by the environment. It cannot exist while we sit in meditation. It has urgent needs to be always in control, always looking for stimulation of the senses, the emotions and the environment—somewhat like my cat.

My cat sleeps almost all day in a deeply, relaxed surrender until night comes. Then he stands at the open door, alert in every fiber, listening, smelling, sensing the world he wants to enter. There is nothing I can see to stimulate him to this intensity, but nonetheless his is an open, intense awareness of any movement, smell or sensory input of dogs, coyotes, possum, squirrels or other creatures. His body is rigid, super tense. If I touch him, he jumps like a taut rubber band in reaction. His focus is totally merged into the environment in which he is about to enter. For my cat, this is the peak moment of his day. Every muscle, every avenue of input is opened and stimulated. Without this delicious input of information to his brain, he, un-stimulated and unchallenged, would go back to sleep.

We are similar in that our chattering mind wants to be stimulated and entertained by something while we are awake. The body wants to move and do something. The eyes crave movement, the ears sound, the nose smell and the tongue taste. The curious mind requires excitement, interest, entertainment to stimulate it and keep it active and alive. Peace, harmony, chanting, oneness with others put this mind—like my cat's mind without stimuli—out of action. There is no role for the ego in meditation.

Eckhart Tolle has clearly demonstrated this ego control of the senses in his recent book *A New Earth*. Tolle explains an aspect of meditation where "when you are alert and contemplate a flower, crystal, or bird without naming it mentally, it becomes a window for you into the formless. There is an inner opening... into the realm of spirit."[9] What a wonderful gift! When the mind is quiet we can enter a spiritual haven. Unfortunately, to the chattering mind, the ego or "Little Ego," meditation and spirit represent a kind of death. Ego dies when spirit arises, so it will fight against this peace with all the skill, deviousness and characteristics of a cornered or hungry animal. Like an inner adversary, almost a separate insane, jealous entity, "Little Ego" enters the peaceful meditation realms and the battle for inner happiness takes on a far more serious challenge.

Unlike my cat who prepares to merge his being into the formless presence of night *fully aware*, the "Little Ego" will not willingly merge with the moment of "now" or spirit that is found in meditation. "Little Ego," full of its own importance, feels its own demise even as the sincere meditator pushes into deeper and longer periods of peace; so this *pain body* struggles like a cunning and devious animal to keep control of the conscious mind—its realm of power. To distract the meditator from the peace within, "Little Ego" will name everything; separate it, categorize it, analyze it, sort it, divide it, compare it, rationalize it, and steal the essence out of what it experiences. It will discomfort the body with itches, sudden urgent needs to urinate, joint complaints, fingernails that need cutting, and then there are noises to be heard, people to think of, lists to be made, anything to keep from diving into 'now'. The "Little Ego," the *pain body*, without the stimulation of the senses must cease to exist.

The Struggle for Control:

So once this inner journey has been taken, once the deeper connection to the spirit within us has been made, a struggle for control of the conscious mind develops. As bizarre as this may sound, it is as if we have a bifurcated mind at odds within us. One mind wants to stay focused on the world and its distractions even though they bring no lasting joy, and another part of us yearns for whispers of inner peace which can bring lasting joy. One is loud and demanding, and the other makes no sound, but merely resonates in silence.

Therefore, this need by the body/mind/ego for stimulation, this constant standing apart from what "is" and analysis by the mind makes deeper meditation a challenge. It is a struggle to pull the mind into the inner realms of meditation as this "Little Ego" pulls us always to the outside world of things and doing. All this begins to rise up into our awareness when we turn up the intensity of our conscious desire to explore the quiet, silent self within.

The meditator who seeks deeper into the core of him/herself confronts the world of repressed rages and injuries, and the "Little Ego's" battles for control; these are the brave ones who have gone through the *dark night of the soul* and have eagerly turned that anguish into joy through meditation. These are the ones who find their inner depths a world as fascinating and satisfying as falling in love or discovering a new country. These can also be people who have never meditated or even thought of themselves as spiritual who are plunged into these depths. Whoever it is who pushes into his or her deeper self finds this is undiscovered territory; it is a maze of unknown dimensions, the new frontier.

For although the inner world of meditation at first seems safe and peaceful to the beginner, as intensity and focus increase, one can find oneself on a strange "pilgrim's progress" meandering into the subconscious and unconscious mind where wide-awake nightmares become grander and more vivid than any in childhood. For this deeper journey there is no preparation, no warning, no map, no guidebook, no destination, no workshop, no course, and no companion. One is entirely a sole pioneer. One is alone, naked, and unable to communicate anything to those who have not yet taken that same journey. This is the path that Chogyam Trungpa warns new meditators not to start at all because of the difficulties, "but if you do, then it is best to finish."[10]

Those brave or innocent enough to take the plunge into their psyches, the hidden inner world, may go through discomforting physical symptoms, battles with the ego, and emotional upheavals for some years; yet the promise of happiness and integration is there as many through history have shown. Meditation is the method of quieting the mind and it is also the method of reaching deeper within to find the roots of happiness. It is the way through; it is the path less often taken; it is the path of struggle and loneliness; however, in my experience it was the path to the truth of oneself, to sanity, and an inner happiness that cannot be shaken. It offers the path to ones' true nature which can be known *at last*. It is the path to knowing why human life is so rare and valued. It is the path to finding out who human beings are in the cosmic arena and what special place we play in the universe.

For the lucky ones, there will be careful preparation with a wise teacher for this experience. This has been the traditional path. I was very fortunate. Along with my benevolent guru came a cosmic guide a Goddess who is the very essence of our selves— the *Kundalini*. When people meditate, contemplate, and push through the mind's antics to remain in blissful states of the spirit, there may often arise a phenomenon as basic as the transformation of the body at adolescence; this is the next stage of human evolution, the awakening of *Kundalini*.

My teacher awakened this within me and set in motion the process of transformation years before I knew what had happened. When Goddess *Kundalini* awakens in us, we have a blissful, uncompromising, wise and all-knowing companion on this journey into ourselves. I was awakened to this power by a great guru who guided me through my "Little Ego" to find something I today call "unconditional peace within," and what he called "The true Self." With the help of my guru and the Goddess *Kundalini*, I took this plunge into my pain body and subconscious; I came back from it integrated with the knowledge of the incredible wonder of being human. This is a state beyond the mind's limitations and, though some may find the path easier than others, it is the realm that can be reached and sustained by that steadfast journey "through." Perhaps it was just as well that I was thrust into it before I knew the full story, like a baby being thrown into the river to swim. I took the plunge and swam to the shore. This is the story of that journey and the miraculous changes that I underwent.

CHAPTER 2

What is Kundalini?

Today more and more people are finding themselves with the symptoms of *Kundalini* awakening having taken, whether they knew it or not, "the plunge." The meditator who inadvertently takes a *Kundalini* Yoga class thinking to try something new, or the person who signs up for a transformative workshop may end up, either during the event or some time after, finding a fire or a snake-like movement rising up through the spine that brings a surge of enormous power and energy.

What has occurred, and what is now occurring with increasing frequency on our transforming planet as more people around the world turn to meditation and yoga, is the awakening of the cosmic *Kundalini* energy—the quickening. In ancient times, this extraordinary good fortune only occurred to few selected initiates after years of careful preparation. However, this awakening is no longer the exclusive domain of religious sects, secret societies or religious adepts. Today the information about this phenomenon is available all over the world; more and more people are activating their *Kundalini* spontaneously or with very little effort.

The energy that may suddenly surge through the spine creates an intense opening; the "god-force" or Holy Spirit is active and flowing through the subtle channels of the nervous system. It is as if 1000 watts are coursing through the 100-watt light bulb of one's nervous system. This is one sign that the *Kundalini* energy is actively transforming the person.

This process has not been widely publicized or taught in the West, and it is still not widely known among doctors today. How can such a phenomena exist within us, be a biological process, create such a huge challenge to our equilibrium, transform our psyche and life, and yet not be known in our Western world? Even though this force is an integral part of every human being, most people have no idea that the *Kundalini* even exists! Yet, like any practical person, they would ask: Where is *Kundalini* located in the physical body?

It is said to be coiled up in the very lower region of the torso, the perineum area between the anus and sexual organs and rises in a spiral, like a cobra rising from a basket. But it is not found by surgery, for it is part of the subtle nervous system. The *Shakti Kundalini* according to Joseph Campbell is a "little female serpent... about as thick as the hair of the boar, white and coiled three and a half times around a symbolic *lingam*."[1] David Gordon White in *The Alchemical Body* concurs that the *Kundalini* as a serpent "sleeps coiled...with her mouth closed over an internal *linga* in the lower abdomen."[2] The hidden, or inner form of *Kundalini* is usually asleep in a small "bulb" of energy that is stored at the base of the spine. According to Bonnie Greenwell, author of *Energies of Transformation:*

> ... after Kundalini enters the fetus and activates the pranic system the residual energy coils 3 1/2 times at the base of the spine, and goes into a dormant state. The mind becomes engaged in the process of living, and we identify with our bodies, our genetic heritage and our mental, sensate and emotional processes, separating from any awareness of the Self, or the Soul or the source of our existence...[3]

For most people this is the extent of *Kundalini* awareness. Joseph Chilton Pearce believes *Kundalini* rises at puberty and mid-life to a minor extent; although we have all had adolescent experiences of heightened emotions, identity crises, overwhelming sexual confusion, and strange soul-like longings, we are never informed that this is our own spirit rising within us asking to be released. The only approved Western answer to this yearning is to see a psychiatrist for medication to shut it down. The modern Western youth often has little choice but to turn to street drugs, alcohol or smoking to numb the inner spirit that will not be denied. What a terrible waste of the inheritance of a human body and this very rare birth!

In India and other areas of the world where this knowledge of *Kundalini* is cultivated, the yoga apprentices practice for decades with vigorous postures and discipline to activate the *Kundalini* energy. Sufi's spin in their spiritual dances and reach states of bliss. American Indian youth go on vision quests alone to find this inner pathway to the soul. African dancers and Dervish dancers create hypnotic states in order to enter altered realities. Chinese martial arts practitioners begin training in childhood to acquire advanced magical skills. Indeed, athletes, dancers and yogic adepts can reach these states through release of endorphins as they challenge their physical bodies beyond normal limits. Any human activity that takes one into realms of ecstasy can enable and support the journey of inner discovery that is the beginning of the *Kundalini* awakening.

Although *Kundalini* appears in many traditions and cultures throughout history, it was virtually an unknown concept in the West in 1979. Subsequently, I have found that it is a universal phenomena, much like puberty or menopause, except it relates less to the development of the physical body, but to the spiritual development of all human beings. I can talk about it and describe my symptoms, but words cannot encompass a definition of what *Kundalini* is or feels like, for it is known solely through experience. Nathan Swartz-Salant explains it succinctly:

> Whoever has known the *numinosum* in a deep enough
> way for his or her life to have been unalterably changed

by it—changed in such a way that they now *see* differently and now experience the center of personality as
existing outside the ego—such a person never *understands* this process. It for ever remains a mystery, one
that he or she has been graced to participate in, and
survive.[4]

My teacher explained that within our bodies is this power found in
all beings called *Kundalini,* which is the feminine holy spirit within; it
lies relatively dormant for most of our lives until it can be triggered to
awaken. The constant bliss and happiness which we intuitively know
lies within the realm of our experience but which is so elusive most
of our lives, can be found as a result of a *Kundalini* awakening. That
awakening will shift our focus from the outside world towards the inner
worlds. The *Kundalini* process transforms us from veiled outward seeking unconsciousness to awakened inward seeking consciousness and
enlightened insight.

It is apparent now according to Lee Sannella, a psychiatrist who
has written a seminal work on what he calls "a form of psychospiritual
energy" the *Kundalini* Shakti, that the "phenomena in the process of
psychospiritual transformation...are constant and universal, tran-
scending personal and cultural differences."[5] According to his research,
Kundalini is integral to the teachings of "Tibetan Buddhism, Chinese
Taoism," some "American Indian tribes, and ...even of the Bushmen
of Africa." It however, was "most carefully studied and conceptually
elaborated" in Hindu India.[6]

Although the word *Kundalini* may appear strange for many readers
and the concept of it even incomprehensible to the Western mind, in
fact it is closer to each person than his own heart. *Kundalini* is closer
than the breath in the body for it is the breather and the breath. In its
dormant form it is the very *essence* of all life. Again Sannella asserts
that the "process of psychophysiological transmutation, most usefully
viewed as the 'awakening of the kundalini,' is indeed a reality... [and]
is part of an evolutionary mechanism... that is intrinsically desirable."[7]

It is this energy, *Kundalini,* that pervades and enervates the world as we see it. Ajit Mookerjee claims that "The coiled Kundalini is the female energy existing in latent form, not only in every human being but in every atom of the universe."[8] He continues, "The arousal of Kundalini is... the basis of all yogic disciplines, and every genuine spiritual experience may be considered a flowering of this physio-nuclear energy."[9]

I have come to experience that *Kundalini* as the scouring pad or force that cleans out the dross and negativity of many past lives. *Kundalini* is one's companion on this journey; She is a Goddess that is the light that lightens and enlightens the path in every sense. She transforms ignorance and misery; She takes away the dread and horror of our deepest fears, guiding the bound soul into the realms of light. I did not realize how powerful and awesome my teacher was, nor how lucky I was to have his support when this awakening occurred. The awakening is a step out of the obsession with materiality into the awareness of our cosmic role as conscious, aware beings.

However, this plunge into the inner worlds can be shattering to the logical mind, the "Little Ego" that has controlled our awareness and kept it focused on material issues. The realm the meditator enters seems to have no rules, no laws, no script. This is unnerving to the logical mind. We are used to depending upon our "consensual reality." We are not prepared for this silence, for this peace, nor for this encounter with our hidden "pain body" selves.

In meditation and chanting or when focused on a creative task it is known that the left and right brains merge. The awakened *Kundalini* joins the bi-cameral brain into one unified channel of awareness. We have been dominated by the consensual reality of the ego = left brain, so most people are unaware that we have any other perceptual possibilities in every-day life except for dreams or nightmares unless they have experimented with psychedelic drugs.

Moving into this unified awareness disturbs our normal reality, and can create some strange experiences. "Even for an experienced meditator, nothing is more unknown than this territory. Anything can happen here."[10] Jung would call this the archetypal realm. We recognize the ancient mythological stories of Greek Gods as insights into this archetypal realm. Carlos Castaneda's don Juan, the sorcerer, would call it the *Nagual*. Others would call it "hallucinations," "altered reality" or "noosphere."

Gopi Krishna famously awakened his *Kundalini* by meditation and wrote extensively about this experience. He says that "When accidentally the center [*Kundalini*] begins to function prematurely, before the nerve connections and links have been fully established... delicate tissues of the body are likely to be damaged."[11] A minor example of this damage would be when one has taken too much stimulant like coffee and one's mind and heart become hyperactive.

Ideally we should be being prepared for this awakening in our youth by knowledge of the *Kundalini*, spiritual practices and careful diet; then the awakening would come after preparation of the subtle body when a person is entirely ripe. Yet such awakenings happen without preparation. A housewife giving birth to a child may activate this center and be totally unaware of what has happened which is what occurred with Christina Grof, author of *The Stormy Search for the Self* and wife of Dr. Stanislav Grof. The experimental meditator who seeks the ancient wisdom and peace within sincerely may activate the *Kundalini* to awaken and begin the rigorous cleansing of his or her subconscious; it is like a car without brakes, unexpectedly this power has taken over one's "self control" mechanisms.

The Heroic Journey:

It can be daunting to the uninitiated, entailing lonely courage and stamina. Joseph Campbell wrote about this historical journey into the inner mysteries of the psyche in *The Hero with a Thousand Faces;* Campbell lays the burden upon each individual to find this path, no matter how insane he/she appears to his society or culture.

> The modern hero,... who dares to heed the call...
> cannot, indeed, must not, wait for his community to
> cast off its slough of pride, fear, rationalized avarice,

and sanctified misunderstanding....so every one of us shares the supreme ordeal—carries the cross of the redeemer....[12]

What hero does not want to heed the call and rush into this experience? Some who hear about this phenomenon want to awaken the *Kundalini* themselves having heard of the amazing powers that arise from it. Unfortunately, this would be foolish and unwise motivation to awaken *Kundalini*. This process is a serious transformation of the mind, awareness, physiology and psychology. It is a hero's journey because, although bliss is integral to the experience, the mind and ego undergo some significant disturbances. It is not a picnic or a comfortable transition for most people. I caution anyone who makes the effort to awaken without the help of an experienced, benevolent teacher.

Advaita:

Although my teacher and many other gurus from India advocated the awakened *Kundalini* as essential to spiritual growth, not all teachers say such a challenging path is required to know our true nature. A less stressful and dramatic awakening method advocated by Ramana Maharshi is *Advaita* or the "Direct Path." He says, "Reality is simply the loss of the ego. Destroy the ego by seeking its identity... it will automatically vanish and Reality will shine forth by itself. This is the direct method."[13] This method does not mention *Kundalini* as required for such understanding and, for those who desire an awakening without the drama and scouring of the dark unconscious, this path would be less troublesome, less painful, and less disruptive. However, there is some question for me whether the people who are attracted to this path have had their *Kundalini* awakened in previous lives, and thus their spiritual centers are already opened. It is possible that in this life, they are perhaps just seeking the final stages of full awakening, for which this Direct Method is ideal.

Sri Nisargadatta Maharaj, a great Nath teacher from Mumbai, also promoted non-duality like Maharshi and was not interested in discussing *Kundalini* awakening as a path to self realization. He said that with the phenomena of the *Kundalini,* "You might also have visions of various gods... but in the process of trying to experience and observe all these things, it is easy to forget the way toward self-realization."[14] I understand this now to be a real possibility as I experienced this same problem. The "Little Ego" becomes enamored of the excitement and drama of the inner scouring process, so the focus is on that instead of the ultimate goal of complete silence and self-realization.

The Goddess:

Thus, even with the *Kundalini* awakening helping along the journey, there are pitfalls for the earnest seeker where the "Little Ego" refuses to release control of awareness; one may adopt a "spiritual lifestyle" and replace one's former habits and mental attachments to material things looking "holy" or "spiritual," but these also become obstacles that must be recognized. So even though *Kundalini* is our helper and guide on the journey, even though She is the transducer of the *Kundalini* power into something our bodies can handle, yet She may not bring full realization; She can clear the path, but we have to make the courageous effort to allow the process and surrender to it. There is still a great deal of self-effort, grace and guidance needed from within and most of all—enthusiasm—before the full attainment.

However, once the *Kundalini* has awakened there is no choice than to surrender, to get on board and experience the ride into the blisses, the terrors, the joys and the nightmares of the unconscious realms to face down any demons that lurk there. There is no turning back from this journey although many wish there were. Fortunately, there are courageous beings like my own teacher and many other revered guides who can tell us about this journey and guide us. Perhaps it is as well that the *Kundalini* gives us little choice once she uncoils. As Elizabeth Gilbert author of *Eat, Pray, Love* so aptly explains, "The search for God is a reversal of the normal, mundane worldly order. In the search for God, you revert from what attracts you and swim toward that which is difficult."[15] This is not a path for everyone, nor would I ever advise it without that person being aware of the journey and at least some of what it entails.

In 1979, I ventured forth into this realm, not because I was brave, although I ended up having to find extraordinary depths of courage; it was not because I had any idea what was coming and wanted to win over adversity, or even because I wanted to be a hero-warrior in some way. I was not even consciously aware of being a spiritual seeker. Yet once my little white snake was awakened, I ventured forth with enormous enthusiasm because of the trust and faith I had for my teacher, and because the door opened first into the blissful gifts and mystical wonder of awakened *Kundalini*.

Joseph Campbell explains this blind enthusiasm, "A hero ventures forth from the world of common day into a region of supernatural wonder; fabulous forces are there encountered and a decisive victory is won; the hero comes back from this mysterious adventure with the power to bestow boons on his fellow man."[16]

I found first the incredible *fun* and discovery that this open door offered me. The blissful spinning around my house, the constant sense of being loved unconditionally by my "other" or "higher self," the waves of joy emanating from my heart most of the time were all great incentives to proceed. My nature as an enthusiastic person as well as my spirit's leap of joy at finding this door open to me spurred me forward. I could not wait to enter this realm, to go through and find the treasure that lay within. Yet like all quests for the "Holy Grail," there are difficulties and struggles to be overcome.

According to Richard Perala, "Earth humans are probably the most complex species in the galaxy. Remember that you took on the greatest challenge of any species—to cut yourself off from all memory of the Source and then try to claw your way back to unconditional love. No other species would be that courageous."[17] It takes courage of a kind that we rarely get to experience or find in ourselves. We venture into a whole new realm of awareness because this precious body, this auspicious birth, is the instrument through which we can know our true nature. The prize is not about powers, new levels of entertainment, celebrity or wealth. The prize is returning to the truth of our innate nature and finding out what a *full human being* can be as a complete planetary soul integrated into the universal soul. For this simple experience, all the difficulties and confusions are worth it; who does not want to move into the next phase of human evolution?

CHAPTER 3

The Time is Now:
Earth Changes

The great teachers tell us that we have now, more than for eons, a golden opportunity to achieve something so rare, so very, very rare—self realization—awareness of who we truly are. In the past people would spend most of their lives struggling to get a glimpse of this. In this era we are facilitated in uncovering the essence of our true nature—what it means to be fully human. We have the opportunity to know ourselves as the stuff of stars and know a lasting inner happiness.

There is good news for us in the 21st Century. Right now the time is especially auspicious as we are living in an extraordinary era. According to John Major Jenkins who writes about the effects of cosmology on human consciousness, "Earth is aligning, via the solstitial axis, with the Galactic Center and the Galactic Anticenter... [that] suggest a very compelling (and ancient) model of human spiritual evolution."[1] Astrologers, both Mayan, Incan, Hopi, Egyptian, Cherokee and Toltec as well as prophecies from other native cultures, point to the good news that all the souls born on Earth now have more opportunity than in past eons to awaken to their true selves. This throughout history has been known as a *"Kundalini"* awakening.

Emma Bragdon, Ph.D a transpersonal therapist, writes about spiritual emergency and *Kundalini,* saying "... spiritual awakening is a natural process of maturation that seems to be affecting increasing numbers of people."[2]

Astrologers say that the influence of Uranus on the planet is having a powerful effect and "there will be an ongoing series of mass *kundalini* risings, no matter the age."[3] Prash Trivedi, a Vedic Astrologer, reports that we are at the Precession of the Equinoxes and several major cycles of time (26,000 years) are converging including the "change of age from Pisces to Aquarius" which all indicate a change coming for humanity. He continues to explain:

> This is the only plane [of consciousness] where we can actually change our consciousness and grow on a soul level. On other planes... you never get to evolve on a spiritual level. So all the entities... always want to take birth on earth to aid in their evolution.[4]

In a journal called *Shared Transformation*, El Collie and C. Kress opened a medium for those with *Kundalini* awakening to connect, and found that "increasingly, the *Kundalini* experience is being reported among people who are not undertaking spiritual practices." And in two years from 1993—1995, 700 people reported being in the "throes of spontaneous *Kundalini* arousal." El Collie states:

> Judging by the current condition of the world, had my own *Kundalini* not risen, I would have doubted the New Age proclamations that we are in the midst of a collective developmental leap in human consciousness. But from what has transpired in my own life,... I have a growing spark of hope that as a species, we are truly evolving.[5]

This was a rough survey taken in 1996. In the time of the late 70's and early 80's when my Indian teacher toured the world, there were thousands of cases of awakening from his influence alone. Ken Carey says, "The earth is rapidly entering a new field of consciousness that is bringing it back into resonance with primal rhythms of creation."[6] He predicts that humanity will experience a "transformation in human consciousness more fundamental than the development of language... a new era is dawning."[7] The spiritual writer, Eckhart Tolle, says, "due to the unprecedented influx of consciousness we are witnessing on the planet now, many people no longer need to go through the depth of acute suffering to be able to dis-identify" from their limited understanding; he continues, "The next step in human evolution is not inevitable, but for the first time in the history of our planet, it can be a conscious choice."[8] What wonderful news!

Barbara Hand Clow, an astrologer, Cherokee, and prolific writer on ancient earth history, says that "the sun is our source of solar radiation (our biological fuel) and the Galactic Center is our source of cosmic radiation (our spiritual fuel)." She continues to say that in December 2012, we will be in direct alignment with the Galactic Center thus in line for a full blast of spiritual fuel and that this "awakening is spiritual because [of] the alignment of the Galactic Axis to the center of the Galaxy."[9] In *Alchemy of Nine Dimensions*, Hand Clow continues, our alignment with the center of the galaxy in 2012 will bring a huge leap of human evolution. "The Galactic Center exists in eternal Samadhi or bliss. High frequencies are slowly building in Earth,... transmuting humans."[10] The evidence seems to be being recorded everywhere.

In astonishing research of world wide ancient and current records, David Wilcock has concluded, "The 25,000-year cycle creates biological and spiritual evolution in sudden jumps."[11] His research connects ancient Sumerian mathematical numbers with the calendar of the Mayans which began recording time 16 billion years ago, and which indicates stages of the evolution of cellular consciousness that are due to end in 2012. According to Barbara Hand Clow, this date thus becomes "the next stage of human evolution."[12] Alice Bailey who channels Djwhal Khul, The Tibetan Master, says that this evolution of humanity "is to bring about the unfoldment of the human consciousness, to institute and bring to men's attention the higher values, and to end the reign of materialism."[13] Indeed, as of this writing, 2013, we are seeing signs of the end of Capitalism as well as Middle Eastern dictatorships. We see climactic and earth changes at a rate unprecedented in past millennia.

Signs of Change:

It is yet to be determined exactly how these changes in humanity will manifest, but the signs on our planet of major changes are unmistakable and according to Paul Ray, Ph.D. of Wisdom University, "Visionaries and futurists have been predicting a change of this magnitude for well over two decades. Our research suggests that this long anticipated cultural moment may have arrived. The evidence is not only in the numbers from our survey questionnaires but in the everyday lives of the people behind those numbers."[14] His research states that there has been an enormous shift in the conscious choices and spiritual awareness of 26% of the United States within just forty years. David Wilcock quotes Dr. John Hawks of the University of Madison-Wisconsin who says that "human evolution is now moving one hundred times faster than any other moment in recorded history."[15]

A recent book by Drunvalo Melchizedek called *Serpent of Light Beyond 2012* directly predicts the changes that are coming to mankind. He explains that:

> At this moment in history, it will be the Kundalini of the Earth that is moving and changing locations, beginning a new vibration. This energy shift will affect every last person on Earth.[16]

Drunvalo is using the word "vibration" but could also be saying "frequency." It seems that whether we wake up spiritually or not, change is upon us. It is clear that the opportunity to embark on this transformation is being facilitated by the Earth, the planets, the solar system, and even the galaxy at this time. It is also being encouraged by the widespread acceptance of meditation and yoga throughout the West. People are open to exploring their inner lives. The dark hold of ignorance and superstition from the Dark Ages is giving way to light, allowance and opening to the spirit. This is indeed the best time in eons to embark on the journey to "realize our true nature." Thus it is even more urgent that we understand what this journey might entail.

The account here is my journey into the mystical maze of my subconscious, alone, unprepared, unaware, enthusiastic, trusting, totally naïve.... but supported, fortunately, with a Goddess of my own nature, *Kundalini,* and the love of a great, great teacher.

CHAPTER 4

The Gift

*"We need the Mother of Soul to play the cosmic game of
life. We need the Mother of Beauty to sing the cosmic
song of life. We need the Mother of Power to dance the
cosmic dance of life."*

Shri Chinmoy

All of this information I was to learn about many years after I was
given the gift of awakening by a guru who was to become my spiritual teacher, a visiting swami from India. I had no idea at that time that
I was being given such a rare and wondrous gift. My teacher was touring
the United States, having spent his life as a swami in India seeking
the truth of his existence and the transformation called self-realization.
Although born into a wealthy family, he left home at the young age of
15, and traveled around India seeking a true teacher who could guide
him to know God. Years of intense seeking and trials took him to the
feet of one great avatar north of Mumbai, India. This being awakened
him and set him on a journey to discover the depths of his being and
the divinity within. Such was the power of his spiritual practices that
my teacher was able to be a lightning rod for God-force to enter into
thousands of people in a process called *Shaktipat*. This God-force he

called *Kundalini Shakti* in Sanskrit; in the West we would call it, "The Holy Spirit."

I did not know then that it was not only rare to be born as a human being, but rarer still to receive this awakening by one's teacher. Why do we need a teacher? Why cannot a human being be born aware of his or her divinity? Why must we fumble around in complete ignorance when, in fact, we have all been given the enormous gift of being human? Much of this ignorance is because our minds have been identifying with the "Little Ego" or the ego as "who we are." This means our mind is working against our true nature, and because the mind is dominant, noisy, analytical and ever-chattering, we do not listen to the inner natural self that is connected to nature during everyday life. Sometimes, if we are lucky, we might have a moment of recognition of this inner self when we are grief-stricken, our lives are in immediate danger, or something cuts through the mind's noise.

Prior to meeting my teacher, I had had some moments like that which I could not explain. When I was about 15, I was delivering papers for my brother, and walking down a garden path one night after a heavy rain; a cobweb heavy with drops had been suspended across the path, just in line with my upper lip. As I moved through this cobweb, the momentary touch of the fragile, wet, silken line below my nose caused my mind to stop, and I was suspended in a timeless state for just seconds. But these were seconds of awe. At the time, I did not have words for this experience and never told anyone, but the memory is still very much with me. This is just one of similar mind-stopping experiences that made me aware of another level of awareness. But until I met my teacher, none of these numinous experiences could be understood or even valued.

Who is privileged to get such a great gift? The great teachers would agree that awakening to one's higher self is a universal stage of growth that has no respect for country boundaries, languages spoken, ethnic origin, physical shape, skin color or even religious upbringing. It occurs when the soul has reached a certain stage of spiritual evolution. So anyone at the right stage of spiritual evolution can go through this, just as it is part of the body's development to go through birth, puberty, adulthood and old age.

Thus an awakening of the *Kundalini* brings us an opportunity to dwell in this natural state, to know a kind of existence that we can only glimpse at or imagine before an awakening occurs. Ken Carey in *The Third Millennium* indicates that it is the human future to live instinctually.

> To simply be. To say the right words without thinking them out ahead of time. To experience the purity of a mind uncluttered by troublesome and misplaced responsibility. To know exactly the right gesture, the right behavior, the creative response for each and every situation. Such are the birthrights of each and every human being.[1]

This harmony and unity is something that, as long as I have been aware, I wanted to experience and be. I knew there was much more to this existence, but no one could tell me what I was seeking.

Adolescence:

During my adolescence I had begun to really yearn for transcendence. Joseph Chilton Pearce proposes that during adolescence, *Kundalini* naturally arises with budding sexuality. He says, "This is the power of God trying to awaken within us to be expressed as our own Self."[2] The authors of *Hinduism and Jungian Psychology* define a perfect personality as " a balanced person. He is inwardly ever in touch with the self and outwardly, in behavior, he remains undisturbed, calm and tranquil amidst the play of opposites."[3] From early in my life I had desperately wanted such a state of being, but I had no idea how to go about attaining it.

Because there was only one possible place to find this in a small town in the England, I went to the church whenever there was an opportunity. From the age of eight the longing in my heart to sing to God was so great. It was one way I could actually feel the connection to something ineffable beyond myself, and it also satisfied a deep yearning to hear certain spiritual music and experience an inner joy. Believing my vicar about the value of certain daily verses, I studied them night and morning because I so wanted to reach a more advanced spiritual level. I thought all day about putting these verses into practice.

One day in that summer of my 13th year, I had a fight with my sister. I had spent months every morning and night reading the prayer verses and pondering their meaning. I tried so hard to put everything into practice. I thought this made me more "holy" and more righteous than my sister and, in the heat of the moment, accused her of being irreligious.

After I had gone to bed, I realized with dismay my self-righteousness and arrogance; I was a hypocrite and seemed to have learned nothing from all my spiritual practice. I could not console myself that I would ever improve and be like Jesus. I was working so hard on being holy and I was getting nowhere. I felt great despair. The whole situation appeared entirely beyond my ability to manage; I was unable to overcome my limitations as a human being. I could not stop weeping as only teens know how to cry. My feelings were powered by uncontrolled teenage emotions. It was overwhelming. My desire for God, for transcendence seemed to have ended in dismal failure. The passion of the ages was in that weeping; it was the soul's yearning from eons, not just this incident with my sister. I was bereft.

The Vision:

In such a depleted and sorrowful state I lay in my bed, getting more and more grieved, and more and more hopeless. It was at the depths of this misery that a flash appeared out of my left eye. A streak of pale light shot out and stood before me about three feet in front, as a two foot, oval shaped light. Within this bright oval shape was the face and energy of a very loving being whom I identified as Jesus, my lifelong companion and friend.

This being spoke to me with the utmost love and said, "Dear Ruth, do not despair. Give up these practices that make you so unhappy and live a simple life. Just be yourself. Just live an ordinary life, and I promise I will return for you in time."

CHAPTER 4   THE GIFT

I sputtered something about, "But I want to be like you, Jesus, and I just cannot seem to do it."

The loving being reiterated again, "Just live an ordinary life like everyone else, and in time I will come for you and answer your wish." And that is just what I did. I slept peacefully after this visit from my dear Jesus. The next day, I was new.

Max Freedom Long, writing about the Hawaiian understanding of our psychology, explains how deep emotional appeals such as mine reach the Higher Self which "will not interfere with our doings, no matter how we muddle our lives... [but] the High Self... longs to help and guide us... until we make the astounding discovery that there is a High Self, and that there is a way to gain its help in living."[5] My earnest search for this transcendence, the rising *Kundalini,* at the age of 13, must have reached this higher part of myself and enlisted its wisdom, for twenty years later I was to meet the teacher who could actually make me grow, activate the full awakening and realize my spiritual quest.

Like magic, this event completely changed my life at that time. I gave up all my pretensions with the hopeless teachings and useless practices of my church and devoted myself to being an ordinary teen with the same joy in pop stars and popular trends as everyone else.

Leaving England:
In my early 20's, I was fortunate to be able to leave England and come to the United States to stay with my sister, realizing a life-long dream. I applied for residency and work. From there I met my Texan husband, and we were able to buy a home near Dallas. By April of 1974, I had obtained my Bachelor's Degree, *summa cum laude,* and had almost completed my first year of teaching. I had a successful, intelligent, kind husband, a lovely little puppy and cat, a beautiful home in a great neighborhood, income to buy anything and to travel, two cars and everything that life could offer a 28 year-old "Yuppie." It seemed I had everything the world could give. I should have been very happy, but when I wrote in my journal, I had many days of deep sorrow and longing for something more. Then a single mystical dream changed everything.

The Tiger Dream:

In late April 1974, a month before my daughter was conceived. I had a vivid dream of a visit by a tiger that filled me with an intensely wondrous love for months after and still to this day. This love was unlike love we share with most other people, even our children. It would be the category of love of God, *agape*.

The dream was prophetic, vivid and real and unlike any normal dream. I know now that this was a *"Shaktipat* dream" whereby I was spiritually initiated. This is a paraphrase of the report I wrote in my diary about that night.

"A Tiger in the Night Dream."

April 28, 1974:

The dream began in my home in England with my family of parents and siblings eating supper. Casually, my father looked directly at me, and with a quiet controlled voice and showing no overt emotions, said, "A tiger will visit you tonight, when he does give him your ring."

No one moved nor ate; a silence descended upon us all. It was as if I had been waiting for this message and now it had come. Everyone looked at me. I felt like the chosen daughter, the sacrificial daughter of Agamemnon, Iphigenia. But I had no fear. I was calm and resigned somehow knowing that what it meant could not be avoided and was inevitable. Strangely, the word "tiger" had not made me think of the animal which kills men and is the terror of Indian villages. The connotation I had was of a large, agile, masterful being, who demanded obedience and loyalty. The feeling was more like the lion, Aslan, in the Narnia tales of C.S. Lewis. So I felt completely secure as I drifted off to sleep that night.

When I opened my eyes, the tiger was there moving towards the left side of my bed. Some power caused my torso to rise from the pillow while my eyes focused upon the magnificent tiger. Seconds only passed as he came to me, yet in that space I registered the immense power of his body, the beauty of his color and the wonder of his eyes. My [wedding] ring was already off my finger and I held it towards him then lay it on a dresser. He watched my actions. His eyes focused on mine, questioning me as if to say, "Are you ready?" and I was lost to him. There was no spoken or given language, yet he was telling me to come to him where he waited at the left foot of my bed. He went into the living room. In a dream-like state, I passed from my bed to the living room without feeling my feet touch the ground. But there the tiger was not a tiger any more; he was a tiger-man. That is, he had the physical presence of a man, yet the spiritual presence of the tiger who had come to me. Once more our eyes locked together, and he communicated the feeling that he meant me no harm, that he would look after me and cherish me. I believed all these communicated things because I felt them within me, and my whole being warmed like liquid love towards the tiger-man. I felt wonderful and joyous before his presence. With this joy he hugged me. I felt myself melt with ecstasy. I have never known such bliss as I felt with him holding me. There seemed to be no bones in my body so gently and tenderly did he hold me, and I felt totally immersed in the powerful love that emanated from him. If I was asleep, and I honestly could not be sure, then I had never known such peace and restfulness and such joy as I knew then in the arms of the tiger-man.

For weeks after this dream the wonderful ecstasy and suffusing love I had experienced from the tiger stayed with me. I had no idea then that it was a very significant spiritual event linked to my teenage prayers, nor that it would change my understanding of myself forever.

For the next month, feeling joyous and loved, I became uncharacteristically playful and flirtatious with my husband. For five years of marriage I had not conceived and thought that we would probably not have children. Yet during that month, I conceived my first and only child. Years later I was able to look back and recognize the tiger's visit as my teacher coming to awaken me from an unconscious life--it was *Shaktipat* by dream.

I recently discovered that my teacher had been visiting Midlothian, Texas that April in 1974 when I was living in a small town only miles from there. How such a powerful dream arose from this proximity is not easy to understand, but in retrospect, it had to have been the connection with him in my sleep.

CHAPTER 5

Preparation

Although as a teen, I had yearned for this spiritual knowledge and bliss, when my teacher first entered my life through the dream in 1974, I was a very unconscious person. I lived like a robot. I did as I was told. I followed a prescription set down by society for "good" people; I was dominated by fear and guilt. I was completely unconscious of who I was outside of my role as wife, teacher, daughter, citizen and so forth.

I had a husband who barely knew I existed because I had made myself a copy of him. The only time I got attention from him was if I did not get his supper at exactly 5 p.m. every night, or if I let one of his shirts get wrinkled. I lived by "shoulds," by guilt and social obligation. I did not choose a life that answered my own inner joy; I had no "acceptable" models for any other behavior. I was told if I lived to satisfy my own heart, I was "selfish." I would be roundly condemned and shamed for choosing to be happy over choosing to follow social convention. My mother had told me that love had to be "earned" by being "good," and that meant doing what others needed by putting my own needs last.

It was some sort of 'Christian redeemer concept' that demanded I sacrificed myself to the greater good. The message was always, "As a woman you are worthless and will not be loved unless you serve others' needs." This was the hidden form of personal sacrifice that I was expected to comply with, and somehow I was duped into believing this by the prevalence of this attitude in my culture. I had no models for anything else even in the 70's. It was an environment that had conditioned me to being a female victim—a slave to others' wishes. All these deceptions and impositions upon my spirit, became just one part of what ultimately caused an eruption of my suppressed life force.

Pools of Tears:

Unfortunately, such was my state of mind prior to the dream, that I believed I was happy then. I had all appearances of living a successful, wealthy, fulfilling life with a luxurious house, professional qualifications, and an upwardly-mobile, intelligent, dependable husband and, best of all, a lovely little daughter. To the *outer mind being*, my life was a huge success. Such was the conditioning and brainwashing of society through church, family and society, that I actually believed my accepting *their* rules and values made me happy. How could I complain to anyone when it appeared I had everything going for me? After that Tiger dream, I began to feel more and more discontent with my "perfect" life.

Sri Aurobindo states, "the central significant motive of the terrestrial existence... is concealed at the outset by... a veil of Inconscience, [sic] a veil of insensibility of Matter hides the universal Consciousness-Force."[1] The truth of our existence then is hidden from our ability to know it. This veil or obstacle to awareness of ourselves as the vast essence of the divine is called "The Ego," or the *outer mind being*. In the world we inhabit, the ego is regarded as all-important. Its desires, needs, future plans and ambitions are what the world caters to and, for daily life, work and existence, this is all that is required.

As Eckhart Tolle defines the ego in *A New Earth,* I was completely "possessed by" my "mind." He says, "As long as you are completely unaware of this, you take the thinker to be who you are. This is the egoic mind."[2] He says egos "live on identification and separation." So there is no room for the spirit. Thus in the world, there is little support for making the ego disappear. The ego or "Little Ego," *the outer mind being,* will do anything and everything to obscure the true Self, our true nature and promote itself as sole hero—sole control.

So this struggle is within oneself, yet not only is that hard, but other people will judge and fight against anyone who tries to live outside the ego. As I found, society not only cannot comprehend this "non-egoic" state, but cannot tolerate this evolving person who seems to exist on another level. It is like a herd instinct to drag everyone down to the common denominator level. Eckhart Tolle says that the egoic being in us may feel threatened by the other awake person as it feels "less" and this diminishes "its imagined sense of self relative to the other." Or the egoic self may then belittle the value of the other, or may even switch into associating with the person to enhance its own status.[3] This is particularly insidious since the person who is envious mirrors the person awake, so the truth is concealed. It is very difficult to awaken and live beyond the ego in an unconscious society.

Neale Donald Walsch has written an extraordinary series of books called *Conversations with God,* and Book 3 has some insights into this somewhat heretical concept. God speaks thus: "The biggest mistake people make in human relationships is to be concerned for what the other is wanting, being, doing, or having."[4] That was all I was doing until that dream came to me in 1974. I had no sense of my own being nor my own needs. I was an invisible shadow person, just living a socially prescribed dream of a "good person." It was all that was expected. Yet I know now there is so much more to being human than this.

Slowly that false self changed after the dream and the hug from the tiger. The façade, the pretense, the false beliefs and false life all began to crumble. When my child was born, the framework of my personality and psyche began to undergo a sea change and to melt into pools of tears. The emotional connection with her, and the responsibility of parenting all brought to light the fact that my relationship to my husband was based on a mutual friendship, intellectual support and common goals, but not on a deep, intimate, emotional or spiritual bond. We did not connect on the soul level.

For over a year after my child was born, I wept daily without any particular cause. It was the start of the dissolution of my ego and who I thought I was. My husband was getting his masters degree and was gone long hours to the library or classes, leaving me alone day after day with my new baby. The weeping was depression that was deeper than I could explain. It was my "Dark Night of the Soul."

On Sundays I would go to the Episcopal Church alone for a few hours by myself and sit in the back row weeping through the entire service. I did not sob, I did not create any drama, but the tears just rolled down my cheeks unabated. No one ever enquired after me. They saw my tears, but they said nothing. Then I would sit in my car and weep and weep before returning home to my empty palace with the preoccupied, absent husband and father. I did not know what was specifically the cause of my tears, yet I could not stop weeping; it was as if my entire rigid, frozen façade self were melting into pools of salt tears.

This profuse weeping went on for months without my husband being aware until one day, after six weekends of dinner parties for him and his office friends, I broke down. For three weeks, I had been taking care of my daughter who had tonsillitis after I had weaned her. The worry of losing her was very real to me, but my spouse seemed completely oblivious to it. Every day she got a little better, but the anxiety seemed to be all on my shoulders. I was expected to carry on with my usual social role of housekeeper, cook, dishwasher, mother, wife and dinner hostess.

During one of these dinner parties, when I had just succeeded in presenting a delicious meal of duck a l'orange with chocolate mousse for dessert, I sat down at the beautifully arranged table with my classic dinner service and matching wine glasses, in my charmingly appointed dining room, and the tears began to roll down my face. Everyone coughed politely, but my tears did not stop. I was not emotional; I was not sobbing or heaving; I was not even making a noise. I was just weeping without stopping. I ate the duck with the tears pouring down my face and dripping into my meal; no one said a word. It was so socially "awkward" for the hostess to be weeping like that without saying a word, that perhaps no one could figure out what to say!

Neither my husband nor our guests had any expressed sympathy, concern or human compassion for me. They ate in silence and left early. I was still left to wash all the dishes and clean up, just one more weekend of feeling like a slave to people that obviously did not care about me at all. If there had been one gesture by my spouse, one arm around my shoulder or expression of sympathy, I think I would have burst like a broken dam, so perhaps it was just as well that no one showed concern.

Wings of Flight:

That night, finally, my husband could not ignore my depression. As was his nature, he saw it as a problem that money would solve, so he offered me flying lessons. He was a private pilot and had access to a military base where flying lessons were offered at a reasonable price. He always felt that I should learn to fly in case something happened to him while we were flying, and I could take over and land the plane. I took the offer as a life-line. It would get me out of the house and a new goal to achieve.

The flying classes were a challenge, and I was the only woman in the class. Some of the Texan men seemed to find it comical that I would want to learn to fly, so their attitude triggered some kind of competitive spirit that forced me not to quit. When I went to take flying lessons at Redbird Airport, I left my baby with a trusted babysitter. I got in my car and said, "Goodbye" to my child, to my husband, dog, cat, house, family and my life. It was like I was dying to them every time I took off in the plane. But my weeping had ceased.

I found a kind of courage that I had never known before in this life. Until I consciously released the emotional attachment to my loved ones, I had a crippling knot of fear in my stomach. How many times I had driven up to Redbird Airport with this knot of fear, yet I never turned around and went home. I would not let the fear win. I just stayed in the car releasing my family, letting each thing go, so I could get into the plane. Only when I had truly let go of them, could I get into that airplane comfortably and take off. This is very similar to the process of meditation where gradually you let go of all attachments to the physical body.

At first when I was flying, I was so terrified of making a mistake and of being killed, that my focus was total and intense. Several times there were near misses with Navy jets, or other planes in my vicinity, which added to the tension. This focus, as I learned, shut off the ego, and allowed me to enter my true state of being. Later, when I gained more confidence, the focus remained, but the fear left as I found myself at one with the plane and delighted to take off and land with skill. I let go of the persona that I had become; I became a pilot soaring into the sky, leaping from the runway, landing smoothly in strange airports, overcoming problems with calculations, wind, gasoline, communications, other planes, manipulating the plane through the air, and returning home triumphant over my fear of death.

I found a joy in this flying and a feeling of familiarity. Sometimes I would land at an airport near a lake and take time to sit by the lake and just ponder. The escape was just what I needed. In my mind there was no doubt that I had been a pilot in another life. My depression lifted. In spite of the skeptical Texan males in my class who expected me to drop out, I passed all my exams higher than they had and achieved a single engine pilot's license. The flying brought me a sense of my worth and depth that had not been there before, even as a very busy English teacher.

I shared with my husband that I felt I had flown a plane in another lifetime because it was so familiar; I knew I had sat in a cockpit before. He scoffed at this and told me never to tell anyone else, or they would think I was crazy. Little did he know just how "crazy" I was going to get within a few years. A month after I got my single engine license, we moved from Texas to Hawaii.

Aloha of Hawaii:

Four years after the "Tiger" dream, we were living in an idyllic village in Hawaii. I had a beautiful three-year old daughter, and a lovely home in a small community close to the most stunning white sand beach in Hawaii. We had left our very elegant house in Texas, pulled up roots and driven across the deserts of Texas, New Mexico, Arizona and Nevada to reach California's coast. I was in love with each state we drove through.

When we took off from Los Angeles for Honolulu in August, 1976, I had no idea how much this move would enhance my life. We had left the Continent of North America and entered the Continent of Polynesia, moving half way around the world from England. The spiritual energy of Hawaii was apparent the moment I smelled Honolulu's air. The tuberose lei given me at the airport sealed the love affair. This was a place I never wanted to leave.

The island magic, the beauty of mountain, trees, beach and sky, the warm weather, the excitement of a new future, dried up the tears. I was in a new place, a new home with great neighbors and a wonderful sublime energy that was Hawaii. I was substitute-teaching part time, caring for our daughter and her schooling, taking care of our 4-bedroom house, and returning to college for a Masters degree at the University of Hawaii.

We lived in a seaside village with the number one rated beach in America. Beauty and color saturated the world we lived in. Our garden produced wonderful fruits of mango, lime, papaya, avocado, tangerine, lemon and exotic perfumed flowers like jasmine, plumeria, and fragrant *pakalana*. I had painted and decorated our simple redwood house with joy and enthusiasm to modernize it. Daily we swam, played in tide pools, walked or sprinted on the stunning, white sand beach. I made new friends, started ballet lessons, went gliding at Dillingham Field, or sailing in Kailua Bay with my husband on weekends, met neighbors, enrolled my daughter in a wonderful pre-school, met other parents and opened up new horizons of life.

I thought my depression had been because I lived in Texas where I had never had many friends and where nature was a hostile desert, harsh and raw, sinister, flat, boring, hot and dry. What a contrast Texas was to the natural warm invitation of the Hawaiian ocean and flora! At that time, I had still not made the connection of my weeping and depression to the "Tiger Dream" and the meaning of taking off my wedding ring.

Although life was happier, I was no longer living an illusion of being happily married at that point. Increasingly with this move to a top executive position, my husband had become shut down, unresponsive, preoccupied and emotionally blocked. In spite of having a beautiful daughter and all that most people long for, he was not interested in fatherhood or having more children. Perhaps he was going through his own depression or mid-life crisis, but we were not communicating. My attempts to get help for our marriage in self-help books, workshops or self-examination were futile. It was a desperate feeling.

Looking back thirty years later, I see it was all a divine plan that he and I were going in different directions. But we were still good friends, and he had agreed to let me finish my Masters degree in order to have more choices of career as a single parent.

Temptation:

Thus it was not really surprising that this almost idyllic life in the bosom of abundant Nature was soon disturbed by a specter I had side-lined in my life since the birth of my daughter. A strange, mysterious, foreign, flirtatious and attractive man from the university was affecting my peaceful, almost celibate life. This fellow student, Bob, flirted out-rageously with me during class and after; he was single, and he wanted an affair with me. This was a great challenge to my integrity; it was temptation in its most obvious form. There was a transformation in me from weeping daily in Texas to feeling vital and beautiful. I came alive.

I was cautious and careful. I took my wedding vows, made in a church, seriously; I sensed in my gut an overwhelming danger to my family if I were to indulge my senses with him. I was not certain of all the reasons why I held back. But one message came through clearly; somehow I knew that I had violated my wedding vows before in a past life and had destroyed everyone. Thus I chose not to fall into temptation. I did not take action on the strong sexual messages I felt from him. I held back, but the price was high for my body. I was a woman in the sexual prime of my life, having just had a child and ready for another but married to a man who saw me as no more than the sheets on the bed. My sexual and emotional needs had been ignored for so long that they had all but dis-appeared. Yet at the university on a daily basis, I was sent unmistakable invitations for sex and more from a very attractive and flirtatious man.

I found myself in a new quandary. I was struggling daily to control my senses and the temptations there. The stress was turning into intense anxiety which all combined to create a great burning fire within—a crucible for the alchemy of breaking open the limited ego. I was being prepared for the more dramatic awakening, for the bursting forth of my spirit.

CHAPTER 6

Mercurius:
The Genie in the Bottle

This complication in the form of an attractive man was the outward sign of the inner conflicts I was suppressing. But the outward signs did not tell of the build up to this point of the stress and conditioning of an unnatural civilized life that pressed on my heart like a ton weight. The volcano that bursts apart after hundreds of quiet years does not suddenly erupt without much straining and groaning, earthquakes and rumbles deep underground. All this rumbling had been going on in my life since the "Tiger Dream" with weeping and unhappiness. Thus it was that this eruption of emotion that came to me on a night in 1979 was but the final act of inner frustration and denial that could not and would not be suppressed any longer. It was a culmination of not just one lifetime of too much conditioning, too much taming, but of lifetimes of limitations superimposed upon a natural inner joy and light I call "Spirit" and what my teacher calls the "Self."

Past Life Recall:

The ostensible explanation for the stress in my being was that I had fallen in love with the attractive foreign student, Bob, in my Master's program at the University of Hawaii, even though I was nine years married with a four year-old daughter. Through daily interactions with this fellow student, Bob, I came to learn first hand that reincarnation was real because it was obvious to me that we had had many past lives in close relationships. While sitting in the classroom, I would see visions of myself with him in different time periods of history. Sitting next to him during the lectures, I felt I was a Mogul wife trekking the Steppes of Asia next to a sled while he sat on a horse that pulled it; he was totally aware of every move of my body and my heart; our hearts beat as one in two separate bodies. Sometimes I would feel myself to be a fat and jolly mother hanging up wet clothes on a washing line in Poland in the 1800's as he, my tiny son, played tag around my legs.

In that classroom in 1979 in Hawaii, lifetimes of memories flooded my being just by being in the same vicinity with Bob. I thought I was really losing my mind as the images continued to play through me like living movies. Nothing like this had ever happened to me before. Even the feelings of familiarity with flying a plane in a past life were nothing compared to this. When I had left England, I had dreamed of his face and his dark complexion.

I had no idea about *Kundalini* nor did I know how I could be re-living past lives while being myself now simultaneously. Such interactions with close past life companions are often a trigger for *Kundalini* awakening as they spark a movement back into the nervous system where these memories are stored.

After class Bob made me feel like the most precious adorable goddess. His eyes caressed my 33 year-old body that was fit and shapely from several years of ballet lessons. There was no mistaking his sexual interest in me, but also he made me feel loved, special and desirable. That feeling of being adored by a man was something I did not feel from my husband. Although I knew my husband loved me, I never felt this magnetic adoration and sexual intensity from him. To my spouse, I was a piece of the household furniture. To the attractive student, I was all things desirable. Thus the pressure to break my wedding vows was great. I called friends and asked them, "What would you do?"

Rising Tension:
They all said, "Have an affair!" Apparently they were all doing that

45

when offered the chance. But in my heart, I knew that path was not for me. I felt sad for them that they had broken their vows, which may have been for them a healthy way to deal with sexual tension like mine. But I had this inner guide that said, "DANGER." I could not do it.

Therefore, I willed myself to adhere to my social role as married wife and mother, and shoved away the idea of being this man's adulterous lover. I said "No" to my animal nature, to the natural spirit within me that sought joy and happiness instead of duty and social obligation. It was a war within. It was a battle against my own nature. Nathan Schwartz-Salant in *Encountering Jung on Alchemy* says that I was seeking the "sacred union" the joining with God rather than other humans, which was "pressing up from the depths of the human unconscious." [1] Indeed the pressure that arose inside me at this time felt to be thousands of years of grief and denial. Arnold Mindell, the visionary Jungian analyst says:

> Our culture tells us: Be civilized, bottle up your true personality, or else let it out so quickly that you explode and go to war. Mercury is the symbol of pressure and tension, the feeling of being bottled up. He is the experience we often have of a tension headache or heart pressure, or of a stomach ache. [2]

Mindell, therapist and genius, quotes a tale from *Grimm's Fairy Tales*, in order to emphasize the importance of this type of stress or pressure in the process of personal development and integration. It is mentioned in *Working with the Dreaming Body*. The story is called "The Spirit in the Glass Bottle." Here it is paraphrased for brevity.

> A university student must return home with his studies unfinished as his father has run out of money. So he returns to the family farm and while helping his father cut wood in the forest, he wanders into a mystic grove. Here while enjoying the blessings of nature, he hears a voice

calling, "Let me out." He is puzzled, but follows the sound to an old oak tree. He buries down into the oak tree and finds a bottle. Inside the bottle is a little creature jumping up and down, "Let me out. Let me out." So the student uncorks the bottle. Immediately out springs Mercurius, the genie in the bottle who expands to a large sized man; Mercurius declares immediately that his task is to "break the neck" of whoever sets him free. The student thinks quickly and coaxes the genie back in by claiming that the genie must prove he was in the bottle as it's unbelievable that such a large being could come from such a tiny bottle. The pride of the genie is activated, and he gets himself back into the bottle just as the student corks him in again.

The genie pleads again for release only this time he promises several boons to the student in exchange for his freedom. When the student again releases the genie, Mercurius gives him the gift of healing and of transmuting plain iron into silver. With this the student can help his father and return to the university, and he becomes a great healer and doctor.[3]

This story is an obvious metaphor for the release of *Kundalini* which is sought after by yogis. The name Mercurius is a cognate of Mercury, the silver fluid used in thermometers that is silver, quick, mirroring, metallic and responds quickly to heat—similar to the character of *Kundalini* in the subtle body. According to the dictionary, "mercurial" means "sprightly, ready-witted, volatile." Mindell calls Mercury, "nothing less than the spirit of the oak tree, the source of life, death and healing.... the wotanic wild, barbaric spirit which was bottled up centuries ago in order to achieve our present level of civilization."[4]

Thus, the bottle holding Mercurius in this story is a parallel to the *Kundalini* enclosed or stored in a bulb at the base of the spine.

Kundalini can be seen by some mystics and adepts as a silver light, just like Mercury. The warning in this passage is that if Mercury is released too soon, there is a great danger. Mindell sees in this Mercury story a metaphor for the suppression of natural behavior and spontaneity which is induced by civilized life. Repressing my desire to violate my marital vows with the student, I felt this bottled up energy as incredible stress in my gut, like a soccer ball on fire.

> Europeans and Americans all have a similar dream. Our culture tells us: Be civilized, bottle up your true personality, or else let it out so quickly that you explode, and go to war. Mercury is the symbol of pressure and tension, the feeling of being bottled up.[5]

He goes on to say that tension is a natural result of this suppression, but that tension is also important as "the ripening of the fruit of wholeness."[6] So this stress I felt was a stage of maturation where my real personality was ready to burst out of its conditioned and socially compliant mask. As Emma Bragdon explains in *A Sourcebook for Helping People with Spiritual Problems,* "Spiritual problems are more likely to occur when a person rigidly holds on to a belief about how life should be and resists change."[7] I was resisting the flow of this loving opening that Bob offered because of my adherence to my wedding vows.

This was creating the same bursting feeling I had had after my daughter was born when I wept so much before I took flying lessons. It was some impulse to find joy that refused to lie down, but continued to rise up within me. It was the same bursting feeling that I got in my ballet classes when we would practice leaping across the floor. I would feel something rise up into my throat like a sort of scream that made me almost lift off into the air beyond normal heights. This bursting feeling would not die down, and I now realize that was the *Kundalini* rising.

When I went to seek relief at a meditation center in 1979, I felt that to keep Mercury [*Kundalini*] in any longer would probably make me mad or die. My desperation was a great spur to bring this release closer.

... if Mercury is not outwitted, as in our fairy tale
Mercury comes out, but could kill the patient. In
practice, this means that by simply encouraging all
tensions and stresses to leave the body, people can
develop permanent physical injuries, or else they can
actually go insane.[8]

Mindell warns that the spirit must be released gradually, "then
feelings come out which actually heal people and help them to individuate."[9] Jung says, "The process of individuation is founded on the
instinctive urge of every living creature to reach its own totality and
fulfillment."[10] This stage of fulfillment also compares to Ken Wilber's
"Centaur," Maslow's "Self-Actualization" and Loevinger's "Integrated"
levels.[11] These are mature states of the ascent of consciousness. This
is the healing boon gained from uncorking the bottle and integration
with the inner life force.

Nonetheless, the dangers from Mercury being released too "quickly
and chaotically" are that people "don't form an imagery or coherent
feeling which the ego can integrate"[12] creating confusion, and even
madness.

Most ordinary people either bottle him [Mercury] up
so long that they die from him, or they let him out,
can't handle the consequences and actually go psychotic. One side of the spectrum is madness, and the
other is vegetative chaos, or illness.[13]

Mindell warns that "modern psychotherapists" do not understand
the "Mercury" element. I believe that our entire culture shuts it off by
denying it in children and adults. Today we even go so far as to prescribe
drugs for this free spirit found particularly in young boys. But spirit has
its own life and will since it truly is the life force within. If we suppress
it today, it must go somewhere. It must find an outlet at some point. Just
like a tree that has had one limb sealed, it will make shoots in another
part of the branch and manifest its growing nature somewhere else.

John Weir Perry, a former professor at the University of California at San Francisco, says that spirit wants to seek release from its entrapment within habits and mental structures. He believes that "Spiritual work is one of liberating this dynamic energy, which must break free of its suffocation in old forms... "[14] The genie must get out of the bottle.

When I walked into a meditation center in July 1979, to meet this awakening experience, I did not know that I was about to participate in an initiation which would send me into chaos, but which held the promise of integration and wholeness. Mindell's words accurately foretell what I faced from my culture.

> Often it is easier to be sick, to suffer unbearable and relentless pressure, or to go mad, than it is to be in the reality of a spirit which brings one up against social conflict, mis-understanding, and the difficulties of being an individual. You see, it is a challenge, a mythical challenge, a proprioceptive pain to be a human being.[15]

I remember feeling as if I had a huge football of black lead in my belly that was Mercury bottled up—it would not let me feel anything except pain. Was I to be saved or destroyed? At this point, I am sure had I known the risks involved, I would still have taken the path I took. The agony of Mercury bottled up and bursting to break loose was more than I could bear much longer.

It was with some anticipation, therefore, that I agreed to go to a meditation center in our village on Friday, 13th July, 1979, with my friend, Cheryl, as she assured me that this would help my stress. Little did she know how well it would work and how this night would change my entire life and that of my family forever.

CHAPTER 7

Shaktipat Initiation

"I saw the world through the darkness of my own eyes and everything looked so dark. Then my Guru applied the lotion of grace to my eyes, and the darkness was removed."

—Brahmananda

On the night of Friday, 13th July, 1979, my neighbor, Cheryl, and I rode in her yellow Volvo a mile from our houses to the meditation center. Cheryl was anxious to share with me the peace and tranquility she had found there. I had a good feeling about the word "meditation" as my daughter's preschool teacher, Anita, had been a meditator, and had been calm and composed in all kinds of crises, so I was already convinced that meditation would certainly help me get some relief for my ball of tension and stress.

In a shady road just off the beach was the pretty single-story home owned by an Italian/American couple, Rob and Lea. They ushered us in with joy sparkling in their eyes. Since I was new to meditation, Rob took about ten minutes to explain how I should meditate and follow the program. I listened carefully. Rob said that I should participate as fully as I could in following the chant which was on tape, and when the tape ceased I should sit quietly and repeat in my mind the phrase, *"Om Namah Shivaya"* any time my mind wandered off into other thoughts.

Then Rob ushered the small group of people into a large, darkened room, with no furniture, the men on the right side and the women on the other, sitting cross-legged on pillows on the carpet. At the front of the room was a large picture of a bearded Indian man with a red dot on his forehead. I felt a little uncomfortable about this picture and decided I would not look at it, nor worry about it since I was there for meditation and the sacred icons of these Italian people who seemed so warm and loving was none of my business.

The program started with a hymn sung in a strange language. Following this, Rob read a passage from a book by the spiritual teacher with questions and answers. He put on a tape, and we started to chant. There was lyrical Indian drumming and some organ music which offset the chant phrases that were repeated, first the tape leading singers and then the audience. It reminded me of the "call and response" of the Episcopal churches where I had sung in the choir throughout my childhood. I found myself relaxing. The language was not English but Sanskrit. I could not make out any recognizable phonemes for quite some time, and then quite naturally, I got into the swing of it. We chanted in call and response with the music melody repeated for two rounds before changing to a related melody for two rounds and then returning to the first melody. It seemed soothing, most comforting and relaxing. Although I did not understand the words, I stuck with it, giving it my all as always. The chanting continued for thirty minutes.

Then a new tape was started with a very slow, almost dirge-like and rather anguished chant of *"Om Namah Shivaya."* This was the tape which would put me into meditation—the "mantra" tape. In the darkened room, I felt floaty and noticed that the tension in my stomach had not occupied my mind at all. I noticed how very relaxed I felt. I felt dreamy and safe. My body started to sway, and sometimes I felt a muscle jerk as if something readjusted. My arms felt ephemeral, gradually feeling stranger in the lower arm, but I could not move them as I felt too relaxed.

The Genie Escapes:

After 30 minutes the tape stopped and there was silence. Everyone by now was in a very quiet and peaceful state. I remembered the instructions to repeat the same syllables silently inside. I was aware then that my arms and hands were dead and paralyzed, like the blood had drained out of them. Gradually my fingers became rigid, stretched out in front as if pulled. Strangely, I was curious but not alarmed.

My breathing got faster, and I had a realization that all the tension inside me would leave me. The tension in my gut was bubbling up out of my mouth, and I found that my head was naturally falling back in order for these bubbles to emerge. For a while it was amusing to feel these bubbles coming out of my mouth. But I started to sob. Somewhat embarrassed and self-conscious, I blew my nose quietly. Then I sat cross-legged again and said the mantra quietly under my breath.

Suddenly my head was jerked back firmly as if by a very strong tug from behind. My throat was thrust towards the ceiling and my head pressed farther back than I ever thought it would go, so that I wondered if my neck would break. I could barely breathe. At the same time my spine stiffened like a rod, so I could not relieve the pressure on my head and neck. The force was phenomenal and totally in control. I stayed rigidly locked in this position while the bubbles of tension continued to rise, bubbling out of my fish-like mouth, my chest heaving in deep sobs and tears pouring down my face.

Fixed in this position, sobbing out of control, I remained thus for at least fifteen minutes until the tension bubbles emptied out. My hands and their rigid, spread fingers were receiving waves of blue electricity. I seemed to be plugged into some enormous energy socket through my hands. I had no idea where it was coming from. Then just as unexpectedly the tension holding my neck released and I curled up into a pile and unashamedly sobbed and sobbed.

It was like having a weeping catharsis in public. Yet I did not care who saw this dramatic sobbing. I was relieved of my tension. I was soaring in bliss. My social concerns had fled. All I knew was incredible relief because the tension had indeed ALL gone. I felt all warm and fuzzy as I used to feel when I had cried as a child and had been comforted by my mother. The group of people in the meditation center quietly left me to recover while they went into another room for snacks. Some were most uncomfortable with my outburst. Some were puzzled. But Rob and Lea were grinning with joy, their eyes sparkling with excitement.

After a while, I was able to stop crying and join the others feeling somewhat embarrassed but not really caring because I was in such bliss. Rob and Lea told me my *"Kundalini"* had been awakened. I had no idea what that meant, but I knew that I felt incredible. They seemed to be thrilled about it. Cheryl was not very sure, being confused and puzzled as were some of the other guests. Rob said, "This is a very auspicious day for you." I really did not pay much attention to his words at that point. All I knew was that I came there as a wreck of tension at 7:30 p.m. and by 9:30 p.m., I was leaving on a cloud. I felt as if I were floating three feet above the ground. I felt "in love" in the deepest way. I felt totally whole. I was an entirely new being in just two hours.

That evening after Cheryl dropped me off, I looked up at the sky really seeing the stars. I felt them all speaking to me as my best friends. I felt such a close affinity to every single star, so that I could almost give them personality profiles. I was equal to the stars, I was among them and I felt them singing to me. At home I sat down in the semi-dark to contemplate what had happened and a fly alighted on my arm. I watched it walk around and then somehow, I knew I could communicate with the fly. So I gave it instructions about where to walk and it did everything I asked. If such a thing had occurred before this awakening, I should have been shocked, but now it seemed normal that I could communicate fully with a fly, and it would do whatever I asked of it.

Something in me had definitely shifted gears or dimensions. I felt deeply in love with the fly, with the stars, with life. From a nervous wreck with a ball of unrelenting tension and an out of control life, in

CHAPTER 7 SHAKTIPAT INITIATION

only a few hours, I had become a calm, divine being at one with the universe. I had no way of understanding anything at that point because all I knew was intense and unrelenting bliss.

Years later I was to find that on the Mayan Calendar, this day sign was *Chicchan* number 9 which is the Sky Serpent or *Kundalini,* and nine is for completion of a universal cycle, fulfillment. On the Gregorian calendar it was Friday, 13th of July. The genie had burst its bottle. I was tasting the bliss of the awakening, without knowing that there was yet an alchemical cleansing process I still had to go through.

CHAPTER 8

The Kundalini Awakens

*"And when you feel God's Presence, you will feel that the
divine energy, the kundalini, is already awakened and
is rising towards the highest."*

—*Shri Chinmoy*

There was no doubt that, in spite of how it appeared to my friend
and the other meditators, I had experienced something very rare
and wonderful in Rob and Lea's house. In 1979 this phenomena of
Kundalini awakening was hardly known outside of the sacred texts
of India or the aboriginal peoples of the world. In the West, there are
examples of this type of awakening power with evangelists who appear
to give healing energy to cripples and sick people, so they are cured
instantly. But most people see this as some kind of anomaly or trickery.
It is not widely understood in our culture that there is some magical
energy available to humanity.

I came to learn that my teacher was the being in the large photograph in Rob's house that I had seen on my first visit. He had recently
come from India to create a "Meditation Revolution" in the West and
spread this yoga as a divine practice for Westerners. In traveling around

the countries of the West, he had developed a network of centers and ashrams for people to learn to meditate in a sacred and protected environment. I had fortunately found one of these centers in Hawaii.

My guru and teacher, carefully monitors, watches over and supervises the ascent of this divine awakening in every student until the student reaches the goal of full god-realization and wholeness. How this is done with thousands of souls or students cannot be explained easily to a Western mind although the laws of quantum physics now can explain it. Years later in my research, I was to discover a clue to how this mystical connection to a saint was possible. The "Einstein-Podolsky-Rosen Paradox" says that if two particles have been "intimately associated and are then separated in space, they are 'connected' nonetheless. If one of them is perturbed in certain ways, the other one is affected *instantaneously.*"[1] It is said that disciples/chelas have had close connections with their spiritual teacher in past lifetimes prior to this lifetime. Thus, the teacher and the disciple are interconnected like a cosmic family.

My understandings came slowly and over many years of experiences, reading and research. I learned to see how, throughout my life, I had been quietly prepared for this awakening, starting perhaps with the vision of Jesus at age 13. Nonetheless, when Rob told me my *Kundalini* had been awakened, I had absolutely no idea what he was talking about. Few in the West then had ever heard of it. It is, in fact, a beneficent boon, a great blessing and a magical gift. A Darrel Irving interview with Gopi Krishna reports, "Every person who is psychic, a genius, or an enlightened sage, has an awakened *kundalini* to a greater or lesser extent."[2]

Caduceus:
There is a familiar symbol of it in Western culture. The symbol for medicine and a common logo on ambulances is the caduceus, the rod with two snakes coiled around it in spirals. At the top are two wings which represent the two petals of the *ajna chakra* more commonly known as "the third eye." Images of Mercury or Hermes show him with this staff in his hand.

Mercury is the symbolic representation of *Kundalini*. As Mercurius in the alchemical process turns lead into silver, so the *Kundalini* turns the human being into divinity. The caduceus in our world is a symbol of healing, medicine, health, and transformation. It shows a central staff with two snakes ascending to a meeting point below two wings with a globe on top of the rod.[3]

The caduceus' central rod represents the central column akin to the spine in the physical body called *sushumna* (a Sanskrit word with no equivalent word in English). No surgeon will find this *sushumna* as it is part of the subtle body. The *sushumna*, our caduceus' rod, parallels the spinal column from the base of the spine to the base of the skull. Just as the spinal column has a structure that protects the spinal cord of the central nervous system, so the *sushumna* is a hollow non-physical, auric structure that offers an ascending tube for the *Kundalini* or light force and within it are three channels. The concept of a vine or ladder is also implied by this rod as described by Shipibo-Conibo Indians of the Peruvian Amazon.[4]

The *sushumna* is identified with the planet Mercury and the qualities of liquid mercury, quicksilver, and volatility perhaps because the *Kundalini* within the *sushumna* appears like liquid light and has characteristics of lightning. People who meditate, yogis, mystics and those who study the Oriental martial arts based upon *Chi* or *Ki* are able to see this light. The great yoga masters were able to assist their disciples with the ascent of the *Kundalini* because they could see where it was blocked or stuck and send their own psychic power to aid in releasing it.

The two snake-like tubes which, in some depictions, spiral three and a half times each around the central rod, meet and cross at the *sushumna* in their ascent. The text *Shatchakra-nirupana* describes the *Kundalini* thus, "She is beautiful as a chain of lighting and fine as a [lotus] fibre, and shines in the minds of the sages."[5] The two outer channels represent the flow of the awakened *Kundalini* energy called *ida* and *pingala* (no English equivalent names). The channel, *ida,* is identified with the left side, negatively charged, feminine side of the body, ending above the right nostril and has characteristics of coolness related to the moon; the *pingala*, is identified with the right side, positively charged, masculine side that ends above the left nostril and has characteristics of heat related to the sun.[6]

As stated earlier, the *Kundalini* is said to be in a bulb at the very lower region of the torso in the perineum area between the anus and sexual organs which is part of the subtle nervous system. The *Shakti Kundalini* is a "little female serpent... about as thick as the hair of the boar, white and coiled three and a half times around a symbolic *lingam*" coiled up like a cobra in a basket.[7] On page 48 of Arthur Avalon's *Serpent Power*, Sir John Woodroffe's classic translation of Indian spiritual lore into Western language, he indicates that *Kundalini* is the static (masculine) element and the body the active/dynamic (feminine) element when humans are unawakened; this focuses the electrical polarity at the physical level. But when *Kundalini* awakens, She becomes the active feminine element and "unites with Shiva [masculine] in the *Sahasrara* Lotus," the crown.[8]

This means *Kundalini* becomes the dynamic partner. The active energy of the *Kundalini Shakti*, a female goddess as two spiraling snakes, wraps around the central *sushumna*, the male, until the two merge in the *ajna* chakra, more commonly referred to as the "third eye" or pineal gland above and between the eyebrows. From there the energy ascends as one to the crown of the head.

The human subtle body becomes the dynamic *Kundalini* herself and Her counterpart is the ever static, divine, Shiva or Lord. It is as if, in the process of this alchemical transformation, the human being is spiraled up to a higher octave of awareness and evolution. In the un-awakened state, the body is the active element, which is limited, but in the awakened state, the higher self or subtle body is the active element and fully interacting with the cosmic dimensions. Ajit Mookerjee's classic text on *Kundalini: The Arousal of the Inner Energy* explains more:

> The coiled Kundalini is the female energy existing in
> latent form, not only in every human being but in every

> atom of the universe...The Kundalini Shakti ...is the
> vast potential of psychic energy...When this Kundalini
> Shakti moves to manifest itself, it becomes dynamic.[9]

This coiling or spiral concept is integral to all living beings. An unmistakable similarity exists between the caduceus and the DNA spiral as uncovered by Jeremy Narby, the respected anthropologist, whose text *The Cosmic Serpent* is significant for bringing the mystical world of the shaman into alignment with the discoveries of our scientists about the inherent nature and unity of everything.

Of the caduceus he quotes Chevaliar and Gheerbrandt who "write, 'the caduceus's staff corresponds to the axis of the world and the serpents to the Kundalini,' the cosmic energy inside every being."[10] He says that this symbol has been used around the world for healing. In China the caduceus symbol is the YIN/YANG logo which is the coiling of two snakes also.[11]

It is this energy, *Kundalini,* that pervades and enervates the world as we see it. According to Ajit Mookerjee, *Kundalini* is "in every atom of the universe," and is "the vast potential of psychic energy, the body's most powerful thermal current."[12]

The awakening process brings the undulating energy up the spine to the crown, clearing out the dross and dregs of unconscious life through all our incarnated lifetimes. So when the inner *Kundalini* is awake it turns us inward to our source—the Divine and all the limitations of "Little Ego" are burned up. It is "the beginning of the spiritual journey" that enables us to enter the inner world. David G. White explains of *Kundalini* that, "She is divine energy (*shakti*) and female materiality (*prakrti*) but she is also a tigress...she is the serpentine female principle within the subtle body."[13]

When I read this, I recalled my "Tiger Dream" from 1974. In 1979, my meditation center leader, Rob, had given me a photo of my teacher, and when I meditated upon it, I saw again that very same tiger who had come into my dream in 1974. It had been obviously a *shaktipat* dream.

Serpents and Snakes:

The caduceus' double snakes have been a persistent symbol of healing in Western culture, but few people would make the connection to *Kundalini* because this spiritual knowledge has been hidden. Jeremy Narby states, "Western culture has cut itself off from the serpent/life principle."[14] In this era, with the discovery of the double helix DNA, the parallels to the spiral snakes around the caduceus are obvious. Jeremy Narby has explored the similarity and believes that, though Western man cut himself off from this knowledge of spirals, it has been rediscovered through the scientific discovery of DNA. His research points to this serpent as "The Great Invisible Serpent, which is causal and timeless, a master of the vital principle and of all the forces of nature... found at the beginning of all cosmogonies."[15]

It would seem that the serpent image is as ancient and universal as human life, and the imagery of snakes and cobras exists in cultures even where snakes are not found, such as Hawaii. In a book on Hawaiian *huna* [philosophy] called, *Recovering the Ancient Magic* by Max Freedom Long, it shows a female *kahuna* with a cobra emerging from her third eye[16] (above and between the eyebrows). This image is identical to that found in the Pharaohs and priests of ancient Egypt. The cobra-appendage emerging from the Third Eye (pineal gland) is obviously a symbol of *Kundalini* awakened. According to Alice Bailey:

> It is the eye of the inner vision, and he who has opened it can direct and control the energy of matter, see all things in the Eternal Now, and therefore be in touch with causes more than with effects, read the Akashic records, and see clairvoyantly.[17]

Clearly these are representations of the esoteric "snake" of *Kundalini* found in disparate traditions all over the world. The rising snake symbol is not just found in the caduceus or coming through the third eye. In India and other Buddhist countries, certain deities' statues are shown with multiple cobras over the crown. The headdress rises over the fontanel and forward over the frontal lobes of the head, like a forward leaning cobra. The ceremonial hats of the Tibetan lamas also curl over the forehead like cobras, as do the head-dresses of Hawaiian royalty and American Indians. These cobra-like head adornments are also found in the sculptures of Greek Athena, Roman Minerva in the Pharaohs of Egypt, and so forth. We also see a similar rising crown in bishop hats from ancient Christianity. The shamans of various cultures and the American Indian chief's all show rising feathers above the crown or, like the Siberian Shamans, antelope horns. Even remote cultures like the aborigine of Australia have this rising plume above the head. It clearly represents a kind of antenna that we might use to receive radio or television signals.

These depictions of cobras indicate the ascendant or elevated consciousness of the person but may also represent the ability to "tune in" to other dimensions. When the *Kundalini* rises into the Third Eye, and then emerges through the crown chakra or *sahasrara*, many higher faculties, including a scalar wave are established. A scalar wave is a type of standing wave; above the crown, it would pick up data at a meta-level which reaches outside of the Earth's or even the solar system's frequencies. This would account for clairvoyance, clairaudience, and the ability to read the Akashic records. Robert Chaney says, "Through raising the kundalini and unfolding the Third Eye one attains great wisdom and spiritual creative power—the eternalness of all things becomes known."[18]

As a result, once this snake-like power emerges from the crown it opens up a whole universe of information and a conscious connection between the human and the cosmic. Bruce Lipton discusses the "invisible forces" that exist in the electromagnetic spectrum which "profoundly impact every facet of biological regulation" including "scalar energy." These electromagnetic waves such as microwave, radio waves, the light spectrum etc, influence DNA and RNA, and alter gene regulation, cell function, hormones, nerves and "protein synthesis." Lipton continues, "electromagnetic frequencies are a hundred times more efficient in relaying environmental information than physical signals such as hormones, neuro-transmitters... "[19] So a being with this scalar wave attribute is going to be able to understand information on multiple levels from all over the universe. Such a being cannot be fooled by lies or manipulation. Dr. Lana Marconi states that "Scalar energy is a 5th dimension healing energy that science can only measure from its health effects." Dr. Marconi continues that people, when exposed to scalar energy, were able to reach transcendent states easily.[20]

The Third Eye:

Thus these rising snakes or feathers indicate access to a scalar wave that enables cosmic awareness after the chakras of the body have been purified by the rising *Kundalini* and merged in the pineal gland or the Third Eye. According to Plato in *The Republic,* "the soul... has an organ purified and enlightened... [the pineal gland]" that makes truth become visible.[21] Manly Hall explains in *The Occult Anatomy of Man* that the third eye or pineal gland, "is a spiritual organ... which is a connecting link between human and the divine."[22] The pineal gland is a mystery to science. It indeed has been shown to have rods and cones like our eyes. Although it is buried inside the brain, it is not actually brain tissue but connected to the throat, and it has been shown to appear inside the fetus at forty-nine days after conception before gender even appears.[23]

Such indications of the rising cobra above the head and the ability to see truth are not easy to verify by typical empirical research methods; however, Carlos Castaneda, apprentice to the Sorcerer, don Juan, does indicate that the power of *seeing* that allows a sorcerer to know instantly the truth of a situation comes from over the top of the head.[24] He also explains that his teacher, don Juan, had something that would come out of his head, "something that was not a double but a horrendous, menacing shape... we call... the nagual."[25] Similarly, these great saints in India with the cobras looming over their frontal lobes were revered as "nagas" which is a Sanskrit word for "king cobra." I have also seen with my inner third eye a huge eagle above the frontal lobes of an American Indian friend of mine as he was doing ceremony. I have also seen five cobras above the head of a friend who was very spiritual.

Since the completion of this *Kundalini* process, I also experience such "knowing" about people and situations where I know without any facts what motivated someone, who they were as a moral being, and how the situation had come about. There is no course that can teach this skill. It has also enabled me to know things about the past which I can heal, and about the future which I can prepare for.

The aura of such a being with an awakened third eye and these cobras emerging over the crown would be much greater than that of ordinary persons, and their positive influence on others would also be profound. This knowledge of the *Kundalini* serpent's role in spiritual attainment has been part of world cultures through history. It is universally found in symbols of priests and saints, so it is clear that the knowledge was available, and yet how many people know of this?

Should this attainment not be something to hail and revere? But sadly all that I have explained in this chapter was totally unknown to me when I received *Shaktipat* in 1979. I had received an inestimable gift, found a magical wonder to being born as a human, yet not only did I know nothing about it, but no information was available to me. I was on my own but for my guru's love.

CHAPTER 9

The Journey Begins

Today more people can relate to *Kundalini* awakening because of the spread of yoga in the West by many enlightened teachers during the Twentieth Century. The traditional methods of *Kundalini* awakening from Indian literature are explained through its great spiritual lineages and literature and many great Indian teachers have come to the West to enlighten us. For me it was more than one event. The dream of the tiger in 1974 started me on a path of purification, and five years later, through a mantra and chanting, I received the spiritual spark of a great teacher.

So as I sat in that meditation center a happy confluence of circumstances occurred to give me this awakening. I was karmically ready, as Mindell put forth; I had reached a state of "inner maturation" by choosing a moral high road that suppressed the wild spirit within, and I had released Mercury, the "barbaric spirit."[1] I was chanting a *chaitanya* or living mantra, a classic device for bringing the two sides of the brain and being into alignment. I was in a meditation center where my teacher's teachings were put into practice and his spirit was invoked. According to the much respected text of Swami Vishnu Tirtha in *Devatma Shakti (Kundalini): Divine Power*:

> The astral force can also be roused by the magnetic influence of other persons. Such great personalities

have their prana and mind on a higher potentiality
and when approached they tend to raise the prana of
others from a lower potentiality to a higher one. The
process may be compared with the flow of an electric current... [that] depends wholly on the will of the
master mind.[2]

I was so fortunate to have been able to find a meditation place close
to my house and a guru of such great knowledge who was able to trans-
mit this incredible experience to me. But all the preparation had not
been easy or comfortable to make me a ripe subject for the cork to come
out and for Mercury to be released. The awakening process is a joint
effort, a partnership. The disciple must be prepared and readied for this
influx of energy, and then, if he or she is fortunate, the spiritual spark
comes and, like the sperm into the ripe ovum, a great transmutation
takes place and a new spiritual entity is born.

I was purified by my weeping episodes after my daughter's birth.
I was tense and taut by my resistance to sexual infidelity and suppression of my natural urges. I had been bottled up with this life force that
demanded release. I was fit from my ballet lessons, so that my body was
primed. All this made me ready when my teacher answered that call
from my soul; when that blue electricity came into my hands during
the *shaktipat initiation*, we were directly connected long enough for me
to experience a dramatic transformation.

Shaktipat:
Swami Vishnu Tirtha says that *Shaktipa*t is "the process of spiritual-
izing a man with the charge of psychic force...not to be confused with
mesmerism or hypnotism, because... [*Shaktipat]* is everlasting and ele-
vating."[3] I was fortunate to be the recipient of *Shaktipat* by my teacher,
a swami from India who toured the United States and the world in the
70's. This set me on a path of the great yoga that "can be acquired only
through the favour of a perfect master... without any effort on the part
of the initiated."[4] Many yogis practice difficult *asanas* or postures for

years to acquire this state, and it had been dropped into my lap by sheer grace. I had received the rarest of gifts, the most incredible boon had come to my life, but only people who have been there themselves could comprehend my good fortune. People who knew me saw that I was different, happier, quieter, more internal; I had transformed, but they did not know how. So began my interaction with world as a butterfly rather than as a caterpillar.

When the *Kundalini* awakens it is a dramatic transformational force. In *Transformations of Myth through Time* Joseph Campbell explains, "As that serpent power enters the field of those sequential centers [chakras] the whole psychology of the individual is transformed."[5] So the movement of this energy up the spine after the awakening is to clean and dissolve impressions and traumas from the subtle body. This is a dramatic cleansing system that will change a person's outlook on life, their way of relating to others, and their world view much as might a near-death experience dissolve a person's fear of death.

Chakras:

The chakras are like spinning wheels of energy or intersections which affect the subtle nerves in their respective sections of the body. They might also be considered transducers which modulate the energy both from the body up to the higher selves, and down from the higher faculties into the body. An adept meditator is able to see them within his or her own body, and that is how the knowledge of their existence has been passed down.

These chakras are like the portals to other dimensions or frequencies. When the *Kundalini* is activated, it cleans out the chakras of negative impressions, or *samskaras*—the ancient memories and traumas of past lives. As each chakra is cleansed by the *Kundalini*, it creates an opening which activates the next highest chakra making that too spin and become cleansed. The common chakras discussed in most modern treaties about them, are these seven. From top down they are *Saharara* (crown), *Ajna* (third eye behind the eyebrows), *Vissudha* (throat), *Anahata* (heart), *Manipura* (belly), *Svadhisthana* (pubic), *Muladhara* (root). There are many books now which show the deeper meaning and cleansing properties of each chakra.

As the mercurial fluid of light spins these wheels and as the *Kundalini* ascends the *sushumna,* different kinds of experiences take place in the nervous system which are associated with past life and present life disturbances that have been imprinted on those nerves. Subconscious fearful concepts, traumas and experiences rise up to the conscious mind like bubbles of hot air. This can overwhelm the conscious mind and make the unprepared feel that they are losing rationality. For as the shining *Kundalini* moves up the central channel it cleanses out all "blocks" in the emotional, mental, and subtle body. How this works is explained by Barbara Brennan:

> Most of us react to unpleasant experiences by blocking our feeling and stopping a great deal of our natural energy flow.... The chakras become blocked, or clogged with stagnated energy, spin irregularly, or backwards (counterclockwise) and even, in the case of disease, become severely distorted or torn.[6]

In our lifetimes we go through experiences good and bad. Each one of these creates impressions which are stored or "sucked up" into our "psychic" storage (subconscious) which is not cleaned out or healed for eons, passing from lifetime to lifetime. Since we know how computer chips are able to store massive amounts of data on tiny nano-sized photographic chips today, it is not impossible to imagine tiny biological cells that store multiple levels of information. Not only can biological cells store massive memories and information, but they can also be impacted and changed by energetic influences.

The biologist, Dr. Bruce Lipton with Steve Bhaerman, in their seminal work on the effects of beliefs on cell formation and reaction, clearly states that "scientific studies over the last fifty years have consistently revealed that 'invisible forces' of the electromagnetic spectrum profoundly, impact every facet of biological regulation." They state, "the subconscious mind is a repository of stimulus-response tapes derived from instincts and learned experiences;... it will play the same behav-ioral responses to life's signals over and over again."[8] These impressions are hidden from the conscious mind, so that we have no active aware-ness they are there, like the pain body. Depression is perhaps a result of this hidden store of pain or misery that we are carrying around stored in our subconscious.

Subconscious:
Thus, it is not magical thinking to believe that our past experiences are still lodged within our subtle bodies and are still influencing us in this body. In India, where these topics have been studied for thousands of years, these quantum impressions are called "*Samskaras*." We might call them the subconscious (below conscious) memories from past lives and experiences since, "The subconscious mind is a programmable 'software' into which our life experiences are downloaded."[9]

The contents of this biological store of past life traumas are not known consciously to us as we arrive in each new life, yet the contents are continuously creating problems and conflicts in each lifetime that perhaps produce more "karma" or debts to pay back. Since this awak-ening, I have learned that any pain is a message to listen to my body, to tune into my heart, to see the cause and hear its message. But not everyone is able to turn within in this way. People have beliefs, ideas and subconscious conflicts within which they often cannot see and resolve. Ken Carey explains that disease "is a subconscious strategy created by those who are spiritually suffering; it is designed to free them from the false gods—conflicting values and ideas—that hold them in their grip."[10] The sense of "false gods" means that we have been deceived into not understanding our true worth and abilities. Is that our "Little Ego", the entity that fights us in meditation?

When we do not know the truth of who we are, when we are oper-ating from one side of ourselves only, we make mistakes because we do not have access to the heart's wisdom. We create trauma and karma for ourselves with an unending story line. This makes a "Catch 22," a sort of ouroboros snake devouring its tail, or an endless merry-go-round from which we can never exit; for without knowing what is in the biological and emotional store (subconscious), we are more or less victims of that hidden, toxic bag of powerful emotions and feelings that we cannot control or understand but which keep on creating conflict and grief for us.

It has been said that 94% of our behavior on any given day is subconscious, and only a small percent of our day is fully conscious. When people give their lives to religious contemplation or meditation, they are making an effort to change this percentage. Meditation is one way of getting in touch with the contents of the subconscious and through the light of inner knowledge, lightening the load of hidden pain. Meditation allows for a gradual change in how we are ruled by the subconscious, the "Little Ego," and the "pain body."

When the hidden pain inside us reaches full capacity, when life becomes unbearable, depressing, joyless and the person experiences "the dark night of the soul," it is in fact a significant marker of a new phase. The reincarnating pattern, the constant rebirth into a new body only to discover the same old tangles, disappointments, griefs, webs of deceit and confusion lifetime after lifetime, is reaching an end. One cannot input any more of this. When it is full to capacity and the smell of its foul contents is disturbing and pervasive, despair, madness, and depression may take over. The pain body's influence is just too uncomfortable. It is the dark before the dawn, so it is not time to escape, but to seek for the light, the answer to the depression within. A person with great luck may finally turn to spiritual knowledge, to meditation, to therapy and to wise shamanic teachers for a way out.

Willis Harmon says, "Access to unconscious processes is facilitated by attention to feelings, emotions, and inner imagery... by various meditative disciplines."[11] These might include Tai Chi, Martial Arts, Art, Chi Gong, Yoga or any practice which takes one out of the confines of the conscious mind, like my flying lessons did. There are many energy therapies now available such as Yoga, Tai Chi, Acupuncture, Hypnotism, Acupressure, NLP, EMDR, Energy medicine, Shiatsu, Meridian Tapping Techniques and Emotional Freedom Techniques which allow people to release some of the emotional charges in the subconscious even without deep meditation. These processes are old and new, have often integrated different healing modalities, and they work. They relieve some of the pain and emotion from this storage bag.

But once that magical *Shakti Kundalini* snake has uncoiled Her head and begun the ascent through the nerves of the spinal column, little effort is required to empty this misery store of its contents. The process is facilitated and magnified, almost at lightning speed by the *Kundalini* although most teachers say the full cleansing does not all happen in one lifetime. If the process is interrupted by death, it will be continued in subsequent lifetimes from the same point.

Once the *Kundalini* is active, good and bad impressions from lifetimes start flying out of the mind and body. In one second there is intense pain and agony causing even tears to come, and the next uncontrollable laughter and mirth. One can feel joy one minute, and then a few minutes later, feel intense fear or even grief without any visible concrete cause. This is the cleansing power of *Kundalini*. Her energy is coursing through the brain's subtle channels, cleaning out any foreign ideas, beliefs and fears that are lodged there. This is the sacred guide and light on the path into the darkness of the subconscious mind.

When the *Kundalini* is awakened, it is God calling us back to our home, unwinding the tape of lifetimes of impressions, and erasing them like a crazy night dream. We can find again the very core of who we are without the conditioning of the mind. What a great gift this is! We suffer here so much because we do not know the truth of who we are. Our powerful subconscious controls our lives. We identify with what is false and with beliefs programmed into us by others or by the superstitions or biases of the past. We are tossed to and fro on the ocean of misery that is full of many lifetimes of ignorance in spite of all our best desires and efforts. No wonder so many people are depressed! No wonder my efforts to improve myself by reading scripture did not work! I began to really appreciate the gift of *Kundalini*.

Thus this cleansing light snakes its way into and through the subtle nerve threads of the body and expels blocks to the flow of pure energy. The past life agonies and griefs appear briefly, as if they are taking a last stand on the stage of opposites before the *Kundalini* transmutes them into light. The genie gave to the student in *Grimm's Fairy Tale* the gift of changing iron into silver; so the *Kundalini* endows us with this ability to change the sorrow and evil of past existences into light and transcendence. It is a parallel process of human alchemy to chemical alchemy.

However, there is a parallel to this fairy tale that brings a note of caution. As Mercurius threatened when he first came out of the bottle, when the person who opens the bottle does not know what he is doing, Mercurius can kill—or at least make a person insane. Everything comes up for review. Every concept of who one believes oneself to be is being turned over like a huge mattress once the *Kundalini* is activated. Our belief system is in for a complete overhaul. For no person is the ascent easy; everyone will experience some intensity since all the latent fears, agonies, hatreds and such of all ones' past lives are caught in one's tissues and these will be eased out by this flowing light (*Kundalini*) in order that one become "new"— literally reborn. The path within is not for the faint hearted yet it brings great hope.

Complications:

With Gopi Krishna, his awakening *Kundalini* traveled only through the *pingala,* the fire channel in its ascent, causing him to suffer interminably. It was only when he was able, after much tribulation, to open the *ida* channel, the cooling side, that he was restored physically and mentally.

> Could it be that I had aroused Kundalini through pingala, the solar nerve which regulates the flow of heat in the body and is located on the right side of *sushumna*?... the idea flashed across my brain to make a last-minute attempt to rouse *ida*,.... There was a sound like a nerve thread snapping and instantaneously a silvery streak passed zigzag through the spinal cord, exactly like the sinuous movement of a white serpent in rapid flight pouring an effulgent, cascading shower of brilliant vital energy into my brain... I was really free.[12]

This is a key reason all wise teachers, saints and responsible spiritual guides do not recommend practices to stimulate the *Kundalini* unless a person is closely supervised by an awakened teacher. Shri Chinmoy is very clear about the dangers of awakening the *Kundalini* too soon. He says purification is essential before opening the chakras, as "Awakening the kundalini power without first being purified is like giving a child a knife. There is every possibility of his misusing it." He goes on to say that the heart center is the best place to focus on awakening the *Kundalini* as it is the most purified, and it will protect one from the dangers of the other chakras.[13]

Sometimes when the *Kundalini* is awakened, strange fears and passions can arise which are similar to mental illness such as schizophrenia and psychosis. Shri Chinmoy, one of the most enlightened speakers on this topic, says "Many people go crazy when they open up the chakras before purification takes place."[14]

Unfortunately, in the West, because of our lack of knowledge of this natural phenomena of *Kundalini* awakening, people react in fear and aversion, and doctors, used to seeing pathologies, medicate with drug control. There may be paranoia, psychedelic visions, psychosis and fear because of the lowering of the veils between dimensions as the chakras open, and the boundaries between oneself and others evaporate; even for the meditators who have been seeking this experience, it can still be disorienting and fearful. We have spent our lives focused on one reality based on many false beliefs, and after this *Kundalini* process, only our true nature remains. We can go to bed with a cold and everyone sympathizes, but woe to anyone whose mind suffers a transformation.

If there is too sudden an explosion of the subconscious material, like Mercurius coming out too soon, it can be overwhelming to the mind and people can become imbalanced. So this is the danger especially for people living in Western countries. Loren Mosher, a Harvard psychiatrist with many years of psychiatric experience states he feels "hopeless about the future of anyone misfortunate enough to receive the label" of "mentally imbalanced" in America.[15]

This adds another element of courage to the exploration of the inner realms. Not only must one deal with the inner demons making their appearance to the conscious mind, but one must deal with the social stigma and interpersonal problems of living with a family who cannot understand what is happening. Awakening the *Kundalini* can be frightening as my family discovered. Joseph Campbell likens the inner spiritual journey to that of a heroic journey:

> And so it happens that if anyone… undertakes for himself the perilous journey into the darkness by descending, either intentionally or unintentionally, into the crooked lanes of his own spiritual labyrinth, he soon finds himself in a landscape of symbolical figures (any one of which may swallow him).[16]

John Weir Perry, Ph.D, in *Trials of the Visionary Mind* understands this difficulty for the serious meditator when he states that "the world the person… was experiencing had shifted from the consensual outer reality to this inner myth-styled reality that tends not to be validated by our culture."[17] We are alone with this inner transformation and unfamiliar territory. John Scudder recounts his *Kundalini* experience as similar to Gopi Krishna's terror in that it was very painful, and the symptoms could not be relieved. He says, "It is as close to dying as a human can come and still survive. I strongly recommend that nobody attempt to open the kundalini."[18] After a childbirth activation of the *Kundalini* and later a meditation intensive, Christina Grof went through a dramatic *Kundalini* awakening.

> Suddenly I felt as though I had been plugged into a high-voltage socket as I started to shake uncontrollably. My breathing fell into an automatic, rapid rhythm that seemed beyond my control, and a multitude of visions flooded my consciousness. I wept as I felt myself being born; I experienced death; I plunged into pain and ecstasy, strength and gentleness, love

and fear, depths and heights. I was on an experiential roller coaster, and I knew I could no longer contain it. The genie or *djinn* was out of the bottle.[19]

The day I left the meditation center in July 1979, I felt wonderful, I was in bliss, I could talk to stars and flies, and I had no more pain in my gut. However, the path within and the journey to wholeness was only just beginning. My Mercurius genie was dramatically out of the bottle. I had no idea what had just occurred, and no preparation for the scouring of my belief systems and ego. All I knew was this inexpressible bliss, so like a love-sick teenager, I plunged in with both feet towards the abyss.

CHAPTER 10

The Ascending Goddess: A Rebirth

"Thirst for rebirth is the desire to be reborn so as to end successive births.... Forgetfulness of your real nature is the present death; remembrance of it is rebirth."

Shri Ramana Maharshi[1]

After my exciting and dramatic evening at the meditation center in July, I returned every night to the two-hour program. I could not get enough of this wonderful blissful feeling that came with chanting and meditation. Nothing before had brought me such consistent joy and happiness. The misery of my marriage faded when I went through the door of the meditation center.

Each night Rob and Leah would tell me more about what had happened to me and try to explain who my teacher was, but it was very difficult to understand how this Indian Guru, who was in Miami at the time, could have anything to do with what had occurred to me in Hawaii. But one evening, Rob gave me a photograph of my teacher, and when I meditated on this picture, I recognized the tiger of my dream in 1974. This was the link and evidence that I needed to understand how this magical connection to my guru could have given me *Shaktipat* on Friday, July 13,[th] 1979.

We carry around a photo of our loved ones for the reason that it conjures up their image in our minds and activates love in our hearts. I realized that the large picture of my teacher in Rob's living room was there to conjure up that connection in everyone who met him. Thus, it was clear to me, I had a soul connection to him that was beyond physical space. This was my guru, my guide and my teacher. Under his care my *Kundalini* continued to rise and with it, the *kriyas* or spontaneous movements of the *Kundalini* energy as it cleansed various parts of my subtle body.

Because I had been so unhappy with my life, meditation and chanting proved a wonderful excitement and an escape. I was suffused with love when I chanted or meditated, feeling intoxicated with God awareness. Besides the two-hour program in the evening, I would meditate one and two hours a day, spending that time in a state of utter bliss and peace. When I was alone at home, I would meditate or dance, twirling and spinning into worlds of ecstasy. I was happier than ever in my life. I felt this rising awareness of how I was connected to everything through love. In this state there was no dependence on others, no yearning for something 'more' from life. Everything had immense meaning and purpose. This warmth and bliss connected me to everything.

Signs of Awakened Kundalini:

Swami Vishnu Tirtha explains that there are many symptoms of the awakened *Kundalini* and the detachment from the physical body is one of these; "the body gets uncontrollable,... you are unable to sit still, your hands and legs stretch out forcibly," and "your body falls to the ground, or begins to rotate like a grinding stone and breath comes not out, the body squatted on floor [sic] crosslegged begins to jump from place to place like a frog, or moves from place to place, or lies down like one dead."[2] I too had some of these experiences but they did not alarm me; they were delightful and thrilling for I knew they were leaving me lighter and happier.

The mantra "*Om Namah Shivaya*" became my beloved friend. This mantra clearly had awakened me in the meditation center and is called *"chaitanya"* or alive. After only minutes of this mantra, I would feel amazing calm and feelings of love and stillness would pervade my being. I felt the syllables create vibrations from root to head. At times it was as if the sound were a living entity, as the vibrations were so powerful, creating heat that felt like love in my solar plexus. I was intoxicated by this easy, free and harmless method of feeling in love with love. Whatever anger or distress I had in my life, I forgot within minutes of sitting down and saying this mantra. My enthusiasm for meditation knew no bounds.

I felt this wholeness coming to my life that had never been there before. Before my awakening, I felt two dimensional, yet now I could feel myself multi-dimensional having understandings and revelations about the Bible and religious teachings that I had never understood before. It was as if all the dogma of religions, ALL religions, truly made sense, for I could see the goal people were seeking beyond all the rituals and strange rules. That goal of each religion was connectivity and unity with all beings. It was truly as if a great helmet had been on my head before, and I could not comprehend what religion or the Bible was about, and now I could see it as if from above, looking down. Now it all made so much sense. Before I was like the man holding the tail of the elephant, and now I was above the animal looking down and seeing the entire thing. This is the power of *Kundalini* awakening the limited mind. This is enlightened insight.

Rebirth:

The changes in my being came about rapidly. Some weeks later, after the meditation and chanting program at the center, Rob showed me a picture with strange patterns. He said I should meditate on this picture. As I looked at the picture, I saw the wavy lines undulate and move in sensual patterns. I was amazed because in fact this was just wavy lines on a two dimensional piece of paper. He called this picture a "mandala" which stimulated my brain. It also stimulated something else in me for I began to feel very strange. I took the picture and quickly returned home with odd stirrings in my belly. I wondered if I was ill. It was as if something were moving and squirming inside me like a large snake in my intestines.

At home, my husband was watching television, so I quietly slid into my bedroom, closed the door, and I sat on the bed in the dark trying to figure out how I was feeling. I had a sensation of discomfort and tension in my belly; I writhed and moved about restlessly on the bed. I felt my spine moving violently back and forth, so I could not stand or sit up. My breaths were deep inhales and exhales that caused my whole body to participate. I felt pressure inside as if something wanted to come out; at the same time, I sensed a warm feeling of expectation and motherliness. But my body continued to spasm and contort on the bed, moving into the fetal position, and my ears tightened up as a conch shell horn sounded in them.

The only way to ease the discomfort was to move in certain ways as the body's intelligence directed. As the movements of *Kundalini* or the *kriya* increased, it became obvious that I was going through the motions of giving birth. With my legs spread apart and squatting forward the pains eased. So I allowed myself to just relax into the experience and observe it. I became aware then that, not only was I giving birth in this *kriya,* but I was also the child emerging from myself. I could feel the popping of my eardrums, sounds of conch shells being blown, my face muscles being contorted as in birth, and my head squeezed, floaty and disconnected. I saw a parade of strange beings like hallucinations from a fever. I knew and felt all the sensations of the child at the same time that I was the mother pushing out the baby. I was panting and sweating, pushing and bearing down in the effort; I was also the one being pushed to emerge out of the womb. I could feel my shoulders being crushed as I came through the womb. I was in every way except physically, giving birth to myself. The Christian evangelists call it "born again." I was literally manifesting this rebirth in a very real and physical manner.

Gradually the new baby me was fully born. I felt exhausted, both as the mother and as the child, but also relieved for the spasms eased. I lay back to rest in a tranquil, meditative state. There was an unmistakable smell of the newborn— the bowel movements smell distinctively sweet having no bacteria—so there is no question that this odor was coming from me as a newborn baby. Just then my husband came into the darkened room to inquire what I was doing, and he immediately said, "I smell baby b.m.'s." As a father, he knew that smell. He put the light on and walked to the right side of the bed and stood looking down at me.

I looked into his golden face from this state of utter bliss, of motherhood and rebirth, and I saw in his face the Buddha, Jesus, his face, my guru's face all morphing into and out of each other. It was such an awesome thing to see, and I was suffused with love for him and for all beings.

I told him what was occurring, and though he would have liked to disbelieve it, the smell was such concrete evidence that he could only shake his head. Later he said that he would like to come to the meditation center with me next time. His curiosity was finally aroused. So he had verified for me that this was no dream. I felt new. I felt reborn. I felt deep peace and satisfaction inside myself. It did not matter whether I was married or unmarried, happy or sad at that moment. All I was aware of was being new and free. This event signaled very clearly my rebirth as a spiritual being. But I did not realize then that it was a much greater event in the cosmic scheme of things.

Involution vs. Evolution:

The Hindus believe that we have manifested into the form of every creature on the planet and have progressed up through the kingdoms of mineral, plant, insect, reptile and mammal to reach the level of "homo sapiens." Indian teacher and former disciple of Ramana Maharshi, H.L. Poonja, explains that we have been "incarnating in 8.4 million species to get to the point of desiring freedom."[3] Thus a human birth is very rare. It is the culmination of many lifetimes of cellular development.

This reincarnation over and over is the "involution," the rotating wheel in a space/time bubble that goes nowhere and that we are all trapped in. We can only speculate on why, for it lies with the very essence of Brahma or God. But Swami Vishnu Tirtha explains that "evolution" is the spiral out of this bubble and return to our "natural" reality which is total unity with the divine. He says,"... through [sic] human body only *moksha* or emancipation from the wheels of involutionary *Maya* is possible," and that even gods must come into human form and "take up the bodies of men" to become evolved.[4] Thus the body is vital to this process of evolution, thus making this birth into human form valuable and essential.

According to Swami Vishnu Tirtha, the ordinary human life is one of "involution" its opposite being "evolution." He compares 'involution' to the potential of a coiled spring, and 'evolution' to the events when the coil spring reverses and becomes kinetic. Thus, the uncoiling of the *Kundalini* serpent at the base of the spine, is the switch over from "involution" to "evolution."[5] The word "evolution" is not used in the Western or Darwinian manner as stages of evolution where the body evolves into higher and more adapted forms. His definition of "involution" involves the transmigration of souls through numerous different bodies as insects, animals and ultimately humans. But he calls this development "psychological" or "psychic advancement." The true meaning of "evolution" is when man is transmuted into his full God self. This comes about through the awakening of the *Kundalini* from which man can realize God or reach "*Moksha*" liberation.[6] It is true evolution when man turns to his source—to God— and his involutionary path, or the transmigration of the soul through many different bodies and lifetimes like being on a roller coaster, comes to an end. The human being becomes divine and as many have claimed, there is a conscious co-creation and choice for man.

Swami Vishnu Tirtha continues:

> ... after the involutionary process has been worked out,
> [it] rests asleep as residual power known to the yogins
> as *Kundalini* and possesses full potentiality of evolv-
> ing or uncoiling the folds of involution step by step
> and finally merging into the Absolute.... Then before
> long even within the span of this very life complete
> emancipation is possible.[7]

It follows then that it is only through the human birth that we can evolve. Even the pantheon of gods has to come into this form to grow.

Only in *human form* can the *Kundalini* transform aeons of incarnations to a life where we know ourselves as the essence of God. The Sorcerer, don Juan, explains that, "We are energetic probes created by the universe... because we are possessors of energy that has awareness... we are the means by which the universe becomes aware of itself."[8] This is why human birth on this earth is so prized and so incredibly valuable to the entire cosmos.

Once we lift out of this bubble of space / time which our minds are locked into, and we return to our true reality, our awareness becomes universal or cosmic; we recognize ourselves as integral to everything and we literally become unlimited, omnipotent, omnipresent, and all-pervading. So not only is human birth rare, but even more rare is the opportunity to meet one's teacher, and even more rare is when the disciple is changed by the *Kundalini* light into the divine.

Gradually the picture was beginning to make sense to me and to make me humbled and full of gratitude. I began to appreciate fully the honor given to me, the beauty of being born human, and the gift my guru had bestowed upon me. But at that time I did not know this wonderful news, and as the joy and amazement turned into unfathomable forays into the fearful realms of my subconscious, I was not aware, nor appreciative of the full meaning of this truly awesome gift. But looking back after my research into this topic, I realize that no matter what the discomforts of *Kundalini* awakening, they all seem insignificant compared to the value of this gift of a human birth.

CHAPTER 11

The Kundalini at Play

"When the power of Kundalini awakens, the whole of the person from the physical plane upwards becomes changed and spiritualized."

Swami Vishnu Tirtha

Whoever I had been in my life up until this day, Friday, July 13, 1979, was no more. The moment of *Shaktipat* had changed the course of my life and naturally, my relationships with that former life were forever altered.

So it was that I left soon after this rebirth for England, my country of physical birth and the place I had always called "home." My husband, my daughter who was four and I were to spend three weeks in England with my family. On our way to England from Hawaii, we would go to Texas to visit my husband's parents. All of this was happening less than three weeks after my exciting awakening and rebirth. A sea change had come over me and they were soon to experience this first hand.

Visit to Texas:

My husband's family loved to play cards or games in the evenings, something I have never enjoyed for it seems to be wasting precious energy and time. I have always had this sense that I have no time for time-killing games as life is too short. But few people shared my feeling; as a compromise to this family ritual, I would sit and knit on the side while my husband, his step-father, and his mother played. On this night in 1979, my mother-in-law, a staunch conservative, began to get angry about people losing jobs to immigrants; while the card game continued, she spewed fear-based racial prejudice in a negative diatribe, her anger and resentment increasing with her temper. Even though I knew this was a projection of her own fears, I have always loathed listening to such racial ranting. After she had decided that Mexicans, African Americans and now she added the Vietnamese, were draining the country of its resources, I felt a certain grief in my heart; as a teacher of English, I have loved and respected many students from these ethnic groups. Anyone who knew the politics and history of America in the 60's and 70's had to know that the Vietnamese were not refugees by choice, and that they were entitled to make a living as fishermen like anyone else. I knew their work ethic was very high, so there was no doubt that they would be successful. But the old me, the ever pacifying, agreeable 'social me,' wanted to find something I could agree with in what she was saying for the sake of being friendly.

Finally, her ranting paused briefly for my contribution to the dialogue, and the only thing that I could sincerely find from my heart that did not endorse what she was saying, but at the same time was a sincere contribution to the conversation was: "I do not have any prejudice against skin color or race, but I do against ignorance." This was my truth and it was spoken calmly and with all my heart.

She jumped up immediately and started to cry. "You mean, you think I am ignorant, don't you?" What could I say? I had not intended to insult her, but it was received as such. I was stating my truth. I was dumbfounded by her reaction. I could not say a word except sit there with my mouth open. Both her husband and mine were speechless, for they had not understood my statement as an insult. She ran into her room and wept for what seemed like embarrassing hours.

Later, I went in to apologize for hurting her feelings. She was on the bed, no longer crying, but looking at me with a strange peace in her eyes. I had spoken my truth and she understood that. It had penetrated her conscience and her heart. She clearly felt no resentment at me. What I had spoken had been so impenetrably true, and she was now aware that what she had been saying was un-Christian. She was a religious person who recognized her own role in this drama. I have never heard her speak about others in this way since and to her credit, she never has expressed resentment towards me for that incident. On the contrary, she always held me in great respect. She forgave me and we never spoke of it again.

Visit to England:

This "truth" serum coming out of my opened heart and deep spiritual center had already affected my mother-in-law, but with my mother it was not going to prove as simple. In England the change wrought by my *Kundalini* transformation was even more bizarre and shocking. We planned three weeks' vacation in England. One week of our vacation we would spend with my brother, his wife and two daughters, my sister, her husband and two sons and my parents in a large farmhouse in Devon near to the coast. All the children were below age nine to the youngest age four. It was to be a perfect holiday for all thirteen of us, a chance to cement as a family and renew the old ties.

Although my mother noticed that I seemed too thin— a result of my ballet classes and very busy life, everything was very much the same on the surface as it had been on other visits to my parents since I had been married. When all the family set off in three cars to Devonshire and the farmhouse, we agreed on a picnic spot ahead of time in case one car got left behind. We found a lush green meadow after a few hours and ate our English picnic lunch under a warm sun. When it was time to set off again, we all changed cars. My daughter went with her aunty and uncle and the other children, and I got into the car my brother drove with his wife next to him, and my mother next to me in the back seat, so we could talk. Unfortunately, she began her usual criticism of me.

In the days before my spiritual awakening, I might have sat there taking this in. I knew it was not worth the effort to defend myself or respond as my answers would be considered irrelevant. I was expected to be silent, to be passive and accept it. No one, not even my father, questioned my mother's emphatic pronouncements. However, with my awakening had come a new sensitivity to my own heart and welfare and an unexpected power. In her statements I registered injury to my own spirit. What she was saying did not align with my own heart's truth, so I felt a pain rising inside me.

Her mind and voice rolled on like an inexorable freight train grinding over all my feelings and sensibilities. It seemed to be a dirge of anxiety-based thinking with the premise that I was not capable of living an adult life, even at 33 with almost two degrees, a successful husband, a career, an adorable child and an upper class lifestyle. I had not been home for four years, yet this is all she could say to me? It was as if she had to catch up on every negative thought she had ever had about me in a four-year interim. She was dumping her "worry" mind entity onto me as Eckhart Tolle would say. This indeed was the egoic mind at its worst, and I was its victim.

As we sat in the back seat, driving through the country lanes of Devon, I listened half-heartedly thinking it would be over soon and she would get it all out, and then I could get into the other car with my husband and not have to listen any more. Whether she sensed she was losing power and ramped up her critique, whether my new state was activating her Pandora's box of pain, I am not sure, but suddenly she had stepped over a line that I could not tolerate. She insinuated that I was not a good mother to my daughter because I was doing too much outside the home. How could she even have any idea of my life when I lived half a world away? It could not be swallowed; it could not be borne in any part of my being. A sort of glottal 'hung' sound came out of my mouth as I felt physically attacked. I knew I was a good mother, listening to my child 's needs and doing everything possible to take care of her for her benefit.

It hit my heart like a fist blow. Something grew like an expanding balloon inside me; it was a fierce thunderbolt which—like a pressure-packed hammer—burst out of my heart through my voice in a way that I had never heard it yell, "SHUT UP."

It was not only very loud and very strong, but with it came the full power of this heart pressure. It was like some beaten down slave who had been asleep for centuries, suddenly rose up out of my chest and struck back with the full force of its abuse in a killer strike. It was some new being from within me that was outraged by the lies she was speaking; it was a role I had never allowed reign before. I felt almost that my guru was coming out of my heart and smacking my mother for her lack of awareness.

I saw my mother shudder and a soul wave passed over her face as, for a split second, some nasty witch-like spirit or entity jumped out. Some years later while taking a transpersonal psychology workshop, I was to see this same image again as the negative critic inside my head that had always stood between me and my creativity. But just for that second I saw this entity leave my mother, and she was just herself then, the little girl from an English forest, free and light. She was so pure and sweet for that moment. But it passed, and then the critic entity came back in and took up residence inside her again with a vengeance.

At the time I did not understand what kind of entity could inhabit someone as loving and good as my mother clearly was in every other way. It was some time later that I learned about these entities that attach to people and make them mean and spiteful. I also discovered a few of my own that had plagued me for years until, through meditation, I tracked their root, identified them and cleared them. I discovered that they hang around humanity waiting for opportunities to "help" when we need some extra boost of energy, or when we are very ill. Then a "Faustian bargain" or contract ensues, where they give us the needed energy or boost, but in exchange they get to play around with an aspect of our personality or vampire energy for themselves. I am sure this was how my mother had acquired this negativity as she had had a hard life.

We all sat there in shock. My brother pulled over, and turned around to look at me in rage. I had no explanation. I too could not believe what just happened! My mother sat withered, vulnerable and shuddering. She and this spiritual parasite had said cruel and unkind things to me my whole life, and I had never stopped it nor confronted her about it. Only the truth power of the *Kundalini* awakening could have given me this courage and the spiritual energy to do it. For that moment her will was not greater than mine. Her domination had been challenged. She/the entity had lost. War was now declared, and she/the entity was not about to lose after a lifetime of control.

The rest of the trip was a mini disaster. My father, brother and sister never quit harassing me during this trip, trying to avenge what I had said to my mother and to make me feel guilty and repentant. As usual they took her side. How could I explain it to them? I did not understand it myself! My husband had no clear understanding of what was going on. He had not heard this yell; he did not grow up in this family dynamic, but he was my husband, and he did try to smooth things over. I had an advocate in my husband, who knew the stories of my life and had always been beside me in support. My daughter at four was also there supporting me in her innocent way. But most of all, I had the greatest power—the truth of my heart— and that was infinitely wise.

It was no mistake that I shook something spiteful out of my mother that day. I cannot help looking back and thinking if there had been honesty in our family dynamic, everyone might have sided with me, knowing how my mother could nag incessantly. But this was a dysfunctional family created by her/entity to keep control and domination. My moving to Hawaii had put me out of range of this control. But my guru had shaken that passive girl out of me who might have cowed before this domination. I was now a spiritual warrior.

Never again would she ever rant on at me like that. My yelling at her and shocking this nasty part of her was a form of exorcism at work, but to my family, it appeared that I was being *"very rude"* to my mother! How could I explain it to them? The *Kundalini* force was acting through me.

They wanted to make me feel apologetic and guilty, but I simply did not feel that. So I said nothing and just put up with the tension. Mother sat as one aggrieved and wronged, never saying a word, but her minions, my father, brother and sister, said it all for her. No one understood the deeper meaning of what I had done, and there were no common words to convey it; my family knew nothing of spirituality, awakenings, energy or *Kundalini*. I knew it was some *will* beyond mine that had verbally "smacked" my mother for her mindless rantings, just as it had my mother-in-law; but in my mother there was no spiritual awareness, no forgiveness, no understanding of the events on a higher or heart level. She could not understand it at all and neither could I.

Return to Hawaii:

At the time I did not realize that I needed to be separated from Mother and her "worry mind" entity for my own emotional health, even though I would never have asked for this method to establish my independence. Who would? It was the beginning of a process for me of discovering that this initiation and awakening was not going to be smooth and comfortable for anyone. I felt that there was a power inside me that was in control, and this inner intelligence knew the truth and was fiercely protecting it. This was like an inner *warrior of truth*.

Who would choose this way to establish self-hood, and integrity? As Mindell states:

> Often it is easier to be sick, to suffer unbearable and relentless pressure, or to go mad, than it is to be in the reality of a spirit which brings one up against social conflict, misunderstanding, and the difficulties of being an individual. You see, it is a challenge, a mythical challenge, a proprioceptive pain to be a human being.[1]

Thus I was shunned by my family, but living half a world away from them, it was not as terrible as it could have been. How could I have borne this condemnation, misunderstanding and vilification without the protection and love of my inner teacher, the *Kundalini* power and guide? It was perhaps the most important event to become separate from the influence of my parents who had no tools to comprehend the journey that I had undertaken, and I had no language to explain it. For years after this, they were all convinced that I was 'crazy,' and from their point of view, they were right.

This is another difficult aspect of *Kundalini* that I was beginning to discover. People who are in denial, hiding their issues will become very uncomfortable around those who are awake or waking up. Perhaps it arouses their *Kundalini* and stimulates the subconscious to open its Pandora's box of misery. This may create discomfort and pain in the emotional body, or as Eckhart Tolle says in *The Power of Now*: "It is not easy to live with an enlightened person, or rather it is *so* easy that the ego finds it extremely threatening." The ego needs problems and confrontations. "The pain-body is demanding feedback and not getting it" from the consciously awake partner, so there is conflict.[2]

Ostensibly this event should have upset me and made me want to quickly return to Hawaii, but I remember this time in Devon as being one of detached, self contained joy. All the time I was there, I felt this great love, peace and connection to my own divine guidance. I was immune, protected by some invisible shield from their personal attacks and I saw it all as a sort of theatre drama of which I was merely observer. I was centered in my heart, and unshakeable in my peace and calm. In the past I should have wanted to die from the shame or guilt, but I felt that I was not the agent of that shout. I was as an observer of it. Something primal inside me had manifested. My photos all show that I was in a type of ecstasy through this holiday.

When we returned to Hawaii from this trip to England in August of 1979, my semester started again and I went back to college for the last two terms of graduate school while my meditation and practices continued apace. I would bring the intensity that had shocked my family to my college work and relationships in Hawaii. Swami Vishnu Tirtha explains it:

> But when a person gets his mind overflowing with blissful Peace and feels the tide of Ananda [bliss] saturating the very core of his heart and feels therein the presence of never-abating divine intoxication, he is then in fact in direct touch with God.[3]

This bliss was reinforced daily by the happiness that came from meditation and chanting. I cannot fully convey here the healing and peace that come from such practices. To this day, I know of nothing that cures depression or unhappiness like chanting. I have read skeptics criticize chanting, saying that it makes the mind go blank and people appear to be zombies. It does make the mind relax and allows the integration of both the left and right hemispheres. The energies of the mind and body are given rest in chanting and meditation, giving a space for healing and peace. People who work non-stop and have no rest from mental activity are the ones to be pitied, not those who chant. When the mind is still, the universe opens to many vistas of potential—the potential of what it is to be a multidimensional human being. When the mind is quiet, our true, blissful nature arises. My teacher would say that chanting gives the mind a stick to climb up and down, keeping it occupied and out of mischief, while the true Self can emerge.

Spinning Episodes:
During my times alone when my daughter was in preschool, and my husband at work, I would spin and twirl like a dervish in utter delight. Even though my body was spinning very fast, I never got dizzy and never fell. Something came to join me that was like a partner. It was me and yet separate from me, so we created between us the ability to spin without being dizzy or flying off center. It was as if I lifted into another dimension where the rules of gravity did not exist. Ancient texts say that with mastery of the vital body, one can fly like a bird. I would spin up into the ceiling. It was utterly exquisite. Nothing can compare to it for joy.

Intellectual Gifts:
Much of my experience was internal in that I found myself happier and more content, calmer and at peace. Sometimes, I would see an outward manifestation of the changes that were taking place, so I could see how these changes were affecting my brain and intellect on many levels. For my graduate classes, I had to prepare a writing assignment

to demonstrate a certain writing method and present this to the class. It was due at 10 a.m. on a Thursday morning. On Wednesday evening when I should have been preparing for this assignment, I made a decision to meditate rather than do the work. As usual I drifted off to sleep in a state of bliss.

At 5 a.m. the next day, I woke realizing that I had only five hours to prepare this teaching lesson. I was not concerned. I picked up the morning paper and noticed a very interesting story on the front page. I sat at the typewriter and in less than half an hour, I had typed out a lesson that embodied all the principles that I had to demonstrate. It just seemed to flow out of me. I drove in early to the university to get some Xeroxing done, and was ready to give my presentation before 10 a.m. It went so well and seemed so well prepared and thoughtful, the other students thought I had spent hours on this assignment. Everyone agreed that my presentation was the best. The professor was highly impressed.

Everything had flowed through me because of the high state that I was in. It was so unusual for me not to fret and worry about such assignments, that I did not feel that this was "me" doing this; I was thoroughly enjoying the experience of watching myself as this new being.

My connection to Bob continued with meeting in our courses and casual meetings on campus. However, I did not feel so obsessed with him after I received the *shaktipat*, because the bliss I felt in meditation was so all-consuming and surpassed anything illicit that he could give me. I noticed that when I would think of love for him, my heart would open, and I would feel great sweetness and ecstasy. But the longing and passion dropped away from me. I had something much greater and it was all inside me.

Resisting Temptation:
One evening after I had encountered Bob near the library, we sat down and had a talk. I told him my complaints about my husband who at that time was babysitting our daughter, and I knew he would be sitting in front of the TV, ignoring her completely. Bob said, "Well why don't you

leave him?" I said nothing for I knew that I could not. It seemed remote and unrealistic. We talked of other things and then as I was leaving Bob said, "Just leave; get out if it is so terrible. Leave your husband." It felt to me like an ultimatum of a frustrated lover. I had never heard him talk like that before.

When I got home that night, sure enough, my husband was asleep in front of the TV and my daughter was alone playing next to him on the floor. It was a scene I was used to, but one that saddened me. So I put my four year-old daughter to bed, and then went to meditate alone in another room. I thought about what Bob had said. "Did I feel so desperate that I wanted to leave now?" I asked myself. I did not receive a clear response; all I felt was confused, so I decided the only way to resolve the issue inside me was to meditate on it.

In meditation, I allowed this question to circulate within me. After a short while, I realized there was no *will* for it. I did not need to leave my spouse to be happy. I knew that I could not leave, for it would violate that "truth" energy of the *Kundalini* inside which was more and more real. Leaving my husband would not get me closer to my heart, for I was already *there*. If I left, I would lose my daughter, and she would end up having to live with my husband who already was not emotionally available to her. It would be a disaster for her, and for me as I would lose her, my home, my lifestyle and my animals. Since *shaktipat,* I was relieved of the stress and tension that I had felt before. I knew that I could stay married and be content because of the bliss of meditation. What more could I have with Bob than I already had? Thus, I did nothing and said nothing to my husband.

Bob perhaps had ulterior motives for directing me to leave my husband. I did feel he was attracted to me, but I also felt he was much enamored of my lifestyle, and that greed was a part of his interest. Thus I pulled back from any move to leave my spouse. When I got up from meditating that night, I knew I was safe from making any crazy decisions. I would stay with my spouse and continue to meditate for my own peace. I accepted my life with him as it was, "for better or for worse." This was also the message I received from reading my guru's teachings. Spiritual awakening is not a valid reason to leave our life and loved ones. However, I had forgotten at that time the dream from 1974, and my dad telling me to take off my wedding band when the tiger came.

I did not see Bob for a week, and then at a lunch-time lecture, I saw him at the back of the room. He looked like "hell." His eyes were sunken, the pupils large, dark and in pain; his face dark and unshaven showed the ravages of great suffering. I went up to him after the meeting and asked him what had happened to him. He did not look me directly in the eyes, and said he had had the 'flu. But something told me that was a lie. He did not speak further, and behind his icy, cold respect was a guarded distancing look. What a contrast to the last time I had seen him when he was eager for me to be divorced. There was no interest in flirting any more. Something in his demeanor had shut down.

When I meditated on his behavior, I came to realize that when he had urged me to leave my husband, and I had not carried out that command, that energy he had sent out towards me like an piercing arrow, did not wound anyone but himself. That is something the Hawaiians understand in their teachings called *Huna*. If a shaman sends out energy in the form of a curse, or command to another, and it is rejected or not received, the shaman must protect himself as the energy comes back like a boomerang. Bob expected me to break up with my spouse, and I did not. So this "poison arrow" boomeranged right back to Bob. What I saw on his face some three or four days after this challenge was the very grief and misery that I and my family would have suffered had I followed his directive. His coldness and distancing was because he knew what had happened; he knew that what he was experiencing was our grief coming to him to suffer because I did not choose to go along with his directive.

This was basically the end of the serious flirtation. We both knew it. I still loved him, but he knew that I was not going to leave my spouse for him, so he maintained his distance from then on and found himself a young, blonde freshman soon after.

Through this connection to him I had come to understand so much of who I was, and who I had been in our past, and I feel that we had discharged the energy that magnetized us to each other in this life. I know that when I emigrated from England, I had seen his face in my dreams, and knew that he and I would meet. Many years later he would tell me that he considered me to be one of the purest women he had ever met. He knew that I had not swayed to adultery even with every temptation.

Later I found out he had also been flirting in the same way with several women on campus, both married and single, and I was by no means the only woman who felt she was in love with him. So this had been a test to see if I would fall into the temptations of sex, deceit and ignorance. I feel sure in my bones that had I succumbed to the temptation he had offered me, had I not held to my vows, I should not have had my guru's blessing with *Shaktipat*. The fire of *Kundalini* would not have ignited.

So these relationships on all fronts were undergoing changes, and I was learning rapidly how to operate with these multiple levels of awareness. I became more intuitive and aware of life and death events happening with other people too.

Smell of Death:

On the 30th October of 1979, I was in the Reading Room for our university Linguistics' Department. Bob and some other students were there, and I could feel his energy like it was my own that day, yet I was not distracted. There was a distinct energy of "death." I could not feel comfortable anywhere in the room. I moved to different chairs several times to try to feel less miserable. Lord Yama, the Lord of Death, was lurking in that room; I knew it and so did Bob. I noticed that when I sat on the side of the room nearest to one corner, it was stronger. Bob too seemed to be having trouble concentrating and signaled without words that he was not sure what this energy was. Eventually I found myself too oppressed by this energy of death, and I went home early.

That night I meditated on this experience and knew someone was going to die, but I did not know who it was. I called my mother in England to inquire about my uncle Percy who had been ill, but he was fine. The next day I got up and put on my blackest outfit and wore a black scarf over my head. I just knew I had to wear black, but since it was Halloween, I thought every one would think I was dressed up. When I got to class the 31st October, the news was out that Professor Ruth C's plane had crash-landed in Mexico City and she had died.

Dr. Ruth C., a Professor of Linguistics at the University of Hawaii, was much respected in the field of Teaching English as a Second Language and was the international president of this professional body; she was much loved by all her students. She was due in Mexico on 31st October, for a TESOL conference in Mexico City where she was due to make a speech. Her office was next to the Reading Room where I had been studying on that evening of her departure, and where she had been gathering up her materials to depart. I often wonder whether she was aware of this "death" energy that Bob and I could feel so palpably that day.

I wondered if I could have said something; would I have been able to warn her of this? It was a very strange thing to have forewarning of someone's death. The sages say clearly that one cannot interfere with God's Will. Was it inevitable that Dr. Ruth would be killed and was it her destiny? It was a very sad time for everyone, but it also encouraged me to trust my intuition and marvel at the new abilities I was discovering I had.

My path, I discovered, was a lonely one that could only be shared with those on the same journey who understood these multiple dimensions. I had begun a journey of cleansing toxic relationships, toxic domination, and control by others and discovering deep levels of myself that I had hitherto not known. All this insight revealed to me the depth and profundity of what a human being can be. This journey of discovery continues to this day.

CHAPTER 12

No Boundaries

"Unity Consciousness lives as the realization that one's true self is no-boundary, embracing the cosmos as a mirror its objects."

—Ken Wilber[1]

It was in the fall of 1979 that the enthusiasm for meditation grew intensely. I was able to meditate for long hours. I read as much about my experience as I could from my teacher's books and talks, trying to understand this process and what had occurred. I was enthralled by everything my teacher taught for it was always the truth— the beautiful, uncontaminated truth. This shone out of his face and out of his books. I took one of his pictures from a magazine and put it on my "*puja*" or meditation table. His face had so much vital energy, but not the teeth. Then someone told me that he had had all his teeth removed and that I was seeing his dentures. That showed me that my vision was not mistaken. I felt the most enormous love for him.

Yet in spite of having the books, lectures and the care of this great being, I did not understand most of what I was going through. Reading books and thinking about this process years later has given me some insights into the process of *Kundalini* transformation. As Bonnie Greenwell explains "The Kundalini process entirely redesigns the structure of the cells, and others see the restructuring of the human brain as an evolutionary necessity made possible by Kundalini awakening." She goes on to speculate that this investigation into the brain chemistry and structure is an opportunity to "expand into a range of wisdom beyond intellectually-dominated dualistic thinking."[2] This restructuring is what brings about the symptoms and discomforts of the awakening. It is also mystery that is not easily understood by the "Little Ego" or mind which we have heretofore depended on to convey "reality," for it is this very mind, "Little Ego," that is the "enemy" of such a transformation. The "Little Ego" has no power over the *Kundalini* process.

Left/Right Brain:

When Dr. Jill Bolte Taylor, a Harvard Brain Researcher, talks about her trauma from a bleeding left brain in her book *My Stroke of Insight* and what skills and abilities she lost and retained, we can begin to see into the silent side of our dualistic reality, in this case, the right brain.[3] What she experienced with her left logical brain non-functioning was similar to what I went through after my *Kundalini* was awakened.

I lost boundaries between myself the shower water and the walls of the shower. I felt the water and my own being were one and the same, as did she. Her right brain did not differentiate boundaries as the left brain would; clearly this process of awakening was in some way bringing the right brain functions to the forefront of my awareness, and in some way silencing the left analytical brain, a reverse of normal awareness. This lack of boundaries Bonnie Greenwell would categorize as "Extrasensory experiences."[4] However, today I would call it "Right Brain dominance" because of the information available through Jill Bolte Taylor's vivid experience of a damaged analytical left-brain.

Since most of my dramatic *kriyas* happened from 1979 to 1981 in fast intensity, I am not able to remember the exact sequence of phenomena that I experienced under this *Kundalini* influence. But this chapter contains an assortment of what might be called cleansings, *siddhis,* powers or movements of the *Kundalini* which cause atypical abilities. Some might call them "god like powers" because they are talents that in our normal state, we do not ordinarily possess.

Journeying in this world was like being in a novel where adventures arose without let up around every corner. Each adventure required courage, skills and abilities that were not part of anything learned in normal life. They almost all required challenges to the logical mind, to one's concepts of how the world was constructed. This chapter describes some examples of these adventures in no particular order. My symptoms and phenomena did not follow any set pattern of development, for *Kundalini* follows her own path within each individual. But William Bodri explains a semblance of a sequence to this process in his book *The Little Book of Hercules.* They are movements of the inner subtle energy which is moving to clear something from the nervous system that is false or erroneous to the light of truth. When that is cleared, the symptoms decline.

I had to deal with these strange experiences, the disbelief and ignorance of my family, and take care of my domestic and college obligations simultaneously. What I needed would have been a quiet cell alone like a monk or nun where I could process through this transformation with a minimum of disruption to others. It is really important to have non-judgmental, sympathetic and kind helpers around who are willing to take care of one's physical needs. However, nothing like that was available to me, so I had to deal with these mind assaults without any preparation, unaware, and very much alone.

No Boundaries:

This category is very broad in that I virtually had no boundaries against anything in the environment, including ideas and influences. The main issue was the sense of boundaries disappearing between me and other people or even inanimate things.

Like Jill Bolte Taylor's dysfunctional left brain, I merged with the shower water and the shower walls. I found myself able to comprehend my dog and cat far better, and I could talk to them both inside and out about their problems and concerns, feeling confident that they understood. I would know when the dog needed to go outside before she even signaled this. I would instinctively know when she wanted to come back in to the house, so I would open the door for her, and she seemed genuinely appreciative. I knew if her water was dirty or she needed more. Even today this is true of the animals I have had. I feel their needs as my own. If an animal is hurt or I see something on TV or a movie where an animal is injured, it goes through me as if I were experiencing it. For this reason I was uncomfortable eating meat and for years afterwards because I could feel the animal's misery from its death and penned up, unnatural life.

Today we know that this lack of boundaries is an attribute of the right brain hemisphere which does not observe physical boundaries. It is also true, thanks to the research into quantum physics, we know that there is very little solid matter in our bodies, but we are predominantly energy and liquid. At parties with other people, I could read their ideas before they spoke. Once it got me into trouble when I spoke the last line of a joke before the person could finish it, as it just came through my head. Everyone thought I already knew the joke, but I didn't.

These disappearing walls between me and my external world included my daughter and my husband, and I knew everything they were feeling all the time. For example, at our kitchen table we had small round stools which had no back to lean against. While we were having a meal at our kitchen table one day, I went and got a chair from the dining room with a cushion so my daughter's back could be supported. My husband wondered why I did that. I replied, "Her back hurts."

He responded. "How do you know?" His question seemed to be rather absurd to me since I could feel her pain so clearly as if it were my own.

I answered, "Well, it hurts her right here." I pointed to her mid back. He looked dumbfounded. He turned to my daughter and asked her, "Does your back hurt right here?"

"Yes Daddy, it does," she replied looking up, not surprised at all that I knew, for children have sensitivity to such things, and she was more than likely feeling all the feelings both he and I had. But what my husband did not know was that I also knew how he felt, and how his suppressed fears and anxieties had an impact on all of us. I knew that his anxiety from his own childhood manifested through his pushing medicine into my daughter for her asthma. I could feel when he offered her a spoon of the red medicine, that he was very anxious, and so with the medicine came all his fear.

Simultaneously, I also was aware of my plants in the house and garden. If they needed plant food or water, I felt it. I did not know how I knew, but it was just an awareness, enlightened insight, as if I were the one needing the water. I was merged with their energies. I was one with the Earth and the environment in which I lived. The awareness I was developing with the rising *Kundalini* was enabling me to receive information that would normally be blocked by chatter or other obstacles to the full intelligence that I was now experiencing. I also feel that this is the true condition of man, to be a steward to Nature, to the Goddess of the planet, and to be merged with the natural world. Fortunately, we know that native Americans, indigenous people who have retained their ancestral spiritual connection to the Earth, do still experience the Earth this way.

Beloveᴅ Companion:

Sometimes this lack of boundaries helped me blend into a divine oneness with "The Beloved" which I believe is the Higher Self, a part of us that splits off at birth and remains watching but aloof and not interfering, like the Hawaiian Huna concept of *aumakua*.

During an especially beautiful, crystalline day in my village, while in a state of immense happiness, I took my daughter out on my bicycle towards the beach which was one block away. I remember the bougainvillea bursting in rich purple in each hedge, the mock orange perfume filling and intoxicating from my neighbor's gardens as I walked next to the bicycle with her in the seat. The sense that there were three of us was very real. A third very warm and loving being strode alongside us. It was so tangible, so loving and companionable. This being felt and knew all my thoughts and feelings and returned enormous fullness. It felt like my very self— the other part of me. I never needed to talk or stay "out" of my center with this being alongside. I felt totally complete and whole.

Later that day my husband took us out to dinner in his newly acquired sports car, and, unlike my usual anxious chatter, I stayed silent the whole time we were driving as I was communing with the companion being within. I remember the warm weather, the familiar neighborhoods as all bringing me support and love. My husband looked lovingly at me, grasped my hand warmly and said, "Today you are as I always wanted you to be, composed and beautiful."

I knew what he meant. My 'old self' was never at peace; my "Little Ego" with its store of subconscious fears and denials was always chattering about something or another and not allowing silences, almost terrified by the space of the present moment. That was the *me* he had known until before the awakening. This moment with him seemed sad then, for I never felt more self-sufficient and whole, never felt that I needed him less than in that space, and here he was expressing his love. Was this how a real relationship should be, both self-sufficient and whole within, yet together by mutual choice? He was feeling for me at that moment that same love energy that I felt for my own inner beloved.

My inner beloved was with me always through this period. When I would spin in my house, it was always a binary event with this being. I was one part of the spin and there was this loving, strong and sometimes stronger being balancing my spins. I did not see anyone with me, but I felt the power of this being as real as any physical touching. In Egypt they have a concept of these "two" aspects of ourselves. According to Jeremy Naydler as retold by Geoff Stray, "The *ka* or double can be seen as "vital force" –an energy body that seems to be equivalent to an etheric body."[5] Was this my companion, my very own higher self? It certainly felt incredibly loving and receptive.

In Carlos Castaneda's explanations of Mexican Sorcery, he is told about an "ally," a presence, "a helper that is nothing and yet it is as real as you and me."[6] He retells a story of Eligio who "was twirled by the allies." And La Gorda explains that the allies "come of their own accord to the sorcerer and spin him... if you had wanted to catch them or entice them to stay with you, you had to spin with them."[7] Clearly this was the experience that I had of being accompanied by a loving being. Was it an ally? Was it my *Ka*? Was I a sorcerer in a past life and this was my companion spirit returning? These are mysteries I cannot answer; all I know is that it was blissful and thrilling.

Changing Frequencies:

In the very depths of the process of cleansing my chakras and the *Kundalini* reaching a certain stage, I clearly recall an experience of dying several times an hour. It was as if I were on an elevator with doors opening on each level. I would fall into a death-like sleeping state as the elevator doors closed and the elevator moved higher; then through the partially opening doors, I gradually awoke to see my bedroom again, but there would be a sparkle in the air that had not been before. The colors would appear more brilliant, more deep and meaningful. Something would have been added to the scene that I had not seen there before, and something dim or dark would have faded away. This process repeated for days whenever I would lie down quietly.

Sometimes it was as if I had died and was re-born hundreds of times a day. I would lie on my bed and drift into an altered state of almost sleep, but not quite—the stage before full sleep. Then moments later I would come back to full awareness, and the world would appear bathed in a gossamer shimmer where subtle changes had taken place. Sometimes it was like coming up from a well of possible worlds, which would shimmer like a mirage for a brief second as my reality formed a bridge of thin micro strings. The strings would 'hold' this 'reality' for but a fraction of a breath, and then it would dissolve or shatter, shaking the ground of my being like an earthquake within. It would feel like disintegration of my whole world in a sinking in feeling. I would feel exposed, naked, without any "reality" or frame of reference and utterly helpless as this process would repeat over and over. Nonetheless, some part of me watched all of it without any fear or reaction.

Then I would drift off again into a doze-like state and again some minutes later I would reassemble the room, and a new "*loka*" or level would have been accomplished with subtle changes of light and vibrancy that could only be detected by the inner eye. This sometimes went on for days on end with these awakenings happening every thirty minutes during my meditations. As I would return to this "awareness" I would see a miniscule mosaic of the scene reconstructing itself before my eyes, as if I were reconstructing physical reality in each second. An analogy to this is the digital television pictures which, when the signal is not strong, break up into small squares like missing mosaics. In the "Star Trek" movies the spaceship would "beam" up people from a planet to the space ship, and it would involve a cellular disintegration of the bodies of each person and then a reintegration when they came up to the spaceship inside a special capsule. This was the process I seemed to be observing every time I would doze off and then wake up. It was the most intoxicating action that played through me without any conscious control.

Much later I came to understand that there are in fact *lokas* or levels (from the Sanskrit meaning which originated our word "location") of frequency which many today would call "dimensional frequencies." I believe that I was increasing my vibratory frequency with these deaths and births, each time I opened my eyes I was at a higher frequency than the previous one. Whereas my 'consensus reality' had controlled my world for most of my life, now it was time for this physical, 'third dimensional reality' to take a step back. These multiple births of my new and awakening consciousness were bringing me closer to this ability to withstand the experience of my true Self. These mini-births were raising my awareness up the ladder towards the ultimate *loka* or place where I could see my own mind as the luminosity that is so revered in Tibetan Yoga, that is so sought after in all yogic traditions. I was ascending towards this realm with every meditation.

Inner Visions:

There were times when I seemed to get lost in the worlds inside my head and become part of them, remembering lifetimes in a particular place or wearing a particular dress. While in meditation but with my eyes open, I would see visions of scenes from ancient India, particularly of Prince Jnaneshwar, riding on an elephant in a parade. In sepia colors, I would see this scene repeatedly. He would graciously wave at me, and I would feel incredible honor. Each time I saw this, while fully awake, it was full of meaning for me in some mythic manner.

It always came like a moving screen in front of my eyes, sometimes in color, sometimes in sepia. I always felt the joy and jubilance of the crowd as if I were there with them again. Mainly these were dream-like visions, but sometimes in the middle of the night I would feel compelled to get up, go to the living room and reenact a scene from a past life. It would be as real as my normal reality, and it would repeat, like a stuck gramophone needle, as I relived it over and over trying to transmute it.

One persistent situation was of being a married wife in a former lifetime; in this reenactment, a male spouse was arguing with me, and in that life, our boy child was peeking around the bedroom door at his father. I was trying to motion the child to leave, as my husband was throttling me on the bed. He strangled me in front of the child. This man then picked up my corpse over his right shoulder and walked down a narrow stairway to a cellar where he proceeded to dig a hole for my body. When he put me into the earth, he piled dirt on me; it fell over my face, but since I had not truly left the body, I tried to brush it off. I would brush and brush and the dirt never came off like the blood on Lady MacBeth's hands.

This same gruesome scene went on for a week around 2 a.m. every night, exactly the same scenario repeating and repeating like the movie "Groundhog Day," until I came to understand how to transmute the ghastly energy of it. Then it stopped and has never come back. I believe that with the clearing of this memory, releasing it and accepting it as over, the emotional debt was balanced, the karma was discharged, so, thankfully, there were no more repetitions of this horrible scene. This reenactment of past life physical events, of returning to scenes from my life or lives and reliving them from a spiritual perspective, seeing both the physical level and the level of spirit in the reliving, has given me many insights into my past and helped me understand the deeper implications of my experiences. I learned so much more about how we experience reality, but for the fluidity of time, I could not have been prepared.

Time Reverses:

Dr. Stanislav Grof writes about his own non-ordinary states of consciousness in his book, *The Holotropic Mind*. "In the state I was in, it appeared to me rather obvious that there could be no such limits in the realm of spirit, since time and space were nothing more than mental constructs."[8] This is what I was learning.

I remember once dropping into an altered state and seeing the clock face as 6:15 p.m. When waking after what seemed to be about 30 minutes, the clock said 5:55 p.m. Time had gone backwards! This was extremely frightening to me. I really felt I was going mad when that happened.

Dr. Dennis Gersten, who wrote *Are You Getting Enlightened or Losing Your Mind?* explains that "time ceases to exist at all" for those who are exploring consciousness. He tells the story of Pepe Romero who was a classical guitar player who instead of playing faster to meet the needs of the music, he "expands the second, he simply expands the second—rather than trying to play faster."[9]

I did not understand while experiencing this how the alteration of time could have happened then, but years later, when I read *Stalking the Wild Pendulum* by Itzhak Bentov, and also *Beyond Einstein* by Michio Kaku, I realized that time can be traversed both forwards and back when we are hyper-aware or moving into higher frequencies.

Itzhak Bentov, who several times met with my teacher, has written a fascinating text that explains many of the phenomena of altered states and *Kundalini* states in scientific terms. He explains this altered time as "the observing mind the entity that correlates and makes sense of the information submitted to it by the brain, was absent."[10] When I saw the clock at 6:15 p.m. I was, in effect, time traveling to the future in an altered state something like Castaneda's *dreaming*. When I awoke at 5:55 p.m. I was returning to my former state of consciousness and catching up with the correct time as my body experienced it. Bentov goes on to suggest that "during altered states of consciousness our subjective, time-space coordinates separate from the objective" measures and "we are rapidly expanding into space... in which there is no limit on speed, in which time is being converted into space."[11]

This was clearly what was occurring to me, but how to convey this to a doctor or my family? How many people could relate to what I was experiencing? Finding out, even years later, however, that there were answers to these strange experiences, was most comforting. Where in my education of Western fairy stories, myths and Greek heroic tales had there been anything to prepare me for the shifts of time? Where in my education had anyone ever suggested that time was part of the "Little Ego" mind, but that a part of us dwells in a timeless realm which can be traversed like a highway into the past or future? Such lack of knowledge is a serious limitation in this strange *Kundalini* world. Every human being needs to know this.

Time Stretches:

I found a quote from Ralph Waldo Emerson that captures my bizarre experience of time seeming like elastic: "Spirit sports with time— can crowd eternity into an hour, or stretch an hour to eternity." I became aware that time was not only relative and could be traveled both forwards and backwards, but it was not even linear. Time for me as a meditator was more like a wave, deep, infinitely deep—going into vertical crevices that stretched moments of time into yawning caverns of hundreds of years— at least that is how it "felt"as my consciousness grew and expanded. A moment could stretch into infinity while I processed a thousand impressions from all around me. I had no shell to keep these out. It was as if I was no-where and no-one. There was no 'I' in this realm. I was merely a computer registering data. I had no identity, no foundation. My "Little Ego" mind could not compute so much information. It was a nightmare trying to make logical sense of everything I was experiencing.

The nearest I had come to this dislocated world was when I had

had a long-lasting fever during a bout of shingles at the age of 13. I had seen strange events in a powerful dream where our kitchen refrigerator had burst into a nuclear explosion, turning everyone in the dream and the room itself invisible, but irradiated by a soft, white light. I had awakened much shocked by the strength and power of this dream; but I did wake up, and I came back to full "normal" awareness. I now know that was probably *Kundalini* bursting a knot in my subtle nerves during puberty. The strangeness of the dream was easily assigned to the fever and so, although I never forgot it, it did not concern me too much. However, this psychedelic meandering since the awakening was not a sleeping dream. It was daily life. I did not wake from it. The further I traveled into this meditation world, the more that my normal reality, my "Little Ego," was shaking in moments of terror.

Meta Processing:

Without boundaries to conserve some sense of "myself" as a separate being, in each second that passed, my conscious mind experienced a thousand impressions which I had to process through a linear mind that could not make sense of this new world. For example, as I could feel my cat's hunger, my dog's need for a walk, the plants need for water, I could sense my daughter's nasal congestion as my own, and simultaneously my husband's needs and motives for everything he did. Simultaneously, I was aware of my shoe not being on properly, my stomach being hungry and of having some loving being sending me "I love you." At the same time, I could sense the ocean, the stars speaking to me in their unique natures; I could also feel the needs of others not present that I loved, the messages of the guides, the presence and voice of my teacher and the call of the Earth. All of this was simultaneously processing through a limited left-brain mind familiar with bytes of information that formed a sequence based in time going in one direction only. No wonder a person going through this is considered mentally ill! A person has to process both realities/views of the world at the same time and boundaries do not exist.

In this hyper-processing state and in desperation one day, I shocked my husband by saying I was going to drown myself to get away from this hyper-awareness. He could not relate to what I was experiencing, and watched helplessly as I left the house leading the dog on a leash to the beach. I had to get "away" from the overload to my processing mind. I did not know what I was going to do, but I just had to be somewhere with less input to my frazzled nerves. I walked fully dressed right into the ocean with the dog on her leash. People were watching me and laughing, but for me it was no joke. I was desperate to find some relief.

The water was warm and inviting me. I was *home*. I felt the ocean like a great Mother saying in waves... "I love you. I love you." It was so loving and beautiful. It was so healing and soothing that I started to cry. I had found some relief from the incessant input of information, but I knew I had to go back to my confused reality. The goddess of the ocean, Yemaya, as gentle and loving as she was, could not entirely take away this assault on my "Little Ego" nightmare, but she and her rich beauty definitely helped that day.

The sensory overload and the input from everywhere making every day seem so long still continued. The sorcerer, don Juan, of Carlos Castaneda's books says that a Sorcerer's,"life is... interminable." He explained that sorcerers "counted their lives in hours, and that in one hour it was possible for a sorcerer to live the equivalent in intensity of a normal life."[12] This was my experience as each day seemed 300 years long. I imagined my guru lived like that and wondered how he could endure the caverns of time. Don Juan continued that when the energy field is shifted, we are able to take in more energy than usual, and this makes us more aware that we are "perceivers" with "more possibilities than our minds can conceive."[13] My left brain could not deal with it, but for some familiar part of me it was perfectly 'acceptable' and almost 'normal' to be processing so much information at the same moment. Yet I have to admit that had I lived in that state any longer, I should have been unable to have finished my graduate work or felt capable of earning a living. This mode of awareness was not viable for the left-brain, rational, "Yuppie," nor for academic life.

The Heart:

But even though my days were strange and confusing, there were always periods of wonderful bliss in meditation. My heart was content and happy even as my mind panicked. More than once in meditation, I could see the heart as beautiful pastel lotus with petals of slightly different colors that moved slowly open and closed in some liquid inside my heart. The lotus faced up from the heart as if my body were the lake it sat in. When certain petals would move, I would feel an emotion, like anger for example. Then that lotus petal would gently lie back, as another petal rose, and then I would feel happiness. I would watch this exquisite undulating swaying scene for hours and understood that the heart's petals govern our emotions, and like petals that move in a gentle wind, they change constantly.

Bruce Lipton states that "in Chinese medicine, the heart is considered the center of wisdom,... in the ancient Vedic tradition, the heart is the mediator between Heaven and Earth." He goes on to explain the HeartMath Institute has found, "The heart is the interface between consciousness and the physiologic responses that generate emotions."[14] I had discovered the beauty of the heart that my guru's teacher had spoken of when he said in the heart there is a sacred city where we should wander. In the heart it seemed to me, there were all the worlds we could see with our physical eyes, all the knowledge that had ever been known, all the reasons and causes of everything. These understandings completely enlightened my awareness.

Poetic union:

At times, wide awake, I was merged into everything: stars, insects, people, trees, even the wind. Once I became the wind and, at the same time, a tree having an intimate love affair with each other. The wind would come and stir my branches to entice me to fly with her, but I would hold still to the ground and keep my role at the mediator between earth and sky. Sometimes the wind would sulk and leave, and I would yearn for that caress among my leaves. It was so real and poetic. It was a delightful, ecstatic love affair. Poetry came easily although the concepts were not always understandable to the logical brain world.

For at least a week in this state, I literally took on the persona of Radha, the wife of Krishna, and I spent endless hours in agony longing for him. Whatever I did, sewing, reading or washing dishes became a beautiful expression of my love for Krishna. It was exquisitely painful, but also rich and healing to yearn so fully for my husband. I had become a Gopi, seeing Krishna everywhere. I remember sewing a rainbow colored dress in this state, dreaming and imagining that Krishna one day would see it. What a rich, meaningful world I was inhabiting! How could anything compare to this wonder?

Instant Knowledge:

My nights of meditation were filled with cosmic adventures; scenes from ancient times appeared before my eyes; revelations of the scriptures and meanings of esoteric books came out of nowhere; greetings from saints and gods were showered upon me, and visions of exotic places were my nightly repast. I would look at the grass of a lawn and see Sanskrit writing in it and somehow know what it meant. I went to the University of Hawaii Asian Library collection and found books written in different languages, and I could read some of them from right to left and somehow know what I was reading. I remember feeling an exultant joy that nothing was hidden from me because of language. Every language and every book was available to me.

Once while in meditation, I went to heaven, a divine place with pastel crystal palaces and lots of white marble steps where genteel, smiling people walked serenely. I remembered when I had been there before. I knew that this place was not my goal now. It seemed a boring place to me, but I imagine that in one past lifetime I had yearned to go there.

Another day in meditation, I flew to a place that I called "Venus." I saw wondrous people of gentle temper and pale blue skin and flowers that were as tall as trees. Their blossoms were the size of umbrellas in colors that I had never seen on earth, even in the most amazing flowers here. The colors glistened with a subtle vibrance that shone out of them, and the flowers waved and nodded in some invisible breeze as if they were always saying, "Yes." Even if I had my eyes open, I could see these flowers and their stunning colors. Many years later, I saw something similar to this in the movie "Avatar" with its blue-tinted giants who inhabited a wondrous garden of beauty.

Kriya Moves:

Kriyas are spontaneous movements of energy pushing through the nervous system creating odd body movements. This could be jerks of the arms, legs, face, head etc. as if someone had pulled a puppet string. Before falling into a doze and as I was waking up again, my body would jerk violently as my leg might suddenly kick into the air, or my elbow give a strong jump for no apparent reason. I felt that this was my spirit coming and going from my body. I had no control over this. I experience this now only if I am exhausted physically before falling asleep. Perhaps it is related to releasing stress in the nervous system; however, it is a common issue with *Kundalini* symptoms.

Tongue Moves:

My tongue would cleave to the top of my mouth and move back and up as if into my sinuses in a feat that I could never do normally. Yogis in India would cut the skin under their tongues to be able to do this. The tip of the tongue is very significant magnetically and seeks a connection to the roof of the mouth activating something like a rejuvenating glandular liquid that is said to drip from the pineal gland. I had no conscious control over this. Research shows that the tongue and pineal are similar tissue. The pineal moves up inside the brain in the fetus as an extension of the throat and tongue, but it is not brain tissue, having similar cones and rods to our seeing eyes. Even today, when I am fully meditating my throat opens up backwards and up towards the inside of my head while the tongue automatically goes upward.

Kumbhak Breath:

In a small room at the University one day, I felt my breath pumping strangely. I sat on a cushion on the floor of our study room, and watched amazed as my belly got larger and larger, swelling into the size of a seven-month pregnancy within minutes. I could not stop this *kriya* no matter how I tried, as my breath just continued to be taken over by the *Kundalini* as it performed spontaneously. My stomach gradually grew into an enormous size, and then at a certain point, I found my legs locked into a yogic lotus position and my breathing ceased altogether. I sat there minute after minute without any panic or stress not breathing in or out. The breath seemed to be held in my bloated belly, and somehow I understood this as my mind became incredibly peaceful and calm. Had I not experienced it, I should never have believed it possible. I did not take a single breath for at least 15 minutes or longer.

I learned that this is a sign that the *Kundalini* or *prana* is balanced within the central channel (*sushumna*). The *prana* balances when breathing stops. Swami Vishnu Tirth states, "involuntary *kumbhak* (filling of the lungs with air) starts beyond control, breath is forcibly exhaled out,... know then that Kundalini has awakened."[15] Ramana Maharshi calls this "*kevala kumbhaka* (spontaneous retention of breath, without attention to inhalation or exhalation)."[16] Both my guru, his guru and many other Indian saints also had large pot bellies which were not from food, but from this *kumbhak* or retention of breath. This signaled that I had control of the breath with leads to control of the mind's restlessness. To this day I can experience this again during long meditations; it seems to rejuvenate me and bring total stillness to the mind.

Noises and Voices:

Throughout this process of awakening, I heard roaring noises in my head like distant thunder and experienced a most radical shaking of the inner worlds. Swami Vishnu Tirtha explains this as a stage in the progress of the *Kundalini* to hear sounds of "bells, conches, drums, flutes, etc., culminating in one resembling thunder."[17] He says these sounds, nada, cause the mind to be overpowered so that the mind becomes empty and calm. The thunderous booming, clicks, pops, cracks, conch shell horns, flute playing and ringing at times were only audible to me, yet the noises were so loud, I could not believe someone else could not hear them. I cannot explain how this occurs among those experiencing this awakening; perhaps it is caused by the *Kundalini* opening up subtle psychic channels or *nadis* that have been heretofore closed. Perhaps these *nadis* are very close to the ear mechanism so it is so loud. I am sure there is a Sanskrit book somewhere that can explain this as the ancient Rishis wrote about all these symptoms in detail.

In contrast to this seeming mystical sound, came voices of some disembodied beings. These may be called "non-organic" entities. Carlos Castaneda's don Juan calls this entity a "dreaming emissary."[18] Don Juan warns these voices often give false information, which I also learned; I learned to only trust the voices that came through my heart. If the voice came three times through my heart, then I knew it was authentic. Many people allow "channeling" of these non-organic entities through themselves like "mediums." Some great teachings have come through this method such as *A Course in Miracles* by Helen Schucman, and *The Return of the Bird Tribes* by Ken Carey.

However, I found these "mind talkers" to be tricksters that could cause problems for me. I learned to ignore the voice or just shut these "clever" voices off. My teacher said only after many levels of realization should one listen to these voices. I have met people who love having these voices in their heads as it gives them some sense of importance. It is unfortunately something the ego enjoys as one can feel a friendly presence that enhances one's feeling of being "gifted" or "special." However, the voices, although seeming to be helpful, are best ignored until their authenticity can be assured.

Spontaneous Yoga:
While sitting on the floor reading a book or watching television, I might suddenly find my body in a strange position. My head would be thrust back into a position called "Fish Pose" where my neck was strained back so my face looked directly behind me with the throat

facing the ceiling. This happened very frequently and when the tension in the neck was released, then I could sit up, but until then, I could not move from this position as the muscles were literally "held" there. This is the same kind of tension in my neck that I experienced when I was sobbing in the meditation center in July of 1979. Many people experienced similar spontaneous Hatha Yoga experiences among the group that I would meditate with. This pose was releasing stress from my neck and it felt really good afterwards. While chanting, I would also do spontaneous *mudras* with my hands in positions that mirrored those of Indian dancers. These are said to reflect various ways that the *Kundalini* is coursing through the brain affecting spiritual progression.

Xray/Double vision:

One afternoon going to a Roundtable Pizza place with my husband and child, I got out of the car and looked up at the green Ko'olau Mountains of O'ahu, but overlaid them were the Himalayas with snow peaks that appeared to be like Mount Kailash, the most sacred mountain in the Himalayas. I was amazed I could see what was actually not there. It was as if the Himalayas were overlaid like a film over the real Ko'olau's. I could see both at the same time; both appeared to be real. I was intrigued and surprised but not afraid. I could distinguish clearly the various snowy peaks of these Himalayan Mountains, see the sunlight reflected on them and almost breathe the crisp mountain air. I was thus virtually in two places at once. It was as real as being there.

Dr. Dennis Gersten asserts that a spiritual vision is not the same as a psychotic vision because the "'normal' person who has a vision doesn't have a psychotic reaction to it." I had no reaction. I accepted this vision as I would any other sight before my eyes. He says further that visions are an average experience for "saints and great mystics... who are spiritually advanced."[19]

Inside the pizza place, we had to stand in line. A tall man in front of me had broad shoulders, and I was facing his back. I could not believe what I was seeing. I saw weapons buried in his flesh in an energetic form, hatchets in his head, spears through his side, and arrows into his shoulders. I could "see" right into the etheric form of this man. As I watched with fascination, I decided to see if I could move these weapons; with my will and intent, I pulled the spears and arrows out of his body and they flew off into space. It was incredibly fascinating, as I had never seen anything like this before. At some point, he turned around and stared me straight in the eye saying non-verbally, "Thank you."

This vision seems to be a sort of supercharged Xray only it is three dimensional, so I can see as if I am actually inside the body in a tiny omnipotent form, or as if the body were a lake into which I could peer. These are called *siddhis* or powers which come with the awakening of various chakras in the body; it is said that when the throat chakra is opened, our imagination becomes reality. When I saw into the body, it was as if I had an open view of the internal organs, called "medical intuitive." It is like seeing with a tiny camera or scope such as the surgeons now use inside people. We know that the body is not solid, and that the distances between the particles in our bodies are astronomically far apart, so that really there is no such thing as "solid." This ability to see on this frequency, as a result of the extremely rapid vibrations in the pineal gland, allows anyone to penetrate and see right into tissue at the microscopic level.

It seems obvious that the Third Eye or pineal gland is sensitive to light and able to "see" at a higher frequency than light waves. It is the "light of the body" referred to in the Bible (Matt 6:22) which says, "If therefore thine eye be single, thy whole body shall be full of light." Robert G. Chaney explains that the pineal is positive, masculine and the pituitary negative, feminine and receptive, so that it directs a high frequency emanation towards the pituitary creating a third form of energy.[20] This is a self-luminous kind of light that enables the eye of the pineal gland to see even if the eyes are shut or there is darkness. It can see any distance to any place.

But, not only does this awakened energy enable one to see beyond physical form, but also to change the things that are seen, such as this example at the Roundtable Pizza; I was seeing the past life wounds of that man, but I made them disappear and leave. It was as if they vanished and flew off. I brought my *intention* to clear these wounds and injuries to his body and that was enough to make them disappear. As each trauma left, I knew it was gone forever. This was one of the boons promised by opening up Mercurius and allowing him to come out—the ability to heal others.

Flying Siddhi:

It seems that lifting off the ground was a *siddhi* that negated the laws of gravity and 'common sense.' I had learned to fly a small plane, but this involved engineering and technology which everyone could accept. But this *Kundalini* flying required no mechanical apparatus, technology or fuel. Just by willpower, I could fly to far off galaxies and visit there wide awake and see everything as if I were truly there. Was I in my body or was it my spirit leaving the body behind?

Late in 1979, I had gone to the Ashram to speak to the swami about the strange experiences of lifting off the ground that I was having, but he did not really have a clue what I was going through. Unable to help, he asked me to meditate in the lovely tropical garden of the Ashram, but this just increased my lack of grounding as it was luscious and beautiful. I held on to a plumeria tree to keep from spinning away; almost immediately, I was in a wheel-less chariot racing into space and visiting the mountain home of Shiva in Kailash which is in the mountains of Tibet. I saw Shiva and his wife, Parvati, in their palace and they greeted me there with hugs and waves. Then I zoomed back to the Ashram garden, still clasping the tree to stay grounded. What an honor it felt to have seen that, for I knew the pilgrimage to Kailash to see Shiva's abode gives a release from karma. It was very auspicious. It also made me realize that my body had not left the tree, but 'I' had left—my awareness or consciousness had travelled to Tibet.

Even though I had found that my body did not go on these flights, I am sure that my body did actually lift off the ground during my spins in my living room. How else could I have been up there in the 15 ft ceiling looking at the patio door and wondering if I would be thrown through it? How else could it be that my dog and cat upturned their heads to look at me? If my body had been on the ground, would they have looked up at me in the ceiling if it were only my spirit there? I doubt that. According to Ajit Mookerjee, there are many accounts of spiritual beings called "Natha" who fly. "There is abundant evidence that their yogic powers enabled the siddhai-yogis to defy gravity... they attained a buoyancy which reduced their body weight and allowed them to lift themselves in space as they pleased."[21] This was exactly what was happening to me, and others I have known who also shared this same tradition of Kashmir Shaivism as a result of meeting my teacher.

What would another person have seen if he or she had been watching me that day? Carlos Castaneda had the same question of Nestor who had been present when Carlos had jumped off a precipice. Carlos is not sure if he jumped in his body or it was just his *dreaming* body. Nestor says, "I saw you two holding each other and running towards the edge,... then I saw you both like two kites against the sky."[22] Nestor in *The Second Ring of Power* describes what it was like to leap off a precipice. "Before I hit the bottom I became so light that I didn't fall anymore but floated. The air went through me."[23] This was part of their sorcery training. How had I learned to do this? It must have been in a past life for nothing had prepared me for this flying, and yet it was extremely blissful and familiar.

When I thought about this feat, I realized that all my life I had felt a similar kind of lifting. I had felt this kind of flying as an athlete in races, feeling this power coming from my solar plexus to force me into the winning position. I never started the race feeling this pull to win, but always it would emerge and propel me to the front of the racers. I still get this same surge of energy when I am in a contest.

During ballet classes when we had to leap across the dance floor, I often felt something very emotional rise up into my throat that felt like it would choke me. As I leapt, I would be suspended in the air, flying, as if I were about to launch into the sky, but at the same time, I repressed the overwhelming emotion that came with this aerial feat. I did not understand it and was afraid of this power. So I did not allow this feeling to take over; but now I understand that I might have exploded with emotion as

I did in the meditation center in 1979. It was the same joy rising up as I would leap across the dance floor. I have seen this same aerial suspension in certain dancers like Nureyev or Cossack dancers, and perhaps they experience that same emotion but without holding it back.

Unfortunately, the timing of these anti-gravity episodes was not always convenient or private. An embarrassing flying incident happened some years later when I was teaching a class at the University. I felt this lightheadedness coming on; I am sure my students wondered if I was under a drug, for my speech was slurred, dreamy and absent. I could barely talk as if my left brain were shutting down. I sent the students home early. I called my husband to come and pick me up as I knew I could not drive home. While I waited for him on Campus Drive, I had to cling to the trees since I knew that I would fly off if I did not. Trees anchored me to the earth in a loving way. How could I explain to anyone what was happening to me? Castaneda's don Juan explains this shift in *The Fire from Within* as my "assemblage point" had moved. "You see, to be healthy and sane means that the assemblage point is immovable. When it shifts, it literally means that one is deranged." He says that a warrior will wait "impassive, untouched, knowing that the assemblage point always returns to its original position."[24]

Even with these flying events, I did not at that time make a connection to the ancient stories of the snake and wings, the flying or feathered serpent of many traditions, called Quetzalcoatl also Kukulcan in Mexico. Also I had not realized the significance of the caduceus' wings which has not only two snakes around the central rod, but two wings at the third eye area symbolizing flight. There is a precious book called *The Secret of the Golden Flower* translated from Chinese by Richard Wilhelm. In this book is a host of subtle wisdom about the process of awakening, meditation and realization. One passage seems to refer to this up-drawing or flying energy.

> ... when one sits in meditation, the fleshly body becomes quite shining like silk or jade. It seems difficult to remain sitting; one feels as if drawn upward.

> This is called: 'The spirit returns and touches heaven.'
> In time, one can experience it in such a way that one
> really floats upward.[25]

This floating, levitation or flying was happening to me when I would spin in my living room which had a 15ft ceiling. There would be days where I could barely keep from leaving the ground, for the ecstasy and bliss were indescribable.

The snake moving in my spine and the ecstatic flying were signs I was under the spell of the flying serpentine *Kundalini* also called Quetzalcoatl. This serpent "is a symbol of the wave movement that emanates from the Tree of Life" according to Carl Johan Calleman, Ph.D, and thus it is an integral aspect of our human origins. He goes on to say that the San people of Botswana say humankind "descended from a python," and that the python can be interpreted as a wave movement.[26] He also postulates this similar activating wave coming from the center of the galaxy in this era is changing and will continue to change humanity with mass *Kundalini* awakenings.

Thus this *siddhi* confirms that there is a hidden serpent, dragon or flying snake within us which is found in all ancient cultures and traditions around the world. Anyone who has felt the snake-like movement of the *Kundalini* knows this is an unmistakable undulating serpent. The bird or feathers are a metaphor for the spirit within man which leaps and flies from the body as this *Kundalini* is activated. It is a reversal of gravity, anti-gravity. I believe gravity is a form of "reverse love" energy, a pushing away from our source. When one is transported by the bliss of union with the divine, this gravity force is overcome, and the love draws us upwards in ecstasy. The propulsion power is via the sexual energy moving upward rather than down. Thus not only do the sexual energy and spirit rise, but also the body rises. "He [the yogi] can make his body as light as cotton or feather.... The Yogi travels in the sky with the help of this *Siddhi*. He can travel thousands of miles in a minute."[27]

These powers or skills that come from the awakened *Kundalini* are called "*siddhis.*" They come to one who meditates as a result of concentration and focus. This can be compared to the power of the Kung Fu master who concentrates his *ki* energy into his hand and breaks the block of wood. It is also somewhat like the focus lens of a laser beam where all the light rays are one coherent wavelength, and the light released is aligned. My seeing into bodies, seeing places simultaneously that were thousands of miles away, knowing the feelings and intentions of my family and animals, flying around my house were all types of *siddhis* or powers.

However, these powers can be a kind of trap that keeps us from pushing through to the freedom which lies beyond all these tricks. The goal is to find the silent "witness" behind all this mind stuff and merge with that. That is freedom. At this point, the events of my awakening were too dramatic, too amazing, too exciting to know that they were actually a distraction from the goal of meeting my true nature. My "Little Ego" was still too actively in control of my consciousness for me to experience its demise and the rising wisdom of my heart. There were still many stages of evolution that I had to go through before I would overcome the "Little Ego" and integrate the mind and heart.

Parallel Universe:

In finding solutions to the physical and emotional issues that arose during this period, I discovered a world beyond the every day, 3-D physical reality of our solar system and galaxy. I discovered that there are parallel universes exactly the same but opposite to the one we inhabit. What is left here is right there, what is black here is white there for example like a mirror. Parallel universes imply that there is another universe where everything is "parallel" to ours— a mirror copy of our universe. Whatever it is, one can interact with this alternate parallel world. What goes on in this universe is also happening there but in the opposite pole or as a counterbalance to ours.

Dr. Stan Grof reports on parallel universes that "often these worlds seem to be located on planes of reality that are parallel to, and which coexist with, our own."[28] I knew from meditation that between or balancing out the two universes was a space that was zero, null and void.

This space could absorb all kinds of chaos and conflict and still remain unaffected. What was a 'plus' in our world was a 'minus' in the parallel world, so they cancelled each other out at the boundary. Carlos Castaneda's don Juan discusses this same experience of a space or hole in the Earth leading into a parallel world. "That world and this world we live in are on two parallel lines."[29]

With this knowledge I solved some everyday problems. Sometimes in meditation, I would feel aches and pains around my heart that were persistent and aggravating. I decided one day to see if I could take the pain to the parallel universe boundary with this universe and neutralize the pain. So I made a metaphorical bundle with a clear image of the pain, added a color and texture to it, then imagined it inside a bag. I grabbed this pain-bundle and zoomed off as a tiny point of awareness into the astral sky as I had done many times while visiting other worlds. I would make an intention to: "Find the opposite" as I zoomed into space. The intention manifested the solution.

Soon, I would feel myself magnetized to a certain area in space, and then a "thunk" of docking into something that was the opposite of my little bundle of pain. I would exchange my bundle for this other energy, and quickly zoom back to my own heart in my body where I would merge this new bundle to replace the old one. By amazing grace, this pain would be gone permanently leaving no trace. I would never have it again. It was a huge discovery and a great blessing. I do not need any scientist to "prove" this parallel reality exists, for I was actively interacting with it.

I wrote an article later about this on my web site; my friends used this technique for healing people, and they agreed it worked every time. They called it "Equal and Opposite." I called it "Soul Salves." A friend who learned NLP years later told me that this was the same concept used in their teacher training. It works, but I can only speculate on the physics, for it is a stretch of imagination indeed. It is just one more of the mysteries of being human. For me it felt that I had taken a little piece of peaceful harmony and brought that into my universe to counterbalance what seem inharmonious. Where we have wars and chaos, our parallel universe has peace and order, so bringing these together neutralizes the chaos.

Blisses:

Besides strange events, there were also days of incredible orgasmic ecstasy where my eyes rolled up in my head. I would sit to meditate on the mantra *"Om Namah Shivaya"* and feel this love in my heart for God. Then I would feel a creeping, snaking ecstasy coming up from the root of my body, through my belly, through the solar plexus and up. This bliss could not be compared to anything else in my life. I found the English language totally inadequate to describe these types of blisses. There would be degrees of rapture that I am sure Sanskrit could describe, but I had few ways to describe these variations of bliss.

It was as if I had travelled in a far off country to everyone else for they lived in the world of seconds of "bliss" occasionally, and I was living in a world of on-going blisses, ecstasies of breath, of body, of spirit, of heart, of vision, of sound, of color, of smell which lasted all day. Always there were ineffable joys bombarding my being, filling my sleepless nights with untold beauty and wonder. Is this how Gods experience reality, I wondered?

So these discoveries, experiences and *siddhis* came, the wonder came, the revelations of my unity with the universe all came and brought me jewels of delicate and subtle joys. I received insights and revelations about the true nature of a human being. We are not bound to the body, we can travel back and forth in time and space simply by intention and imagination; we can ride time like a wave into chasms with multiple awareness of events, beings and Nature around us; we can intend and imagine ourselves or others healthy and well; we can intend to heal and it happens as co-creators. We can love and thus become multi-dimensional, changing the planet, the solar system, the universe at will. All this was making it clear to me that our "true nature" as humans is a whole lot more than I had been given to believe.

CHAPTER 13

Dying While Living

"... I see the death image as almost always signifying the death of the limited state of being, of the previous state of the ego, or of the insufficient personality."

John Weir Perry[1]

One of the classic symptoms of *Kundalini* awakening is a distinct and ever-present awareness of death. I had heard my guru speak about "dying while living" and had always wondered about this phrase which kept going through my head and heart. What did it mean? How could I be dying as I was living? There came a point where I made a decision to explore this further. Some months after *Shaktipat,* in a deep meditative state, my conscious mind wanted to know about death. I planned an experiment which seemed logical and reasonable. I thought about it carefully and decided to create an opportunity to taste an experience of death. I had no fear or qualms. I felt supremely protected and safe with my teacher's guru and my teacher very present with me on the inner planes.

Experiment:
Making sure I was alone, I went out into the garden and allowed myself to fall backwards onto the top of my head. I was totally relaxed as I

fell under the tangerine tree in our yard. Lying inert, I went into a very death-like inner spiral. I spiraled in and in to a tiny space in my heart *chakra*. I saw these spirals as different colors and like a rainbow vortex, they circled smaller and smaller and my being became smaller and smaller until I was only a single point of consciousness, sitting in the center of my heart.

Flies came and walked all over my face and body, but I remained in my death-like state, frozen and not concerned by the flies. I was completely aware, but I was as one in a coma, for I did not move. I could hear birds singing, I could smell the mock orange and *pakalana* in the bushes, and I could feel the hum of the air alive with life. No one disturbed me while I was there, but if they had I should have just pretended that I had been napping. I lay in a highly conscious inner space. I felt the flies on my face, had awareness of time and who I was, but I was NOT alive in the sense that my body was inert almost paralyzed. After what must have been about fifteen minutes, I *willed* myself to return. I came out of the spiral the way I had gone in through a rainbow spiral of color deep in my heart, and I filled my body with life again. I got up realizing that this experience had given me some valuable knowledge about death.

It seems interesting that I chose this way to experience death for the top of the head is the most stressful point of the body in birth. It is also where the hair on the head spirals, the fontanel. Perhaps there was something I needed to relive in order to experience real life again. For it was actually life I had found. No school or lessons could have taught me more about life and death than this experience.

I learned that day that death was just a portal or a doorway into another garden of life. One's death is not an end but an entrance to more and more spirals of life. I learned that it was truly life that endured through the death of the body... and that life loved itself and controlled the entire picture of living and dying. I was profoundly changed by this experience and though it may have seemed foolish from a logical stand-point, from my view, as the experiencer, the meaning of this experiment was perfect. I had learned what those who have near death experiences feel as they come back renewed and changed.

Years later I was to witness an animal, a bat, in hibernation shown by a thermal camera to be lifeless and inert, yet when it awoke gradually heat came to its heart and then the rest of the body warmed to life again like a widening spiral. It reminded me of this experience in my garden under the tangerine tree. What amazing things I was discovering in this *Kundalini* adventure.

My Magic Wand:

I walked into the house feeling euphoric and peaceful, but then I came more and more into my bodily sensations and had to admit—I had a raging headache. I tried to bend over to load the dishwasher, but had to stop for the pain in my crown was too much. I looked into this pain from within my mind and sent my *Kundalini* to the center of it. How I knew how to do this I have no idea. But it was as if I had a sort of magic wand inside the very base of my body, and I could send energy, laser-like to any place in my body and heal it. At first the pain reeled with even more agony as this energetic hose focused on it, like a blast of water almost, but I persisted in directing my "force" into it. This seemed to evaporate the pain, and it just disappeared as if folds of love were healing each painful part. The pain was gone in less than five minutes, and I went on with my day.

Many years later I read that my own teacher had done similar experiments to this in order to discover if death were real. I read in *Trials of the Visionary Mind* by Perry that this death trip is actually an effort by one's spirit to die to the old personality and framework which is being shed like a snake skin.[1] The theme of death becomes part of the renewal process with the *Kundalini*. There is a need to re-feel death and birth again to determine new meaning for these. There is also the element of rebirth or even a kind of reincarnation into the same body through these experiences.

Because of this and other bizarre things happening to me, I moved myself out of our bedroom into the guest room, and this caused my husband to get very suspicious. How could I explain to him what was happening? I did not understand how to explain it to myself. The distance between us widened, and he spent more time at work. What I did not know is that without being in his grounding energy field at night, my spirals into the depths of my subconscious just accelerated.

The *Kundalini* facilitates the unraveling of one's past life sufferings, and enables the tape of all one's lifetimes to unwind. As the mind is cleared of more and more of these strange creatures, dreams, fears, tendencies, so other ones beneath come to the surface. It is like stirring up a soup pot where all the heavy things are at the bottom. As one stirs, so the issues come up to the surface to be exposed to our conscious awareness. I believe it is the bliss experienced in meditation that allows the dark memories and fears to feel "safe" rising up from the depths of the hidden mind to be healed. It means that most "normal" people are walking around with a subconscious full of these strange companions who are hidden as long as our focus is on everyday 'departmentalized' awareness and living without inner reflection.

It is well documented that people who experiment with hallucinatory drugs find out soon enough that the crowd inhabiting their heads is not always friendly. This can lead to a lifetime of haunting, paranoia and misery because they are not prepared for this journey into the depths of their psyches. This is another reason that it is wise to have a teacher who him or herself has gone through this journey and emerged on the other side.

But on the other side of this digging out the subconscious was the dark side of my own past lives. I was to find that I too had haunted others, and the price was revengeful energies that haunted me and turned all the bliss into hell. During some phase of my involution through various bodies and lives, I had been a sorceress and had employed elemental energies in black arts to carry out evil intentions against enemies or opponents.

Karmic debts:

The energetic debt to these elemental entities does not go away just because we change bodies. If we have a debt to pay for services rendered in one life, then the elemental energies will come to us in future lifetimes to get repaid, like the cosmic Mafia. Just like the subconscious mind, these elementals have no limitations in time. Time seems to be a factor of the human mind, and they are outside of that. They come to claim their energetic debts without regard to when these debts were incurred, to who you were then, nor to whom you are now. In Castaneda's *The Art of Dreaming*, Carol explains "Something nearly, nearly got me." And concludes her experience as "inorganic beings collecting their dues."[2] I concur that they just want the bill paid. If we have used them for black magical arts in one lifetime without having repaid them in kind, they will indeed come for the balance in any lifetime where the opportunity arises.

Learning this helped me understand why we do not always see justice working in our world. Executives or thieves who steal, lie, and fraudulently cheat others of their money, walk away with millions of dollars that leave thousands without jobs or in hardship, yet we witness these frauds go unpunished by the law. It appears unfair to the victims and observers, but even if a person is not punished for crimes in this physical life, he or she will still have to pay the victims back and receive punishment in a future life. Of this there is no doubt. Who knows how it will be paid back? Perhaps it would be repaid in a lifetime of slavery to each victim, perhaps as an abused child of another victim, perhaps it could be condemnation to a murky hell world, or perhaps as a mistreated pet, or a soldier maimed in the war. We just cannot know how the law of karma will play itself out, only that it is inevitable and merciless.

So this is the greatest form of justice; however, whatever comes to us will be some repayment of our karmic debts, whether they be good or bad. The brilliant and gifted engineer, Itzhak Bentov, explains consciousness in cartoon-like drawings to make it more comprehensible. He says that "Manifest Creation... is a tight structure, a hologram, with all parts interrelated. This is the basis for the law of karma or the principle that to every action there is a corresponding reaction."[3]

Dear reader, when these karmic energies hit me, it was as if a 50-ton truck had run over me. I could not move. I was paralyzed. I could feel no life or joy anywhere. It was all I could do to exist. I could barely cook or clean; I could not exercise or even eat. I was only able to take care of my daughter and husband and get their meals almost like an automaton. The duty to them gave me some kind of energy to get up. When they were out of the house, all I could do was to lie flat on my bed, drained and exhausted from morning to night. I was feeling all the negativity that I had inflicted on others only magnified. This was paralytic depression. Such an experience would instantly reform any black magician, or any person putting out mean and negative intentions to another would instantly cease their meanness, for all of it MUST come back. It comes as a dark wind that sucks the very vital force out of the soul. Could hell be any worse than this total lack of life force? Such is the price we pay for misusing power and abusing others.

It was a number of months I suffered in that state, dragging around, taking care of my home and family without any life energy, before gradually I began to return to normal. One thing that always brought me back to myself was chanting and meditation with a group. Whenever I could, I would go to the meditation center as if my life depended on it, and I would sit down feeling absolutely horrible and worthless. The chanting would begin; I would get lost in it, allowing the music, the drums, the singing to reverberate through me; the meditation would conclude the program, and I would open my eyes to a "normal" me again. It was incredible how that helped me. Just a few hours a week of feeling normal kept me going towards that state again and helped me survive. Without that, I do not know how I could have continued to live my life.

I was beginning to wonder if I could truly make it through the process of cleansing my past lives and karmic debts. I had started out with such joy and bliss, but now this process was dragging up the muck of my subconscious; it was certainly not easy. The journey into my psyche was negatively affecting my family life, but I was riding the *Kundalini* train, and there were no stations to get off. The best I could do was take a rest from meditation for a while and allow the energies to calm and cool. I asked everywhere for people who knew about this phenomenon, but none did. Who could relate to it? Only one person came close—my spiritual teacher—who was in Miami; I wrote to him about my craziest experiences; his reply always said it was "auspicious" and to keep doing my practices. At the time it was hard to see that as a valid response, but now of course, after spending years pondering this event and seeing my own evolution, I realize what a huge gift he gave me.

The Bardos:

On my desk as I write are two beautiful Tibetan paintings of "White Tara" and "The Healing Buddha." Around White Tara or *Amitabha* are many deities with six arms and three heads some riding strange looking animals. Some of these are the deities that visit a soul that has passed from human life which is in the *bardo* or "transition" between death and the next incarnation. I learned it is important to become familiar with these deities before one's death because during that period, how one reacts to and how one meets these entities in the passage through this *bardo* (gap or space between states of consciousness), determines one's next life or possible enlightenment and freedom from bondage.

Spiritual traditions, based upon the understanding of the phases of death and reincarnation, prepare a soul for this vital transition period. The highest possibilities for being released from the endless cycle of births and suffering, of involution, and misery are made at this transition point of dying; thus religious education *should be* about this major crossing point. "By following the training of these practices, it is actually possible to realize these states of mind while we are still alive."[4] I was realizing these states of mind at 33 years of age while I was strong and young enough to bear it.

According to *The Tibetan Book of the Dead,* lack of knowledge of what to expect in the *bardo* between death and rebirth, and lack of spiritual knowledge can lead one into "hell and...unbearable suffering through heat and cold from which you will never get out." If one does not understand the different experiences of the mind as they present themselves after death, one could end up as an animal being "tormented by boundless suffering."[5] It is vitally important to know about the phases of death as with the right teaching, one can leap to an advanced level and avoid the hell realms just by knowing and studying this information. This lifetime *bardo* is the period in which we must prepare for this important transition time.

Christian Missionary:

My teen years in the church earnestly searching for enlightenment seemed like a waste of time after I learned this. I remember being at my Church of England Catechism ceremony on my 15th birthday, yearning to be a Christian missionary to take the word that Jesus is the only true way to ignorant African children who had never known Jesus. I thought then that I understood enough about the subject to teach others. But nothing I had learned in all this study had given me one insight into the state of my own being. Nothing I had learned was preparing me for my transition or for transcendence. Nothing I had learned had uplifted me or transformed my character. All it had done was re-inforce socially compliant expectations to make me "good" and willing to sacrifice my own needs for everyone else's. It had made me self-righteous. I was certainly not getting enlightened; I was getting more entrenched in an imperialistic doctrine of the superiority of this "faith."

At the age of 15, I was pathetically and arrogantly ignorant of the truth. I realized now how a little knowledge combined with self-righteousness is a sophomoric and dangerous thing. I had to face the fact that virtually nothing in my Christian education had prepared me for this awakening to my natural spiritual life and the importance of preparing for my death. The church teaching was all about Jesus' sacrifice and pain for me, whereas my role was to be ignorant and unaware; let someone else bear the responsibility for me. It was about dependence on another, by "borrowing" Jesus' body and energy. But thanks to my guru, the truth had come through an amazing dream and the birthright of my humanity could not be suppressed any longer.

One positive thing has occurred to me from this experience in my church. The Church of England does not inculcate fear and dread into a child's subconscious like that of some religions. As Joseph Chilton

Pearce affirms in his book *The Biology of Transcendence,* "The Christian accusation of sin is part of the very fabric of our culture... It underlies our whole legal and legislative fabric and convinces us that without law and its justice, society would run amok... [and] is a major heresy of our or any age."[6] Having met people from certain "sin-obsessed" religious groups, I have seen their struggle with true spirituality, which is "non-denominational," completely aligned with Nature, and beyond any exclusive church affiliation; I see that my awakening was considerably less stressful ideologically than it was for them; I did not have a subconscious full of guilt, fear and threats from everlasting damnation or hell fire. I had my culture's and parent's fears, negativity and anxiety as everyone does, but it was not pounded into me with the authority of "angels," "god" or "heaven."

So I am grateful for this church system that was established by our conflicted Henry VIII, and which I now see allowed the people of the United Kingdom to have a freedom from a hell-focused conscience, freedom from oppressive religious dogma, and freedom from mental straight jackets that were a key to our country's common sense. This religion did not support my true spiritual evolution, but it did not prevent it.

With my *Kundalini* awake, eighteen years after my Catechism, I was grasping great principles of the soul and understanding things that had been secret doctrines for thousands of years. I was entering the veil and hidden maze of my psyche and making real progress. I could feel a light was truly there for me at last. The *Kundalini* was lighting up areas of my brain, transforming all the life-denying concepts that had kept me tamed and compliant. I just "knew" what the Bible lessons meant without having to get any "interpretation." I understood the underlying goal of all spiritual practices and paths; it felt that my whole being was transforming as great truths were coming forth. What a huge gift I had been given. A great turn-around in my life had taken place.

Luminosity:

Aware therefore, of the valuable information in this little book, I made a practice to read *The Tibetan Book of the Dead,* even though it is obscure in places and not easy to understand. I discovered the answer to my obsession with death. The experiences I was having were similar to the trials and tribulations of the stages of dying—the *bardos*. I was going through them while I was young, alive and conscious, while I had a teacher helping me with the power of the *Kundalini*, and while my body was strong and vital. As I read Sogyal Rinpoche's wonderful explanation of the *Tibetan Book of the Dead*, in *The Tibetan Book of Living and Dying*, I found this clear statement:

> By causing the winds to enter and dissolve in the central channel through the force of meditation, a practitioner can have a direct realization of the luminosity or "Clear Light" of the nature of mind....In this way the yogin is imitating what happens at death; when the knots in the channels are released, the winds flow into the central channel, and enlightenment is momentarily experienced.[7]

This was a revelation. It was the most wonderful news I had had in my life. I began to put together the words my teacher had told me about "dying while living," and realized that what this whole "Meditation Revolution" that my teacher and his guru had started was to give Western people, *real* knowledge of how to depart this world of misery, something they could do to improve their chances of getting out of "*samsara*" or the cycles of hells that their ignorance subjected them to over and over again.

Few Western models had demonstrated to me this ability to "die while living" because it was shrouded in secrecy. Those in our culture who were awakened and aware were considered odd such as poets, madmen, artists, musicians and so forth, like William Blake or St. Theresa of Avila etc. This secret may have been taught only in hallowed protected practices of closed brotherhoods probably because of the immense power of this opening. But through my teacher and others coming to the West and spreading the news, thousands were being given this chance to know the truth of human existence. The gates to knowledge were opening to all of us alive at this time. These teachers knew that this time period was one where many could be given the chance to awaken, and they were giving as many souls the opportunity as possible. I wondered if this could be indeed the end of the Fall of Man under which we have suffered since the Garden of Eden?

How valuable my awakening was turning out to be! Now I began to understand that verse by Gautama Buddha about the value of a "rare" human birth. The mazelike puzzle was beginning to make sense.

The great transpersonal psychologist and founder of the International Transpersonal Association, Stanislav Grof M.D., agrees that experiences of altered "consciousness" from taking drugs, having near death experiences, or transpersonal crisis are described in the *Tibetan Book of the Dead*. He says that, "These ancient descriptions were not taken seriously by scientists until recently, when modern research in experimental psychiatry and thanatology confirmed their authenticity."[8]

Samsara:

Apparently there are series of "lokas" or "*bardos*" where one meets different levels of the mind. With each day after "death" one meets a deeper level (*bardo*) of entities or aspects of the mind which are often terrifying, but which are part of our deeper mind during life, whether we are aware of them or not. These appear to be similar visions to those on ancient rock art from thousands of years past. As one's spirit ascends towards the next life, these layers or levels of fears and demons appear to release and take a last stand on the stage of one's mind. They are ghoulish, fearful, dreadful in every way, but they, like the entity in my meditation, are not *real*. Any kind of reaction of fear or attraction would draw the departing soul into that level of awareness and the possibility for spiritual freedom would be gone. Should one freak out, become terrified or filled with desire to run away, then one is assured another life on Earth to fall back into another cycle of misery—*samsara*. The instructions are very clear:

If at this time when the fifty eight blood-drinking deities emerge from within your brain and appear before
you, you know that whatever appears has arisen out
of your own radiant insight, you will immediately
become a Buddha inseparable from the blood-drinking deities.//O child of noble family, if you do not
recognize in this way, you will be afraid of them and
escape, and so go on to more suffering.... You will feel
terrified and bewildered and faint. Your own projections will turn into demons and you will wander in
samsara. But if you are neither attracted nor afraid
you will not wander in *samsara*.[9]

The *bardo* or period between deaths called "living" is when these
important teachings should be introduced and studied by everyone. I
realized that my teacher's awakening was not just about my finding bliss
and meditation, but it was to give me the chance to release the accu-
mulated detritus in my subconscious mind and know my true nature
while I was young, strong and could bear it. In some reports there are
21 levels of the mind that have to be overcome to know the silence and
light that is full of peace.

The inestimable value of my *shaktipat* was beginning to be revealed.
Instead of having to experience this in the period after my death when
I might be old and worn out, I was going through the maze of these
aspects of my mind while alive and with a guru guiding me. I was not
weak, but as strong as I would ever be. I was not entirely alone, as I had
a guide taking care of my process, and I had the bliss that came with
the *Kundalini*. I came to realize that the *Kundalini* process was like
a short cut through the dying process. Gradually the meaning of the
guru's words began to make sense; I was actually "dying while living."

Pandora's Box:

As my meditations deepened, it was like the layers of an onion peeling off.
And as these layers got to deeper and deeper levels of the subconscious,

the experiences became even more bizarre and surreal. Strange entities appeared as I went further and further into the recesses of my subconscious. This is part of the mind's panoply of characters, parasites and entities gathered and acquired through all the lifetimes. William Bodri in *The Little Book of Hercules* says these entities are part of the "impure illusory body."[10] It seems that the more light I created in meditation, the more it shone into the darkest caves of my subconscious mind, and these creatures could see me, and I them. Pandora's box was opened!

These strange entities who were appearing in my meditation were the unfoldings of my deep mind. Lifetimes of murdering, being murdered or tortured, of deception, blackmail, betrayal and all the panoply of negative events that can happen to a human being are locked into the mind's ancient memory. They do not go away because when the truth comes, we find out that there is only ONE being of awareness living through us. All our "attacks" of others are actually attacks on our highest, most beloved Self. This memory comes along attached to us in each lifetime like a hitchhiker or a parasite. The *Kundalini* is the cleanser that pushes them out like a roto-rooter or like sausages extruded from grinders. As the warnings in the *Tibetan Book of the Dead* state, these ghastly entities "only arise out of the spontaneous play of your mind."[11]

Not having any knowledge of this process, that play got to be rather frightening for me. While meditating in my usual time, place and posture, a particular creature popped into my awareness. I saw it in a ghost-like form before me, but it was alive and moving. It stood before me unafraid, and not at all shy. It was ugly, hairless and grotesque with lumpy, reptilian greenish skin and a forked tail. It would have a sort of grimace on its face, something like the huge, fat slug-like being in "Star Wars," Jabba the Hut, only with little horns everywhere. It stood before me with its arms folded in the most arrogant manner and indicated that it was waiting for me to get into meditation and feel arousal as the *Kundalini* rose, so it could suck off my sexual feelings.

I stopped meditating immediately; I felt sick and violated by this creature who said its name was "Begneth." I recognized this name as being of some Kaballah origin, and wondered if I had acquired it in a past lifetime. Anytime I would meditate from then on this creature would appear snickering and lewd waiting for my feelings to arise.

I fretted about this and worried what to do. It seemed to trigger a memory of camping with Girl Guides in a field in England when I was 13. That summer, we had had a severe drought. I had to hike half a mile alone with two buckets to get water for our camp, and trudge over these withered, cracked and dried-out fields, climb over a fence, and go around a very old, derelict mansion to get to the water tap. The fields had cracks that were 6" wide and seemed to drop into infinity. Never had England had such a dry summer.

I remember being very wary of this old, abandoned house with its boarded up windows, overgrown garden and eerie silence; but what was even more sinister was in the space between dreams and awaking at that time and repeatedly on and off since then, I had seen this same creature peering at me as I walked across those fields. This creature in my dreams had always been watching me with leering, voyeur interest it seemed. Later in my life after much therapy, I was able to remember seeing this creature when I was being sexually abused at the age of four; it had been feeding off the energies of that experience. I had been truly terrified then by this creature who had every appearance of the devil himself to me at that age. I went catatonic with fright. It created a great scene for which I was blamed and from which I came away thinking, at age four, I had done something very wrong. So here he was again, bold and brazen.

I rifled through all the books I could find to see what to do about this interruption to my quiet meditations. After a few days I found something in my teacher's books that told of the *darshan* or vision that certain beings would give a meditator. These beings may not always appear to be friendly or welcome, and may be grotesque attached entities from my past. I read that they could not harm me unless they had a physical form; they come out of curiosity to see one of us humans in their realm; the creature may have come to suck off my rising *Kundalini* energy when I began to meditate.

Maybe if I had been exposed to the Tibetan images I have since seen in murals, or read about the Hindu tales of the *Ramayana* with all the creatures and demons that Rama fought, I might have been prepared for this. Like the ghost I had nightly seen in my bedroom as a teen, seeing such things was considered an imaginative illusion in my culture. Although this thing was not "real," as it had no physical form, still it was talking to me as an independent entity. I also had to face the fact that because the creature came in this way to my personal space, there was no escape from it. It would always be just there, disturbing my peaceful meditation and joy. It was somehow attached to my very own mind.

For me this was a confirmation of other dimensions within the realm of consciousness. Most Western people exist nicely cocooned in third dimensional consensual reality, and rarely see ghosts or beings from other realms. We are entrained from childhood to ignore anything like that; our dreams or nightmares where these creatures reveal themselves are dismissed as fantasies of our imaginations, not worthy of concern. Yet they are part of our hidden selves, our past lives, our collective unconscious, occupants of our subconscious, our ancestors and even beings that co-exist in other dimensions with us here on the planet. What a great deal I was grasping through this awakening.

I learned that it was also my fear, feelings and sensations that this creature was most anxious to ingest. Years later I read in the *Book 3* by Neale Donald Walsch, "God" states that "What you resist, persists. What you look at disappears."[12] But then I had only my teacher's books to help me. Finally I found his quote saying that the creature just wanted my energy or attention. I understood that the best way to deal with these beings was to ignore them and give them none of my emotional or sexual energy. I had to remain indifferent and unemotional, completely detached. If I had sexual feelings or emotions like fear, then it would appear. I had to get the message into my head: "No fear, no food," so I could keep my feelings calm and give this creature nothing to "eat." It did not mean "pretend it is not there," nor did it mean "push it out of my mind," or "suppress it," but to just acknowledge it was there and give it NOTHING in the way of my emotional energy. Having had the practice of detaching from my family in 1976 when I was learning to fly, I knew how to let go of the energy of fear.

Devilish Darshan:

When this creature appeared again, I was not afraid; looking at it squarely, I dispassionately and firmly informed it that it could visit as long as it wished, but that it would get rather bored, since I was not going to have any emotional or sexual feelings. About two weeks later, after having had mostly uneventful meditations without any strong emotions, I heard a sickening voice calling, "Ruth".

I answered, "What?"

It was Begneth. "I'm leaving you, " it stated with a malignant sneer.

"Oh you are?"

"You are so boring now. I have to find someone more interesting." It stated this as if I would be disappointed and be offended! What irony! It left and has never returned. Good riddance!

In don Juan's explanations of sorcery to Carlos Castaneda, he also mentions such "inorganic beings" and says the secret is "not to fear them." You need to send the message, "'I don't fear you. Come to see me. If you do, I'll welcome you.'"[13] He indicates that too much attachment to these creatures will interfere with ones' progress towards ultimate freedom.

An authentic American Indian healer, called Jade Wahoo Grigori has written a most enlightening article on such inorganic negative entities which he calls "spiritual parasites;" this should be required reading for any therapist or psychologist. With his permission, I share this gifted understanding. These entities create family abuse, even chronic fatigue syndrome or mental derangement. Such parasites attach to families and lineages, being passed down from one family member to the next generation ad infinitum... until someone like Jade can exorcise them. Jade is able to remove them through American Indian ceremonies which are ancient and proven. His web site article explains, "By removing the Parasites, and allowing the autonomic system to once again take up its normal task of maintaining the integrity of our own health and welfare, we rapidly move towards a condition of renewal and stability. We experience freedom!"[14] After it is removed, that energy it was stealing is restored to us.

The Grim Reaper:

Soon after this Begneth incident, with my eyes open one morning before I had even gotten out of bed, I saw the "Grim Reaper" standing at the foot of the left side of my bed. It was a skeleton under this dark hooded gown, and carrying a tall scythe. In all of literature, this is the symbol of death coming. But I did not feel fear. I stared intently at this creature because even though its appearance was grotesque, the bones were vibrating with a shining energy that reminded me of my guru's energy. I was more curious than alarmed. I said, "Shiva, is that you?" It paused and then melted into the wall invisible again. I laughed. It seemed to be a test to see if I had learned this one about apparitions! But it signaled a victory for me over something that since those days when I was a teen, had haunted and controlled me. My fear of ghosts was gone.

William Bodri explains this stage of seeing the "bone chi" of the body as an important stage of *Kundalini* which he says it to teach the person something about the purification process of the bones. Seeing the bones alive, or as I saw them vibrating with life force, is an important signal that a difficult part of the purification process has been accomplished.[15] So it was a signal to me that I had purified the bones of my body.

Since then, of course, I have seen many apparitions both from my own life and when working to help others. The appearance of these beings can look grotesque, but beneath all this ugliness and fearful appearance is an illusion and beneath that, an aspect of God vibrates.

Possession:

Other strange events occurred after this realization. Sometimes I would be aware that a being had come while I was meditating and inhabited my body in a form of possession. Often this lasted only a while, but once it lasted for a few days, and I was unable to clear it. No one but me seemed to know about this possession. One being appeared to be a very strong, bossy, male who had four heads and four arms. Dennis Gersten, an insightful psychiatrist explains, "Spirit possession may sound like mumbo-jumbo to a Western-trained scientist, but we have to acknowledge that possession is recognized in every other culture around the world."[16]

When this being came into my body, I was aware, but unable to speak, for it would be speaking through my voice. It was bossy. It would tell me what to do. Because I was aware I had four arms, I would carry my cat or daughter around and realize that I was not using two arms to hold them as I imagined, but I was only using one "real" arm. I would also feel I had three heads, and could see left and right if I chose. I understand these deities, like the ones in the *Tibetan Book of the Dead*, had always four arms and four heads. I would feel as if I were looking out to the left or right, as the one facing out the front spoke. But 'I' as me, could not speak as the "entity" would dominate my voice controls. I could hear it speaking, yet it was my voice but not my intentions. I could not explain this to anyone for they would be afraid of me. Furthermore, no one seemed to know I was not *myself*. It was very alarming not to be able to explain to someone that I was not me, but someone else.

A friend of mine in the neighborhood knew about possession, and I went to see her to see if she could help me. She could see the being clearly as a male, but she was unable to shift this being out of me. So I went to see the Swami from our spiritual Ashram. He was sure the entity was Lord Indra, the Lord of Heaven who has four heads and four arms. He was excited about it, but this visit did not help me either as the Swami did not know what to do. I have subsequently found that this too is a stage of cleansing of the body in the *Kundalini* process. It signifies the "Conjunction" stage in alchemy when the two become merged or "two in spirit." Finally I wrote a letter to my guru who was in Miami, and long before the answer came, somehow energetically, he knew of the problem, and I was released from this dominating spirit.

This is why the spiritual guide is so important.

I realized, humbly, that my experiences were quite tame and insignificant by comparison to my guru's experiences. This to me was a sign of the importance of having a teacher overseeing one's progress. This was one person who truly did understand the loneliness of being on the hero's path. How can one give enough gratitude for such a friendship and caring? It is inestimable.

As weird and strange as all this was, once I concluded it was all for my benefit, I became less afraid. As I understood that these frightening and challenging episodes with strange demonic beings, elemental spirits and various testing experiences were saving me from having to go through this during death, I accepted it more calmly. B.S. Goel who himself experienced the *Kundalini* process from Sathya Sai Baba explains, "It is through this grace that one can face one's own death."[17] And Sogyal Rinpoche discusses this ability to see the other realms and states:

> Six realms of existence are identified in Buddhism: gods, demigods, humans, animals, hungry ghosts, and hells. They are each the result of one of the six main negative emotions: pride, jealousy, desire, ignorance, greed and anger.[18]

I had learned tremendously useful information from this exposure to the demonic entities. My indifference had been the secret to getting rid of Begneth. Had I freaked out and expended all kinds of energy to get rid of it, it would have probably remained, and may have even ended my progress in meditation. This often happens to people who have no awareness of the other realms of reality. My resistance would have strengthened its hold on me.

I had learned that *not reacting* was the secret of traveling into the numinous realms. And *not reacting* was also the secret of traveling safely through the *bardos* of my mind at death. This was useful knowledge. This was something I could never have learned in my church, but this was knowledge I could take with me into future lifetimes. It was like a great jewel to know just this much about demons and other realms.

In spite of what I had experienced in the early days of the awakening, this *Kundalini* event was not just about blissful ecstasy and talking to flies. It was about learning the dying process while I still had a body. It was about learning about the mind and cleaning it up so that the "luminosity" the Tibetans talk about could be seen before physical death and could guide me through the *bardos* or hells of the mind.

Not only had I got this rare gift of human life to be in the "lottery" to receive this knowledge, but I had been given this knowledge to transcend physical death. Thus this meant that the gift of immortality, so long sought after by man since the mythical Gilgamesh, was found through this process. The pieces were beginning to fit.

The full nobility, wonder and beauty of true human life was becoming apparent to me gradually. Being a human being meant I could go through the experiences of death and dying while fully alive in my body. It meant I could visit other realms, meet other "inorganic" beings that existed on other planes or *lokas*. I could heal people's bodies; I could travel to the parallel universe and find healing for my pains. I could travel in "time" and know amazing things simultaneously. I could feel the connection to the source-of-all and actually change the course of my life by use of intention. This then is why we have sought life as human beings.

It is as if being human, we automatically get a lottery ticket to immortality and evolution! Thus, I was more enthusiastic than ever for meditation and more in love with my spiritual guru than ever.

CHAPTER 14

The Rising Kundalini: Rapture

"As long as the individual self thinks it is separate from Brahman, it revolves upon the wheel in bondage to the laws of birth, death and rebirth."

(Svtasvatara, Upanishads.)

The meditation and blissful spinning, the visits by entities, the almost paralyzing depression the deep crevasses of awareness that seemed like eons, the strange possessions, mystical abilities, and all the panoply of the inner world continued to be my reality even as I was also a wife, mother and student. Moving out of my husband's bed, I lost the grounding he had given me, and I began to spiral to higher levels of awareness spinning into other worlds. At the same time I had less and less of a boundary between what was my daily life and what was my inner world.

My third eye was clearly active since I could see the pineal gland tapping like a morse code machine towards the pituitary as if it was feeding information to my pituitary gland. Bobbing up and down like a rapid praying mantis, it vibrated at a very high rate. I see these two organs as they appear quite far apart across the mid-brain in anatomical drawings. However, since the changes frequently occurring with *Kundalini* affect emotions, appetites, sleep and so forth, it makes sense that the pituitary gland, stimulated by the pineal, would be affected and releasing related hormones. I could not find anything more apt to explain this idea than the lovely picture of Minerva, painted by Mihran K.Serailian. The title is "The Opening of the Third Eye." Below the picture the artist has stated:

> This painting of the head of Minerva shows, in part, the activities of the pineal gland and the pituitary body at the time of the phenomenon commonly termed 'the opening of the Third Eye.' The Kundalini fire is seen rising upward through the spinal canal into the pons of the medulla oblongata. The golden light radiating from the base of the brain, at the back, gradually increases in size and intensity until it forms the nimbus, or halo of the saint. The pituitary body is here shown surrounded by an elliptic rose aura. The pineal gland... the Third Eye of the Mysteries...is here depicted as blue in color and surrounded by a radiating blue aura... The tiny vibrating finger on the pineal gland points directly toward the pituitary body. This finger, vibrating at a very high rate of speed, is the actual cause of true spiritual illumination.[1]

The tapping of this finger of the pineal gland sometimes got faster, and it was clearly visible to me inside my head; to this day I can see it when I meditate. According to Robert Chaney, from the pineal towards the pituitary there is a "tiny hairlike protuberance vibrating at tremendous speed" which is a "rate so rapid one cannot even conceive of it."[2] In my opinion, this is why through my third eye, I could see into bodies and cells because of this frequency that was beyond any Xray machine we have yet developed.

Sexual Desire:
One of the unexpected experiences in having an awakening of

Kundalini is the impact it has upon ones' sexuality. Sexual and spiritual energy are one and the same in the base of the spine, as the sexual energy is what drives the spiritual awakening and spiritual illumination. With love for God, love for my family, for Bob and my teacher in my heart, I would meditate or chant; very soon I would feel strong sexual desire rising. If I would try to appease this strong desire myself, it was ineffective because it did not reach where the true desire came from. I would be still actively unsatisfied and unappeased. It was clearly not about sex with a partner, although the feeling was identical.

The tension of my suppressing natural sexual urges, since it is in the same vicinity as the coiled up *Kundalini*, had burst the knot, opening the *Kundalini* coil and caused the energy to rise like a cobra out of a basket. Some people say it is like a match lighting kindling. The spark (the guru's power) comes and lights the fire if the kindling (the disciple) is ready. Many people find that once the *Kundalini* begins to rise, there is an incredible fire and desire for sex, but this is not always true. For me it was true. Even today, I can feel that sexual pull when I meditate and when the *Kundalini* begins to undulate through my body. Thus it is clear that it feels like sexual desire, but it is *not about sex*.

If we understand what is actually happening and accept that it is the beautiful love of Goddess and God, of Shiva and Parvati, of Divine Mother and Divine Father, we can know this bliss ourselves. If we allow it to turn down into sexual desire for a human partner, we may have some temporary pleasure, but the energy will be wasted unless having children is the goal; we cannot use this same precious energy to transcend for it has been spent. There is only so much of this light that we can use to transcend the mind and open up the chakras. So how many lifetimes do we waste this precious gift within ourselves and not use it to surge beyond the physical limitations of the body?

Thus it is important to control and conserve the sexual energy and guide it up to the higher chakras. In the many religious sects this restriction has been most severely put upon men to conserve their procreative energies by being celibate. However, it is true for both sexes although it has been said by many scholars, the demand in women is different to men.

The work of Mantak Chia is helpful for men and women to control and conserve this energy. He offers exercises to channel the energies where they are conserved, yet still enjoyed. What could be more familiar to most people than this warmth and longing for joining with another? This then is the same feeling that the Goddess feels for her Lord. Allowing this desire to be directed towards the heart instead of towards a partner yields a path towards the bliss of blisses.

This inner rising desire was more subtle, more blissful and ecstatic than in any sexual encounter. It was my own *Kundalini* pulling up towards my crown to join "Her" partner, Shiva in the *sahasrara* or crown. The male and female aspects of my spiritual being were being drawn together like magnets, and it manifested as a wonderful inner desire, warm and healing. This warmth is on a scale so much more cosmic, so much more beautiful, deep, fulfilling, erotic, complete, love-filled, exquisite, enduring and blissful. We do not have words to express this in English. The bliss that comes is magnified thousands of times beyond normal sexual intercourse that lasts but seconds. But it really was not for "sex" that this sensation was aroused. It was for "union" with the divine within my own body.

I wrote many poems during these months of altered awareness and arousal to my inner male/female union. This one shows the sensual but also beautiful feelings I was feeling:

"Within the Heart"

Within the heart is God's space.
It echoes yearningly through endless births
Until the aeons churn the weary soul to God again.
The heart opens as a lotus flower
Which in a trembling moonlit realm
Enjoys timeless openings of unfathomed joy.
All is bliss in God's space.
There is no lack or satiety
Nothing within nor without...
Only God.

(Ruth Angela. Nov. 1980)

If I allowed this magnetic arousal sensation to just be or exist without reacting, it would grow deeper and sweeter, especially if I meditated
in the cross-legged posture. If I did not do anything with it nor try to
appease it but just witnessed this, then I could feel the sexual fluid
rising up through the stomach, up into the chest... as it rose through
the *sushumna*, the nerve column of the center of my body, up through
the different chakras. As it rose it would bring the most amazing bliss
and love. We only have a few words for bliss in English: rapture, bliss,
ecstasy, joy, nectar, elixir. Yet I felt endless ripples of *blisses* that were
not all the same, but were infinitely varied and subtle as this fluid
would rise within me. I could feel the *Kundalini* snaking up through
my body bringing an unbelievable nectarean pleasure. This pleasure
belongs within all of us as human beings. One taste of this and the
world would change instantly for everyone. We would know we are all
Gods. This is our birthright. It is a biological inheritance like growing
up and becoming an adult. It is nothing to do with religion or rituals,
but everything to do with turning inside to the heart and finding our
own bliss within. We own this as part of our birth.

Inner Bliss:

I distinctly remember a 48-hour period of intoxication where I was in
a constant state similar to on-going orgasm where my eyes were rolled
up into my head. I went about my daily duties. No sex was involved.
There was no human partner to this ineffable inner bliss. It was just
the exquisite snake of *Goddess Kundalini* rising within me seeking for
her Lord, Shiva, in the crown of my head. I was solely the two aspects
of the divine, Shiva [male] and Shakti [female], drawn together within
me, and generating this incredible intoxicating bliss. I would feel totally
at one with everything and everyone.

I did my housework and chores; I tended to my family and household, but silently because I was drawn inside to this inestimable wonder.
We have no language, no metaphors for this experience. I was truly a
herm-aphrodite—the combination of Aphrodite and Hermes—Shiva

and Shakti united as one being within myself. What could be more freeing than to find one's beloved within one's own being? What a great secret I had found for my own joy. How liberating to know my beloved met me *within my own being*.

I heard my guru talk about this intoxication of the saints, how their eyes would be rolled up into their heads and they would not speak for days, and I was also experiencing it for myself. However, though I am female in my body, I was very aware of the invisible lingam (phallus) at the base of my body around which the *Kundalini* had been coiled. Invisible to the eye or surgeon, nonetheless, it was a "phallus" or "lingam" and it would grow stronger as I meditated. It would point to the crown of my head like a flashlight beam of wondrous power. When I had fallen under the tangerine tree and needed to heal the pain in my head, I had used this *Kundalini* 'fountain' or magic wand to send the *Kundalini* into the pain, and it was healed in minutes. What great and wonderful secrets I had found! Human beings, who have reached a certain stage of spiritual growth, can attain a hermaphroditic state within the body and heart through the awakening of the *Kundalini*. The pictures of Tibetan deities appear with their female consort wrapped around them in coitus called "*tantra*." These are representations, not of two beings, but one being who has found this inner goddess, or in my case, this inner lingam/phallus.

I think of how many people go through so much suffering to have a few moments of orgasmic experience with a partner; I think about the deviations and perversions that the ignorant create for this same all-too-brief experience of intercourse. It is an amazing gift that even such a brief sexual orgasm where this energy goes downward into bio-logical function can bring the man and woman a beautiful miraculous child. What is also amazing is the upwardly directed sexual energy can bring on-going orgasmic pleasure and wonder. For I knew this state as my own being for extended periods of time, without anyone else involved, without any genital stimulation or body movement, without any dependence on someone else. I was both my own male and female unified. There is nothing comparable to this incredible rapture. This was a jewel of being born human.

The statues of the Shiva-lingam are worshipped widely in India for this core meaning of oneness within oneself. It is the very power center of unity with one Self. Many yoginis (female yogis) cease to menstruate with the onset of *Kundalini* awakening because the sexual energy ceases to be funneled down into biological uses such as producing eggs and preparation for fertilization, and it is directed up towards the *sahasrara*, or crown. The strength of this upward pull from the base chakra to the crown pulls the sexual fluids up to the crown where the energies are united at the third eye. Such a person is called *"Urdhvareta."* Pulling this energy up to the third eye enables one to have the kinds of *siddhis* that are called clairvoyance, clairaudience and so forth. So the sexual energy is incredibly powerful in enabling us to have babies, but also to birth ourselves into the realm of Gods. We humans can experience the union of the Lord and his Consort within ourselves.

In this state I went about my daily life in perpetual ecstasy. From this point the *siddhis* of spinning and lifting off the ground, seeing into people's bodies, healing by intention, seeing other worlds, reading Sanskrit in the grass, seeing ancient scenes, feeling time as endless, finding time going backwards, flying into space, being able to read people's minds, knowing on a multi-sensory level what my entire surroundings were experiencing, being able to see 360^0 at once, reading books in seconds through my hands, merging with water, seemed to be still manageable to my left hemisphere logical brain. I could still function in the world and carry on my normal life. But when I moved into even higher states, my rational mind, my chattering left brain, began to break down and leave me completely.

CHAPTER 15

The Crucible

"Fire is the test of gold; adversity of strong men."

Seneca

For those who have never been through a major inner struggle or battled inner demons such as jealousy, anger, addiction or depression, it is hard to convey the difficulties of the deeply personal struggle. There is no map, no training manual to refer to. All one has are one's instincts, one's wits, and one's lessons from past lives to counter the dark places in one's psyche. The terrors at meeting the custom-made, panoply of mystical creatures from the subconscious derived from our deep fears and traumas, can seem to be a living nightmare. I get letters from people going through this *Kundalini* process, and their fear and confusion is evident. I can only assure them, as my teacher did me, that it is transitory and will pass as the cleansing process comes to an end.

Ego Disintegration:

In the yearning for freedom and transcendence, just as in our dying process, we do not know what that journey will bring. All kinds of subconscious and predatory entities lurk within us, hidden in the convenient and survival-based denial of the ego. When that Pandora's box is opened by the uncoiling *Kundalini*, we have no idea what will come to our consciousness to be cleared. Jung quotes the *I Ching* as saying, "When yang has reached its greatest strength, the dark power of yin is born within its depths, for night begins at midday when yang breaks up and begins to change to yin."[1] Christina Grof explains this state as "the domain beneath the everyday layer, the vast pool of the unconscious which contains unknown possibilities" and which "intrudes into ordinary awareness."[2] She goes further to indicate that this experience can become a "colossal battlefield where a cosmic combat is being played out between the forces of Good and Evil, or Light and Darkness."[3] This battle becomes a spiritual emergency—a struggle to maintain mental, emotional and spiritual equilibrium for many people on this path.

Emma Bragdon, Ph.D. has written about spiritual emergencies which can occur as people deal with the rising *Kundalini*. "The inner world of a person opening to life myth is replete with dramatic archetypal images that portray profoundly significant themes to the person."[4] And John Weir Perry writes extensively of this mystical journey and the mythic images that appear. He says, "Madness rouses a myth-forming, visionary state of the psyche in which the Eros principle becomes awakened."[5] His definition of the Eros principle is an awareness of the interconnected nature of everything and of relationship to others; this refers to the lowering of boundaries between oneself and the environment which, he says, is "not validated in our culture."[6] He also finds that "messianic visions" all over the world, show similarities which suggest that the "psychic healing process with its regular mythic structure" creates a renewal and healing for both the individual and the world.[7]

But in studying the process of patients undergoing this renewal process, he finds:

> The world the person... was experiencing had shifted from the consensual outer reality to this inner myth-styled reality that tends not to be validated in our culture... we [must] learn a firm trust in the capacity of the psyche to discern the way it must take to integrate or reintegrate itself.[8]

True it is that, as the *Kundalini* cleanses our nervous system on the inner journey, the process continues whether we desire it or not; the mythic world becomes the "real" world; but it is so new, so strange, so unpredictable, more illogical than any dream as daily life takes on the archetypical characteristics of a myth. We become Alice in *Alice in Wonderland* falling into the rabbit hole. But though this inner domain resembles the myths studied in school, there is no school which can teach the raw, unaided courage which one must find second by second through this journey.

As Joseph Campbell states in *The Hero with a Thousand Faces,* "fabulous forces are there encountered."[9] This journey is a form of death spiral where one descends into hell itself. Greek and Egyptian myths all speak of this descent into the underworld. Indeed, this is the death of Osiris before the resurrection.

Such a profound change takes place when the powerful *Kundalini* is sparked into full power inside the human entity. No longer are the boundaries distinct around oneself; no longer can one define what is "mine" and what is "thine." The two merge. One becomes merged with the environment and intimately a part of the hearts, emotions and well-being of everyone around one. The constructs of the egoic sense of self disappear. The mind or ego must surrender its control of the body and become something it fears most to be...."egoless." There is terror in this understanding and a great resistance.

The Tibetan teacher, Sogyal Rinpoche says, "Yet the ego is so convincing and we have been its dupe for so long, that the thought that we might ever become egoless terrifies us... Ego plays brilliantly on our fundamental fear of losing control, and of the unknown."[10] One person who experienced this loss of ego in a painful way, describes it thus:

> The arousal of Kundalini is like a big earthquake when everything in the personality of a person is shaken and many things in it fall like pins... Suppose one is living in the tenth storey of a building and the whole building is uprooted and falls suddenly...[11]

The term for this breaking is not surprisingly, a "nervous break-down," a term used for hundreds of years. Yet the language says what it is. It is the breaking down of the nervous system that has been living in a paradigm of false beliefs. My weeping uncontrollably in the church just after my daughter was born was definitely one of the symptoms. But it goes deeper than this even when we are referring to the *Kundalini* awakening. It is like the entire structure of the personality, of mentation, of values, of beliefs and one's very foundation of being is overturned, like a giant mattress. *Kundalini* wipes out these lies and false ideas, leaving us stranded in a world we have not known before, in which we can find almost no support.

Jung writes about what happens when people begin to explore the hidden side of their psyche, the *yin* side in Chinese understanding. When Westerners try to meditate and take up practices such as yoga which moves the subtle energy, Jung says that, "The conscious mind raises prolific objections, in fact it often seems bent upon blotting out the spontaneous fantasy-activity in spite of real insight."[12] He refers to the conscious mind almost as a separate entity.

Surrender:

So no matter how much of a manager of reality this left brain is in normal existence, when the *Kundalini* comes into the human organism and vibrates everything at a higher frequency, the logic and false belief systems we have depended upon, must surrender control and give way to an integrated being where both brains work as one from the heart. This is why the process is difficult, painful and transformative. Joseph Chilton Pearce in *The Biology of Transcendence,* states that "direct connections between the emotional brain and the left hemisphere are sparse."[13] Pearce goes on to quote Paul MacLean and Arthur Koestler's opinion that this problem of "nature's failure to knit the left hemisphere firmly to the emotional brain [is] a fatal error."[14] Pearce continues this idea, "The left hemisphere and its hypothetical interpreter have no direct connections to that central intelligence agency made up of the heart and emotional systems."[15] So the left brain or mind has been dominated by the "Little Ego" a sort of dictator of time and details, with constant chattering and obsession with future or past but not *present* and, tragically for us, not connected to our higher mind—the heart.

The right brain has no language but a "still small voice" which is our in-born intuition. It is drowned by the dominant focus of 'here and there' and words, an unrelenting input from the chattering left-brain. Meditation and other techniques enable us to hear that small voice within, to listen to our hearts and to quiet the mind. We then have the ability to bring these two brains into synchronicity and thus balance, and the *Kundalini* process integrates them by transforming the energy of the body. This is what a full human being becomes. However, it is not without a very strange battle to overcome this "managing" brain, this dominant dictator that is very much in control of our conscious life since most of us believe ourselves to BE the mind.

Pearce states that the right hemisphere "with its rich connections to the two lower brains, is involved in new learning."[16] This is the brain that makes the random bits of information you gather about a topic come together in a synthesized, organized composition or theory. This is the brain that will make connections between symbols or events that appear to be random or new. It is the poet's brain. It is the feeling brain that empathizes. This is our idea giver, our dreamer, our creative ability. It is the artist or architect's mind that sees color and shape. It is also the connection to the spirit that gives meaning and depth. Yet, significantly, this side of the brain does not use language, but operates in "images" or symbols. It is silent. It is also the emotional brain that gives us compassion, creativity and art. We need both hemispheres to operate together where there is no domination of one over the other.

The *Kundalini* power opens up the deeper heart, all the chakras, and integrates both left and right hemispheres so that the individual operates with the integrity of his or her whole heart and whole brain connected to the cosmic energies. When I was spinning and flying in my living room above the dog and cat and seeing into other people's bodies to pull out energetic weapons, this logical brain was absent. The bliss I felt overruled its power. This blissful merging of the two brains meant that my rational left brain, the "middle self" or "parent" of the Hawaiian *Huna* vocabulary, was no longer running the show. This language-oriented mind was pushed out of decision-making and visited other dimensions without too much concern. Yet it became terrified by the disappearance of time when time slipped forwards and backwards and into caverns. William Blake, the British poet who clearly had experienced this same awakening, wrote:

> To see a world in a grain of sand, /
> And a heaven in a wild flower, /
> Hold infinity in the palm of your hand, /
> And eternity in an hour.

He had experienced this loss of time without manifesting any fear. But for me the loss and wobble of my sense of time came with terror. For it seems that the left brain is key to our awareness of time. Was the ego's very existence based in time?

Resistance:

I began to sense there was some kind of resistance within myself to this ecstatic process of integration. Could there be something "dual" within us that tries so hard to prevent us from entering the realms of meditation and timeless peace? Why would not our entire being desire to be in bliss and peace? It appears obvious that something exists masquerading as "us" which is against our best interests. Whatever we might call "it," it has the power to create great discomfort when the *Kundalini* is awakened because obviously the two cannot exist in the same being. Was *time* the key to its hold over my consciousness I wondered? Was that why the fluidity of time started a spiral of fear?

I came to the conclusion that the *Kundalini* power of truth *reveals* this rebellious aspect of our being and once light is shone on it, the rebel must die. It is like a totally artificial "self living within us. The Goddess wipes out the liar, the rebel, the fake being that has inhabited our very mind and constructed our reality *in time* for our entire lives, and in so doing, that world constructed on some imaginary entity—crumbles and falls. There is no rock on which to stand. This was where the terror arose within me. R.D. Laing explains this stage, "The person is plunged into a void of nonbeing in which he founders. There are no supports, nothing to cling to... that retain a link with a world long lost."[17] Wilhelm explains this tenuous state and the societal effects of embarking on this journey inside also.

> If the values are not retained, the individual goes over to the other side,... from sense to nonsense, and even from rationality to mental disturbance. This is not without danger.... The Westerner who wishes to start upon this way [meditation], if he is truly serious about it, has all authority against him—intellectual, moral, and religious.[18]

So not only do we have to deal with this rebel "Little Ego" within which is wily and sly at hiding our true selves, but we also will find no comfort or relief for this struggle in the real world we inhabit. Nothing in our society supports letting go of this "Little Ego." The whole society is based on feeding it. To clear it out would seem to be an extraordinary task which our dear Goddess *Kundalini* undertakes for us. There is the battle. There is the struggle.

What is it that undergoes such a dramatic change with the influx of this higher force or power called *Kundalini* which is the active feminine power of God? Is it just the ego sense of 'I,' "Little Ego," or the false self without a foundation in real "life"? These are questions that it seems the Sorcerers of ancient Mexico answered but shared only among themselves until Carlos Castaneda wrote about the topic in the 1970's.

Foreign Resisters:

These Toltec explorers of consciousness found there actually is a "foreign" element controlling our minds and awareness of time, and it takes up residence behind and within in our logical, language faculties where we are imprisoned in its reality—a thought-dominated time capsule—our left brain. They discovered that there are certain "fleeting shadows" that are our "companions for life." This predator, according to don Juan, came from the "depths of the cosmos and took over the rule of our lives. Human beings are its prisoners."[19] He called them "Mud Shadows" for they have a certain weight, they fly and they appear on the ground like fish shaped shadows. They are partly visible to humans, and some children can see them.

When I read this account of Castaneda's "Mud Shadows" or "Flyers," I immediately recalled reading about a very strange experience of the shaman Michael Harner in his book, *The Way of the Shaman*. While he was undergoing a dramatic *ayahuasca* experience in South America and on the verge of death, he sees that his thoughts are given to him by "giant reptilian creatures reposing sluggishly at the lowermost depths of the back of my brain." I have seen this same slothful, toad-like creature in the back of the mind through seeing into people's energy fields. It looks like the creature in Star Wars, Jabba the Hut.

Harner goes on to explain he was given a vision of such creatures arriving during the prehistory of the planet escaping from their own predators. They dropped from the sky as "large, shiny, black creatures with stubby pterodactyl-like wings and huge whale-like bodies... [to become] the true masters of humanity and the entire planet. We humans were but the receptacles and servants of these creatures."[20] This human predator who is influencing human behaviors for its own use has hidden itself very well.

My discovery of this explains a great deal of the strange behaviors that I was experiencing for which there was little to no support nor explanation in my culture. How many people would know of such a creature taking over our minds; and how many people would know that when the *Kundalini* Goddess awakens that she exposes its presence and kicks it out? She returns us to our natural state, our true nature. This struggle unbeknown to me was about to take place.

The Matrix:

More recently, we have been exposed to this concept of ourselves being controlled by predatory entities in the movie series called "The Matrix" which shows control of people's reality being activated from the back of the head, like this sluggish creature seen by Michael Harner. In the movie the control disconnect device is a large electrical plug in the nape of the neck. The ones who disconnect from the Matrix have the ability to move faster than time, to fly, to be aware without thinking, to know the future and to be able to fight like superhuman *Kung Fu* masters. These would be the "true humans" who have disconnected from the Matrix or reality control frequency. Did the movie's author know this fact about our being controlled and the full powers that humans have without the predator on board?

I know many that have watched this movie over and over because they too sense that there is something profound that they need to understand. These similar accounts cannot be coincidences but point in the direction of secret, masterful manipulation of human consciousness. These reports come from the depths of shamanic exploration and expedition. They give us warning of the struggle that takes place when we turn within and face this wily predator whom our awakened *Kundalini* will displace. Castaneda recounts don Juan's explanation of the disparity between human intentions and our actual reality:

> Think for a moment, and tell me how you would explain the contradiction between the intelligence of man the engineer and the stupidity of his systems of beliefs, our ideas of good and evil, our social mores. They [the predators] are the ones who set up our hopes and expectations and dreams of success or failure. They have given us covetousness, greed, and cowardice. It is the predators who make us complacent, routinary, and egomaniacal... They gave us their mind... [they] inject into... human beings whatever is convenient for them."[21]

"Glowing Coat":

This is what we are up against as humans. We apparently have something very special for these predators which don Juan describes as "a glowing coat" and we are the "only species that had the *glowing coat of awareness* outside of that luminous cocoon." These creatures eat this magical gift of ours as it grows around us and as don Juan says, "There is nothing you can do about it." [22] This glowing coat is our magic, and our amazing abilities as human beings like "Neo" in the Matrix movie, and like me flying in my living room in 1979. Kryon says that humans are the "ONLY creatures who have Almighty God inside them,... The creator is in you and you don't even know it." [23]

So this "Little Ego" is not so little, not friendly to us, not easily disposed of, and certainly not willing to give up its dinner for us to become free. This is far more serious than just overcoming certain habits and tendencies when we discover this horrific truth about our life as humans. Don Juan, the Mexican Sorcerer, says that we have to use discipline and meditation to the point where we become unsavory to these creatures and they leave us alone then our "glowing coat" re-grows. Our self–reflection "is the only point of awareness left to us as the predators create flares of awareness that they proceed to consume in a ruthless, predatory fashion." [24] My assumption is the "flares" are emergency situations or moments when we are shocked, in fear, highly emotional and so forth such as my trauma at age four. These "flares" would be the emotional trauma as an outcome of wars, fights, conflicts and distress.

The Rulers:

Even in ancient times these predatory creatures were known, although the information about them had been hidden for 1600 years until 1945 when the *Nag Hammadi* scriptures were discovered and translated. Though the Roman church has questioned their authenticity, there is plenty of verifiable evidence of the texts' value to humanity in discovering how our energy and god-given talents and energies have been stolen by such creatures who, in those days, were called "The Rulers" or the "Archons."

The rulers turned to Adam. They took him and cast him and his wife out of the garden.... The rulers threw humanity into great confusion and a life of toil, so that their people might be preoccupied with things of the world and not have time to be occupied with the holy [sic] Spirit.[25]

This puts an entirely different perspective on the story of Adam and Eve. For one thing, it is not God who throws Adam and Eve out of the Garden of Eden, but the "Rulers." How differently the entire story becomes based on that one fact. Many sources indicate that "Edin" was a city or region belonging to Sumerians in Mesopotamia. The serpent (*Kundalini* or Holy Spirit) countered the plans of the Rulers to keep man an ignorant slave, and gave man some special knowledge. Could that knowledge and gift be now coming to fruition as the numbers of awakened souls on Earth has increased? Is this present era, with its incredible parallel legends, myths and calendars among disparate tribes and continents, the age when the serpent's knowledge, the Holy Spirit, overcomes this ruler and restores mankind to our full place among the gods? This is my hope for the future.

No wonder the teachers tell us to meditate and watch our thoughts. In the witnessing of the mind's behavior we are watching the predator from the cave of our "true nature." The longer we stay in that cave, the more likely we will gain control over ourselves, our minds, our bodies and our consciousness.

The Root of Truth:

In another section of the *Nag Hammadi* texts, the envoy of the one True God, an angel, comes to Norea, daughter to Adam and Eve, who, when she had been told she had to sexually serve the "rulers," calls to [the real] God for help. The angel tells her:

Do you think these rulers have power over you? None of them can overpower the root of truth, for on behalf of the root of truth a figure [the perfect human will]

has appeared in the last days, and these authorities will
be restrained. These authorities cannot defile you or
that generation [the Gnostics or spiritually awake], for
your home is with Incorruptibility, where the virgin
Spirit dwells, who is superior to the authorities of
chaos and their world.[26]

The "root of truth" is the *Kundalini* at our root, the Holy Spirit
where the "virgin spirit dwells." The *Kundalini* will appear in the
"last days" of history according to many ancient cultures. (see Chapter
Three.) Thus it predicts that the Biblical "fall" from heaven is about
to come to an end. Such a transition time is discussed by David
Wilcock in his book *The Source Field Investigations*. He explains that
the "real purpose of the negative forces are simply to help us evolve in
consciousness; but they were never intended to win—and never can
win." From an old Zoroastrian scripture he explains the end of time
prophecies:

When all the creation that was created by the Lord
will come to an end, and every man will go to the
Great Judgment of the Lord, then the times will
perish; there will not be any more years or months or
days the hours will not be counted anymore.[27]

Wilcock continues to describe ancient accounts of The Golden Age
when time has ceased and we all participate in the universal peace of
God. If these many predictions are true, it indicates possibly that the
domination of our minds and our sense of time given by these Flyers,
these Archon, or predators is about to end.

This era according to many ancient sources is called the "End of
Time," and who has controlled our obsession with time up until now
but these mind predators who have inhabited our left brain, language
and logical thinking abilities? The message from these ancient accounts
from the First Century and before is that if we become preoccupied and
engage with the Holy Spirit, *Kundalini,* we learn of this domination

and control and we escape it. The snake of *Kundalini* is that "root" in the presence of whom this *beast* must perish.

The Mind Exits:

So here I was on the edge of an abyss for my "Little Ego." Yet I had no idea what was coming because I could only be in the process and I had no idea of any of this knowledge which I am imparting here. My "Little Ego" panicked when I had reached a point where the waves or caverns of 300-year-time moments caused my logical, controlling mind to falter and shudder. In these spaces, time ceased to have meaning; it was no more; it was the bliss of eternity. There were no boundaries, no rules, and no restrictions on my consciousness as it flew freely through "infinity." "Little Ego" ceased to have control when I opened up my being to "no-time." This fluidity of time made the left brain dominated mind lose control. My joyful leaps and adventures with *Kundalini* were pushing this predator away, but it would still come back hoping for one more meal of my "glowing coat," until finally it fled, and then as don Juan explains:

> That's the day when you have to rely on your own devices which are nearly zero. There's no one to tell you what to do... for the real mind that belongs to us,... after a lifetime of domination has been rendered shy, insecure, and shifty... the real battle of sorcerers begins at that moment.[28]

Another person experiencing the drama of this time when the conscious mind drops away is B.S. Goel: "The sense of "I" goes into such a turmoil that one simply feels lost... that day the Kundalini is aroused a most basic nervous breakdown takes place."[29] My basic belief paradigms, comfortably built up through my upbringing and my rewards for logical behavior, that had allowed me to operate throughout my life in a successful and thriving manner, were now being shaken at their very roots. It is as if the floor drops from beneath one's feet. Gopi Krishna says, "The old personality disappears from the scene and a distorted one emerges lost to the norms of behavior and sense."[30] So this is a phenomena that is common in this *Kundalini* process. The ego, or false mind, is a fiction that creates fictions that must be gradually or directly erased if the true, authentic human being is to emerge. We become like the animals we were born, or like very young children before speech again; we have no clever rhetoric and vast vocabulary. We are innocent as in the Garden of Eden. We are truly naked of clever words, artifice and logic.

At this crisis stage the *Kundalini* has cleaned out the muck of our subconscious which has been programmed with false beliefs influenced by this predatory "ego" sense. Bruce Lipton Ph.D. has eloquently explained the connection between our belief system, our experience of life, and our physical health in his book *The Biology of Belief: Unleashing the Power of Consciousness, Matter and Miracles*. Lipton shows exactly how a belief system can directly change a cell within our bodies. He asserts that "the self-conscious mind is extremely powerful."[31] Unfortunately, these belief systems may "seem" to be logical to us when they are acquired, but most of them are instilled in us from other people's perceptions, like our society, our parents, or through the direct influence of these mind predators. "Not all our learned perceptions are accurate."[32] So there are in fact a great deal of false beliefs lodged in everyone's minds, but such is the nature of our dependence on these beliefs that we cling to them even when logic would indicate their insanity.

When this feminine Goddess snakes through our cells that have erroneous information locked into them, all that is false must be expelled in the face of this higher truth energy or light. We are the very body of Goddess *Kundalini,* so when she awakens in us, She cleans out the false "dirty chi" that has created our "fake" reality. This is why our bodies undergo dramatic *kriyas* or movements when *Kundalini* pushes through the subtle channels of our nervous system. Where She meets a false belief, a block of the energy pathway, She pushes right through it. If this is in the arm, the arm will jerk. If it is in the stomach, we may have diarrhea; if it is the face, the muscles will twitch. If it is in the mind, we will go through some memory or trauma which can come and go in just minutes. This power cleanses like a "roto-rooter" gets out sludge from the drain.

These blocks or dams that interfere with the flow of *Kundalini* light are belief systems or programs which my teacher called our "conditioned mind," and thus something has "conditioned it." Our mind's "parasite" and false information have created these false concepts in us to make us compliant, submissive, tamed, but all these have to go in order for us to become aligned with the Goddess *Kundalini*, aligned with the very truth of the Universe.

The pre-conditioned ideas that I was "limited wife, mother, daughter, teacher, limited body" etc. all had to be destroyed or transmuted in order for me to know myself as a drop of infinity; one with the divine One. Sogyal Rinpoche summarizes this:

> So ego, then, is the absence of true knowledge of who we really are, together with its result: a doomed clutching on, at all costs, to a cobbled together and makeshift image of ourselves, an inevitably chameleon charlatan self that keeps changing and has to, to keep alive the fiction of its existence.[33]

Eckhart Tolle asserts in *A New Earth* that the voice inside our heads "*is* the voice, is the thinker, is the observed mind. It could almost be looked upon as an entity that has taken possession" of us.[34] Here it is again from a modern teacher, that idea that the mind is a predator. He concurs with my findings about how time freaks out the mind in *The Power of Now* when he says "Time and mind are inseparable. Remove time from the mind and it stops."[35] He clearly explains the nature of this "entity" as fearful and obsessive. "The underlying emotion that governs all the activity of the ego is fear, the fear of being nobody, the fear of nonexistence, the fear of death."[36] Tolle calls it, "an entity made up of emotion" with its own "primitive intelligence, not unlike a cunning animal... which thrives on negative thinking."[37] This corresponds to don Juan's explanations of this manipulative, and anxiety ridden creature, the "Flyer or Mud Shadow," inhabiting and controlling our minds. This fearful animal, always afraid that there will not be another meal, that it will be discovered, that is eating and stealing our light energy is what, tragically, most of us believe ourselves to be.

But this is not the truth.

All these nightmares can be expelled by the *Kundalini* truth serum.

Therefore, I was finding my struggle for enlightenment was not only against social ostracism, not only against external forces or evil obstacles, but against my own mind's controller. It is a battle of wills, the will of God and the inexorable pull to merge us into the ocean of union, versus the will of the parasitic being that wants to keep on fooling us that it is in charge of our own life and destiny, and that it is a mini-God. Where do we begin to wrestle this fearful, illogical, set of false beliefs that is our very own mind? Our limitations in this form as human beings require that we get help, some extra higher energy, benevolent source to overcome the pull of the senses and the mind. We need *Kundalini* the fierce goddess of the universe, but it is also important to have a teacher in human form who has found this "true nature" and who has trodden this path before and thankfully can see the road ahead.

The Subconscious:

The subconscious and the logical mind have been falsely programmed by church and society to make us believe that we are all sinners who are "bad" or "evil" and do not deserve to be called holy or divine. This imprinting makes it almost impossible for us to have a valid understanding of ourselves as divine. How powerful is this subconscious belief? According to research by Bruce Lipton and Steve Bhaerman in *Spontaneous Evolution*, the subconscious is "one million times more powerful than the self conscious mind." However, it is unfortunately nowhere near as creative with skills only equal to that of a "precocious five-year-old." Sadly, about "95 percent of our decisions, actions, emotions, and behaviors are derived from the unobserved, unregulated processing of the subconscious mind."[38] This is what is running the planet, your life, and the billions of other people here.

The Kundalini Code:

Is this the best we can be? Human beings who have the divine "glowing coat" surely are designed for much more fine, noble designs and accomplishments. But first we have to overcome this limitation, this struggle with the predatory mind/time creature, and our own lack of awareness of our true wealth and inheritance. According to Gangaji's guru, Poonjaji, we have been cheated for 35 million years at that game. But the game is changing. Thanks to a code in our DNA that awakens now, there are reports that *Kundalini* awakening is rising in humanity. Thanks to the discovery of these ancient texts telling us the truth of how we have been taken down or fallen, we are waking up to the truth. The strong power surge of the *Kundalini shakti,* the magical alchemical spirit, can override this deep conditioned hold on our beings. She can wash away the illusions and beliefs which hold us in limitations, and free us to the highest possibility of our potential as humans so we can become all that we were intended to be. And this struggle to free ourselves is perhaps the most thrilling and amazing emergence of the pupae into the butterfly ever witnessed. But like any emergence, there is a death of that old self, a struggle that continues until complete establishment in the highest state is reached.

For one who has lived lifetimes at the mercy of the conditioned mind, this process is the ultimate terror. The mind must surrender itself, give up that control, retreat, and allow the "conscious being" the "human being" integrated and whole, connected into the spiritual heart to step into a world of unity with others, harmony with the environment, and oneness with the divine.

Therefore, when we walk through that doorway to the spiritual realms, the ego or controlling "foreign" mind must surrender to the full heart that is our doorway to the divine. This surrender to that which is unseen, felt and mystical would be like jumping into an abyss for the ego. This is the void from which many retreat in terror. I knew nothing of this when I entered that meditation center in 1979, and my "Little

Ego" would never have gone so willingly had it known that its demise and death throes were coming.

CHAPTER 16

The Abyss

"The destruction of the world in a great apocalypse is the opening theme in the making of many new myths."
                                        John Weir Perry[1]

And so the acceleration of bliss, mixed with strange and fearful apparitions continued until I reached a state of awareness called *Turiya*, or the Fourth State. *Turiya* is an advanced state of awareness beyond such states as waking, sleeping or deep sleep. It is called the fourth state because the other states are part of every day life, but this state comes when the *Kundalini* has reached a certain stage of ascension. This is a state that yogis spend years of intense practice to obtain sometimes called "conscious Samadhi." Yet it came to me without any special effort.

Turiya State:
The *Turiya* state became more apparent to me at night. I would lie in bed and my body would be completely immobile, but I was conscious with my eyes open through the entire night. During the night, I was registering consciously, but I could not lift my leg off the bed, nor move an arm if I wanted to. It was as if I was an eye observing or a witness inhabiting this body, but not really part of it. The real "me" was using

the body like a shell. Castaneda explains this as "dreaming" which don Juan says is the "*not-doing* of sleep. And as such, *dreaming* affords practitioners the use of that portion of their lives spent in slumber. It is as if the *dreamers* no longer sleep."[2] In this state I was in fact in a space where my "energy body" had learned to move by itself beyond the body and "thoroughly out of their [The Flyers] reach."[3] I was not thus tied to my physical body, but had become an independent energy being, my original condition before birth.

In spite of the unstable alterations in perception and visions, the *Turiya* state is much sought after by yogis who are probably prepared for the changes by intense training and instruction. Sages call it the "sleepless sleep." *Turiya* can be described as the "Spirit having the human experience" since the mind is transcended and the body seems like something heavy and almost inconvenient. The benefit of the *Turiya* experience is the ability for our awareness to see clarity in *all realities* and beyond.

According to scriptures, the waking state is the first state, the sleep state is the second state of awareness and deep sleep the third. In all these states of mind something is awake and aware registering everything that we experience. It is this ever-conscious state that knows upon waking in the morning if we have rested well or had fitful dreams. Instead of going into the sleep state, one can also slip into another place or gap between these states and enter *Turiya*. In the *Shiva Sutras, Turiya* or *Turya i*s defined as:

> The fourth state of consciousness [is] beyond the states of waking, dreaming and deep sleep and stringing together all the states; the Metaphysical Consciousness distinct from the psychological or empirical self; the *Sakshi* or witnessing consciousness; the transcendental Self.[4]

When in that state, I would "wake" the next day, and my body was fully rested as in normal sleep, but I would have been consciously aware the whole night. My sense of 'observer' did not sleep, but my body was rested. In John White's book *Kundalini, Evolution and Enlightenment* the Singh Khalsas write about sleeping and the *turiya* state explaining that one sleeps for two or three hours in this state and then "deals with all his subconscious pressures during his early morning meditation." This process eliminates the need for dreaming and requires less "sleep."⁵

This is when my dreams accelerated, the visions of entities increased and I started to lose a hold of "normal" life and consensual reality. What I understand now was that not only had my rational mind (Ruler) disappeared, but by not sleeping in the normal way and processing all night, I was burning out of my brain and tissues certain subtle trace minerals, metals and nutrients that are needed to keep the brain functioning fully. The chemistry of my mind was altering and my diet could not replenish it. I was not aware of what food would replenish the brain. I had read that anyone going through this process should eat nutritious food regularly and frequently. Although I was experiencing the *Turiya* State, I was not established in all the states of consciousness. In the *Siva Sutras* it explains the following:

> This Sutra says that the fourth state which is the natural state of *atmic* consciousness should be maintained in all the three states of waking, dreaming and deep sleep.... The present *sutra* exhorts the Yogi to be on the alert and not lose his hold on the 4th state so that it may permeate the three states in all the stages—initial, intervening and final.⁶

Truly, this was a clear manifestation of the ascent of the *Kundalini,* and that in itself was an enormous benediction; Jaideva Singh states that "turya is integral awareness i.e. it is always aware and conscious of all three states... it is completely free... being pure consciousness and bliss."⁷ However, as wonderful as this attainment was on the spiritual level, I was not truly prepared. I was not educated about what to expect, and I knew nothing of the great gift that it foreshadowed.

Thus it was from this point on that my awareness began to become lost in the *Turiya* state day and night. I began to exist more in the altered states than in the day-to-day waking state. This is the time when people in other cultures or religions where this phenomenon is recognized would be taken to a small room and cared for 24/7 for some weeks or days as the case may be. Or as in India, such a state would be revered, honored and respected. A faithful devotee would take care of a person in this state, making sure that his or her body was properly cared for with nurturing and replenishing food.

But for me there was no comprehension of my state of being, no respect for it whatsoever, and indeed, there was no understanding from any quarter within the society I lived in. I was on my own with diminished logical abilities and comprehension of what was happening. I look back and see that the control of the predatory mind, "Ruler," had "fled" leaving me unbound to my normal consensual reality. I was operating as pure spirit, like a child without complete awareness and control of the consensual reality world. It was as don Juan described when the "Flyer" leaves our mind, and we are left without logic and we become idiotic.

Although in the 60's there was great interest in research into psychedelics and the effects on the brain, for political reasons much of that was shut down; scientific investigations into the brain chemicals which activate visions, and psychedelic experiences in particular are not easy to initiate. However, Dr. Rick Strassman has recently published his research into DMT, which he calls "The Spirit Molecule." This research is still on-going, yet there is a link between pineal production of DMT and psychosis experiences that may be initiated by meditation, creating visions, sounds and other worldly psychedelic experiences.

Pineal Gland:

One of his chapters focuses on the pineal gland and its role in regulating melatonin, producing DMT (Dimethyltryptamine) and affecting psychedelic states. "The most general hypothesis is that the pineal gland produces psychedelic amounts of DMT at extraordinary times in our lives... [conception, birth, puberty, death etc and] it provides us with the vehicle to consciously experience the movement of our life force in its most extreme manifestations."[8] Such life force is of course the *Kundalini*.

Strassman explains that more research needs to be done to show the link to spiritual experiences and visions. His research explains that higher degrees of psychosis correlate to higher levels of DMT. This may explain why patients in the 1960's with schizophrenia who received pineal gland extracts which contained "anti-DMT" experienced improvements.

Meditation or prayer also can elicit deeply altered states of consciousness; I was meditating for several hours a day without a special diet for such intensity. At times in meditation or just before sleep, I would see some lights coming towards me, even with eyes open. These twin lights would be so brilliant and bright that I would become afraid as they approached like car headlights getting closer and closer and larger and more penetrating. They would rise up like the sun around a curved horizon, getting brighter and bigger as they rose. It would begin to feel like torture to keep staring at these lights inside my head, so I would panic. Gradually I learned not to fear this light, for I was sure it was the light spoken of in the *Tibetan Book of the Dead*. I was operating on a level beyond which my left-brain could begin to understand, and yet some part of me was reveling in all this deeply symbolic meaning.

Pineal DMT production could underlie these mystical or spiritual experiences. All spiritual disciplines describe quite psychedelic accounts of the transformative experiences, whose attainment motivate their practice. Blinding white light, encounters with demonic and angelic entities, ecstatic emotions, timelessness, heavenly sounds, feelings of having died and being reborn, contacting a powerful and loving presence underlying all of reality—these experiences cut across all denominations. They also are characteristic of a fully psychedelic DMT experience.[9]

Thus changes in my brain chemistry from my intense meditation practices were spiraling me away from "normal" reality into other mystical realms where common sense and logic played no part. In an ashram or temple, the teacher would know the diet for such intense practices, but I knew nothing of this.

This spiral lead me to a place I can only call "The Abyss."

The Abyss:

The "Abyss" to me was a place of terror; however, for those who have been there, it is the place of truth. Kunihiro Yamate writes in *The Way of No Thinking,* that this place is "Space Consciousness" which is "our real self."[10] Itzhak Bentov, a self-inspired meditator, was familiar with this phenomenon of falling into a void. He writes an analogy with what he discovered to be the truth about this in sketches and diagrams. Upon reaching the end of the tube of light one sees to one's amazement that the being there is oneself... totally at peace. "The whole thing explodes! There are no bodies, just the void. You have become the void. You *are* the void."[11]

So I was approaching this void or abyss, but unfortunately, without the background and training of what to expect. I did not know what this was, so I felt I was sliding into a bottomless black hole. The 22nd Sutra of the *Shiva Sutras* page 78 says: "By uniting with the great lake (the highest Shakti herself) (he has) the experience of the Supreme I-consciousness which is the generative source... of all mantras."[12] I wrote a poem about this which tries to capture this experience:

The Inner Waters

by Ruth Angela

Inside the cavern of my soul
Is a black pond
Of lightless melting ether.
There is no light,
Yet luminously I swim in warm feeling fluid.
Being without name,
Speaking without sound
From echoes inside.

Abandon beckons you;
You swim here too,
And silently we move.
The silken liquid
Over ancient limbs murmurs and soothes.
In depthless dark I swim surrendered
Without form
And know my SELF.

(© Nov. 1980 by Ruth Angela)

A compassionate clinical professor at the University of California at San Francisco, John Weir Perry, discusses the psychotic state that I was entering. He says in an article in *Spiritual Emergency,* "visionaries undergo the shattering experience of seeing the world dissolve into a chaos and time whirls back to its beginnings... when a transformation of one's inner culture is under way, dissolution of the world image is the harbinger of change."[13] I was approaching the state where everything would appear to fall.

When the final break with the predatory but logical mind came, it was the wee hours of a night in mid November of 1979. I was one spirit without logic or sense. I was like a little five-year-old child in an adult body pulled to action by "feeling" states not common sense. I felt a strong calling or impulse to get up from my bed, and taking a blanket around me, I drove away from my village towards Honolulu. In normal states of mind, I might imagine myself somewhere, but my body would stay in the bed. But this was as if my imagination had *will and intention* and now travelled with the body along like a suitcase. The imagination, will and body were all acting as one. I said nothing to my husband for in this state of mind, there was only the need to respond to my *will* and my urges. Thoughts of caution, consideration of others did not inhabit my mind because the mind's controller, the parent, was gone. I was now in a depleted other state. I was in another world beyond such considerations.

The Primitive Will:

I had not slept in normal sleep for weeks. Every night I was processing in *Turiya* state all the visions, past life scenarios and entities coming and going, so that I really was losing touch with reality of everyday life. John W. Perry states that the "truly transformative death... is an autonomous and archetypal process among ritual images, as movement of the spirit in the realm of myth and ritual."[14] This is what I was experiencing. I did not rationally choose to act out this drama in the middle of the night. I was operating without full awareness of how this would appear to others. I was just following an impulse from a primitive, yet powerful inner urge.

At 5 a.m. I drove through the deserted city and every traffic light turned green just as I reached it. At that moment I felt as if I were on a special mission in another universe, so everything seemed to be magical and profound. I found myself drawn towards Tantalus, the small extinct volcano above Honolulu which has a long winding road to the top where there are spectacular 270⁰ views of Honolulu. I have only good memories here of picnics and meditations, and the loving energy of trees, wind, sunlight, sweet smelling ginger plants and the vista of the ocean. I drove slowly up the winding roads as the sun began to dawn, and I parked overlooking the city of Honolulu wrapped in my blanket.

Disaster Visions:

I stayed there for a long time seeing things that now I know were not "there," but I saw them just as I had seen the Himalayas that day at the pizza place. I watched in fascination as movies began to play out in front of me. In a sepia overlay, I saw a tidal wave that was over 1,000 feet tall, slowly approaching the entire island from the south. In endless replay it came inexorably again and again. I watched it looming like a sinister transparency superimposed over the everyday reality below which was not as bright and third dimensional as it normally would be. I saw the tsunami coming over and over, towering above the city and the university like a Hollywood animation. After one wave had swept over the island, there was another towering over the dwarfed city of Honolulu.

There was no emotional fear, no sense of danger, for it was an overlay like a ghostlike warning. Yet I could not take my eyes from the horizon to the south.

As I processed these visions, more scenes played out in front of me which seemed to have incredible importance to mankind. They were scenes from the Bible. On the grass below me, I saw a scene of a black bull slaying a white lamb right there and somehow this conveyed a deep symbolic Biblical meaning. I have read that others experience this drama in similar death myths; at the time it was so important what I saw, but when I remember it now, I cannot put into language what was so important. I saw colors, black and red and white as having amazing importance and meaning. Perry emphasizes that "In this state every occurrence seems to conjure up a multiplicity of meanings."[15]

I saw in the sky mosaics of meaningful pieces being shifted and sorted into different scenes of great significance, yet I could not speak it into language. To my spirit, every picture was an epic of great meaning. At some point, overhead, I saw a small plane with a woman pilot take off from the Honolulu airport, and I knew she would land in the water in Maui, so I did something magical to protect her which I cannot now explain. But the next day there was an article in the paper about how she crashed into the water, and was safely rescued.

In this strange trance, I began to drive round and round Mt. Tantalus on its winding road that snakes from bottom to top and then from top to bottom with hairpin turns and over-reaching, tunnel-like tropical forests on each side. Since it was a workday, few people were around to see me. I must have looked like a homeless person, disheveled, in pajamas, without makeup, my hair unkempt, with the blanket around me and my strange out-of-body appearance.

I did not feel I was in my body at all. I felt I was now an angel. I do not remember eating, going to the bathroom or taking care of my bodily functions that day. After most of the day in this non-logical dream state, seeing these sepia movies, I noticed I was weak and hungry, so I began driving down Tantalus on the winding roads to return home. I had no sense of anxiety about my daughter or husband, for I was living in a time warp, where time and my life as it had been did not exist. There was no logical mind operating. Everything was being driven by a primitive will outside of time.

As I descended around the 180° sharp, hairpin corners of Tantalus, dogs seemed to come out of every driveway and bark viciously at me, as if they saw something alarming. Something about my appearance freaked them at every corner. They ran into the road barking and trying to attack the car. I had driven that hill many times and never seen a dog, but suddenly these dogs were everywhere.

The Ayatolla:

I looked into the rear-view mirror and understood their distress. I did not know my own face. I looked dreadful in every way. Staring back at me was the most anguished, grotesque-looking Ayatolla Khomeini, the cleric from Iran who had inspired the Iranian Revolution and the kidnapping of many Americans in 1979. This was a face of evil, yet it was *my face*. I had reached a state of crisis with some inner demon, a state where the hero encounters a "dragon" that is "one's own binding of oneself to one's ego... it is your ego clamping you down."[17] I was truly in despair by this view of my own face. This horrible entity was possessing me and seemed to be keeping 'me' out and forcing its way in. I began at last to feel fear; I was in physical trouble. I was getting desperately hungry and weak. How much time had elapsed, I am not sure, but I found myself coming back to awareness in the rush hour around 3 p.m. I had been gone almost a whole day.

Nuclear Disaster:

As I drove up the mountain on the Honolulu side of the Pali Highway to return to my home on the Windward side of the pass, I saw the entire island a sulfuric yellow as if a nuclear bomb had gone off and left everything destroyed. As I drove in broad daylight back to my home, I saw corpses of animals everywhere. They lay on the ground as empty yellowed skeletons. The mountains were yellowed and devoid of green with ghastly empty tree skeletons. A dull and lifeless, insipid pallor hung in the air. There was no more lush, green foliage of the tropical island. Everywhere was empty, dry, desolate, and bathed in yellow, sulfur, sickly light as from a nuclear fall out. Don Juan explains to Carlos Castaneda that this yellow fog is the realm of "inorganic beings."[18] He indicates that this color is a realm boundary.

There is another reference to this sulfur yellow in Castaneda's *The Second Ring of Power* where La Gorda is explaining the world of the guardian who lives in this "yellow sulfur world." The guardian represented a barrier to entering other worlds or realities, and only those with sufficient power could pass it. Apparently in this episode, Castaneda in his "second attention" state of mind was not able to go past the guardian into this other world, and it "nearly killed" him.[19]

Could this also be the yellow light of the "skanda" of the third day after death found in the bardo of "*Ratnasambhava*" in the *Tibetan Book of the Dead*? It says when you "see the sharp, clear yellow light,... you will be terrified" but you should "recognize it as wisdom."[20] It was perhaps what Perry explains psychotics go through in the disintegration of "the structures of the old self-image and world-images" creating dreams or visions of "nuclear explosions."[19] Though this was all terrifying, I felt detached from it, as if I were in a theatre watching a movie.

Now very weak and wondering where the usual me had gone, I drove home carefully, for I had no strength and I was not fully in my body. I had to hold the steering wheel very carefully so as not to lose control of the car. I was feeling so weak and not in control of my muscles; I could barely sit up straight or have the strength to keep my foot on the brake. At one point going down the winding descent of the Pali Highway, I pulled off into a runaway truck lane covered in gravel and waited until I felt more in control. Eventually, in growing hunger and panic, I reached home like this still in my pajamas.

Ego Death Struggle:

My husband was there distraught. The whole day had gone and he had no idea where I had been. He could not go to work and leave our daughter alone, so he had stayed home calling everyone who might know where I had gone. I did not know how much time I had been gone. All I knew was I was exhausted and feeling close to dying. I begged him for food. I tried to explain what was going on, but how could he understand? He had no knowledge of spiritual emergency, and even those who should know did not know. He had no idea what to do.

I was falling fast into a bottomless hole and knew it. There was no one to understand, no one to show any sympathy. He thought I was playing a fantasy game and I could snap out of it. I lay on the sofa in a deeply troubled state. I tried to communicate to my husband that I needed good, nourishing food. I was very hungry. I knew food would balance out my brain which was spinning into this abyss. He made a meal of meat and potatoes. It helped me gain some strength and I could relax a little.

He called my friend, Carol, to see if she could help me. Carol was living a life as an ascetic in a one-room apartment, traveling around from place to place picking up jobs, so she could focus on her spiritual life. She wanted to be a *sadhu* or monk, and made us feel she was knowledgeable about spiritual matters, but she really knew nothing about my emergency; she just seemed to speak nonsense to me. She tried reasoning, but she was addressing the wrong side of my brain for that logical mind had fled. She tried yelling and punishment; it was completely cruel and unnecessary. She had never seen *Kundalini* in this form. As spiritual as she thought she was, she had never had anything like this happen to her.

This is true for many who claim to be advanced meditators or spiritual teachers. Unless they too have gone through this, they are likely to have no idea what to do in such a crisis. She tried to scold me and treat me like a child. It was meaningless. Though their reaction to my behavior was understandable, it did not help me.

They were reacting to my ego and not my spirit or my heart. Nothing she said related to where I was. In this condition I just needed someone to hug me, to reassure me that I was not going insane. I needed solid nutritional food. I needed a complete lack of judgment and a total embrace of compassion. For me this was the battle for my soul. For her and my husband, I was acting crazy and should be scolded into change. It was terribly lonely and shattering for me. Could they not see my desperation? If only they had been kind to me at that time and not reacted as if I were a naughty child. If only they had listened with compassion.

Thus their statements transmitted to the absent "parent" that had left, did not reach me at all and only made me more desperate and lonely. John Weir Perry says, "At the very time when one needs loving sympathy one finds oneself... alone," with those who "make one conform to the ways of the former self and former world."[21]

They could not see my terror as I fought off this dark entity, the Ayatolla that I had seen in the car mirror, looming over me like a shadow that seemed to get stronger and stronger; my efforts to fight it back took all my strength. It wanted to swallow me up into itself and I knew without doubt that 'I' would be annihilated if it did. I knew 'I' would cease to exist if this darkness, this abyss were allowed to come into me.

Trauma Emerges:

These experiences I now know are considered classic in "ego death." The psychologist, R.D. Laing, explains, "Loss of ego may be confused with physical death. Projected images of one's own mind may be experienced as persecutors."[22] What was happening to me was a release of something in the subconscious that was so terrifying to me that I could not face it, and it was returning to be integrated into me again. This memory of terror seeing the demon from age four, when I was catatonic and yet scolded, was so hidden inside me that most of my life I could not penetrate the veil I had put over it. But with all the meditation, the ecstasy and love I was feeling, this anguish and hurt was coming up to the conscious mind to be healed.

The little four-year-old me who had been banished into a dark well of fear, was coming up the well and calling to me. But this little voice with its message of horror at seeing the devil could not be believed by the proper, civilized part of me which would not believe it. It had to be denied fiercely. This trauma was coming back as something I did not want to believe, something so awful to my conscious mind that it had to be denied, projected into something else— the Ayatolla.

As a child of four, without knowing better, this traumatic event of seeing an entity that looked like the devil, had created a false belief then that I had done something so terrible that I deserved abusive treatment. This is how children understand the world. I had no idea what I could have done that was so awful, but this logic did not change my childish belief that I was "very bad." I have subsequently spent many dollars and hours in a therapist's chair to be able to explain all this now. But even knowing it, does not heal it. I highly recommend the book by Yvonne Kason, M.D., *Farther Shores,* for dealing with the emergence of traumatic memories. But no such book was available to me, nor my caretakers in 1979.

The healing comes when a higher vibration energy releases the pain from the deep subconscious belief, and it comes up to the conscious mind to be emotionally released, accepted and integrated. The healing can come when we are no longer controlled and suppressing our spirit. The healing can come when there is true love to salve it also. We have to have a higher frequency energy to heal. These healings come when the *Kundalini* kicks the ghouls out of their hiding places—in my case this terribly frightening memory of a childhood trauma when I suspect "Begneth" first appeared. Thus when this shame approached me looking like the Ayatollah, I did not recognize it as "me." However, it was a part of me that had been lost and denied, and it was yearning to return 'home' to be healed. This whole episode and drama was an opportunity to reconcile with a damaged part of my psyche.

What had happened to me at the age of four was too terrible to allow into my conscious belief system, so it was shunted out into a dark place somewhere in the ethers and a dark veil was put over it from my conscious mind. As I was meditating and bringing more and more of my "lost" self to be healed and cleared in the *Kundalini* light, this part of me which was pushed far away had begun to draw near to my conscious awareness like a rubber band which had been stretched far and was now releasing its tension. It was dark and ugly because it had been scorned for so long. It was grotesque, strong from being pushed so far, and in pain from being cast out, denied in the darkness "away" from "me," from light, from comfort for so many years without love. Yet it was 'me;' it was my own life force and spirit that had been denied. I had superimposed the face of the Ayatollah onto this "denied aspect" because this man had an ugly, stern face and was creating great fear and anguish for people in Iran and America in 1979. He was also on the cover of *Time Magazine* that was sitting on our coffee table. He was the projection of this dark place hidden inside me.

On that day in November of 1979, the energy of this denied part of me, the earnest need it felt to be healed and loved after being rejected and miserable for such a long time, was stronger than my need to push it away. Max Freedom Long who writes about the Hawaiian system of *Huna* puts it clearly. "The middle self [logical mind] is easily driven out of the body through a temporary or permanent injury to its nervous centers."[23] Long says, like don Juan that, "Allowing the low self [self without mind] to control the body is 'dangerous because it lives under the domination of the animal world where things happen illogically and as if by accident.'"[24] He goes on to explain that "One of the ways in which the low self forces its wishes on the middle self is through engulfing the middle self with a great wave of emotion."[25] Thus my middle self or the logical mind, the mind given by the predator, that was obsessed with controlling time had left, and I was functioning under the domination of the low self, the primitive animal world.

A good example of such behavior is when people get drunk and do illogical, dangerous and destructive things. This low self was in charge during that crazy day. It could not drive well, it did not get food, it did not take care of my bodily functions, it made decisions without planning, it was easily exhausted, it seemed not to care about my child or husband's feelings, and it had no awareness of "others," being wholly preoccupied with survival in the face of this impending 'annihilation.' When I read this book *The Secret Science Behind Miracles* by Max Freedom Long this information came as a vindication of my crazy experience, and I understood what had happened with new compassion for myself.

The Grofs in their classic text on the "spiritual emergency" state that, "Approaching the moment of the ego death might feel like the end of the world. Paradoxically, while only a small step separates us from an experience of radical liberation, we have a sense of all-pervading anxiety and impending catastrophe of enormous proportions." This is putting it mildly. But they go on to say, "When the individual... decides to let things happen, he or she experiences total annihilation on all levels... everything that is important and meaningful... seem to be mercilessly destroyed."[26]

What I did not know was that this fear was the ego, the artificial "me," the predatory creature that has been controlling our minds for millions of years, facing its own death. If I had realized at that point that 'I' was not the ego, perhaps I could have allowed this darkness to engulf me and been reconciled to it, but all I knew was terror. I had to fight it with all my strength. To not fight it, to not win, was unthinkable death or certain madness. Over the years I have found out that this trauma at age four happened in November, and this final understanding ended years of depressions that always came in November. It took me 20 years to dig out the details and release the horror of that event.

The Guru's Mercy:

So there I was lying on the sofa fighting with an entity that only I could see, trying not to allow it to enter my being, feeling as if it would annihilate me, and my poor husband was trying to figure out what to do. I have no recollection of sleeping that night, but the next day, he made a call to my meditation leader, Rob, who immediately called my teacher in Miami. My guru's message paraphrased was:

Do not panic; this is a stage of the process; it is auspicious. He did remember my *shaktipat* the previous July. He instructed that the doctors should not to give me any drugs, and most importantly, that I was *"a good girl."* My guru also gave Rob instructions to do a special chant for me, the *Guru Gita,* which was scheduled for the following night. All the meditation group would have a special chant just for me. This information helped me so much to calm down. I was still very weak, still very afraid of this entity, but I felt the love, safety and protection of my guru. I knew I was in good hands.

The Doctor:

This same day my husband took me to the office of a psychiatrist in Honolulu. While we waited in the waiting room, I found a newspaper report of the woman in the plane who had ditched off the waters of Maui, but she had managed to swim to shore and was safe. Clearly I had not dreamed that part of my experience the day before. I knew somehow my intervention had saved her life. Who would believe that! In the psychiatrist's office nothing seemed to make sense to me. I was still disconnected from my body in a daze. John Weir Perry explains, "the activity of the mundane world is positively painful to people in this state of arousal."[27]

The psychiatric doctor was unperturbed by the drama of my account. I told him about my meditation, my experiences and how I was almost annihilated by this evil entity. He listened without any emotions or show of feelings. He was very matter-of-fact. He did not even blink at all the drama of my fight with the demon that was trying to destroy me. At some point I told him about this little child's voice I heard telling me about a terrifying vision of a demon from when I was four, but I did not accept it. I explained that I had no memory of that and did not believe this voice. He coolly looked me straight in the eye and said, "Why can't you believe that idea? Why do you reject this voice from inside yourself? If your child's voice is saying that, why not believe it?" I was shocked that a doctor would say that at first.

"It is not something I want to believe." I sputtered slowly.

He countered, "But what difference does it make? It was something that happened, but it is not happening now. Why would you not believe the voice coming from inside you? Why would you believe it is lying?" The logic was so amazing. He gave me permission to trust my inner voice, something I had not done for years.

At that point I started to come back into my body and felt a change;

I needed to use the bathroom. This was the first time that I had been aware of my bodily functions for days. I let my mind wrap around this idea of accepting my little child's voice as truth, and I realized that it did not affect my core being. I felt the deep anguish of it in some distant part of my being, but my mind seemed at that moment to accept it without fear. What if that were true? I am alive and that trauma happened years ago. Big relief came with this acceptance. He recommended a prescription and no more meditation. It was the beginning of healing and integration which did take some years to complete, but this was a turning point.

This was the total of what this psychiatrist who cost my health insurance a great deal of money could do for me in this state. Yet even though it does not seem much, it was what I needed. I had permission to accept the long-denied message. I was able to endure it, watch it, feel it because, as awful as this message portended, it did not destroy the very core of my being. My heart was safe from the dreadful impact of the message, and my core heart was where I truly lived, as I had found out in my experiment in the garden.

John Weir Perry explains that "psychotic states can be cleared up quickly if there is someone to respond to it in an honest and warm way, and often the "thought disorder" can melt away.[28] Fortunately for me this is what happened for it is now 30+ years later, and, in spite of the fact that the psychiatrist was sure I would return to his office again and again throughout my life, I did not. Clearly he was ascribing my symptoms to a psychotic pathology he had seen in others, but he was not aware of this psychotic episode as a healing crisis that the *Kundalini* had created for me.

Even for a top psychiatrist, these bizarre effects of meditation were not understood in 1979 by psychiatric medicine. How could he understand the radical cleansing that *Kundalini* could undertake in a person's psyche? A psychiatrist would see psychotic patients with true mental disturbances returning over and over throughout their lives, so how could be believe that such an event could be cleared up in one event? There was little known and even less understood about this phenomena of *Kundalini* awakening in Western psychology at that time and even today, it is not easy to find mental health practitioners who understand it. Thanks to the work of Dr. Stanislav Grof and others in the field of Transpersonal Psychology there are pockets of true understanding of the spiritual process called *Kundalini* awakening today.

The Guru Gita:

I am now certain that another reason for my atypical recovery was the immense benediction that my guru gave me—another precious gift. That next night my meditation center friends chanted the *Guru Gita* for me at Rob's house. This is an ancient chant of 181 Sanskrit verses said to be from the *Shree Skanda Puran*. This section is a conversation of great love between the goddess Parvati and her Lord. My guru had it translated and published as a major text for his disciples. I had never chanted it to that date, although I had heard of it, and I later was to find chanting it myself that it cured just about all the crazy symptoms I had had.

As my friends chanted for me in the meditation center, I lay in my bed at peace all night feeling the waves of their love coursing through my very sensitive nerves. It was like a great white, peaceful balm pouring out waves of soothing love. It seemed to move through my nervous system like the waves of a great ocean of healing. How to describe such a thing when one is in such a nervous state as I had been? It was pure nectar. I no longer needed to fight the demon that had been the Ayatollah because that trauma was soothingly integrating and melting into oblivion.

I woke up the next day completely calm and normal. This transforming chant, my guru's blessing, the psychiatrist's admonition to accept my own voice from within, all came together to bring me a deep acceptance and back to my fully aware, conscious mind once more. I woke up as a different person. I was on the other side of the abyss. I had integrated something huge that I had pushed away at the age of four into dark regions of rejection.

Gangaji:

Many years later, in 1992, I was to meet Gangaji, a teacher from Ramana Maharshi's lineage in Honolulu. I told her about this abyss and the demonic Ayatollah and she said, "You should have jumped." I was shocked at first by what she said, as I was so sure I would go mad if I had surrendered to it. But now I understand what she meant, and she is right. The fear was my ego afraid of death, afraid to learn of the horror I had buried in my subconscious. However, the acceptance of this "dark" and "denied" part of my psyche was achieved more and more over the years and with it an integration and healing. It also brought forgiveness and energy releases from having suppressed it for so long.

I returned to my classes and in spite of the drug the doctor had prescribed, I managed to get through my exams. The crisis had passed. Within a few weeks I took less and less of this drug, and in months I stopped taking it altogether. On the last visit to the psychiatrist he told me I had had a "psychotic episode." I asked him what that was, but he did not have a definition of it. The definition for psychiatrists at that time was, "diseases of unknown etiology."[29] Basically, they had no clue. This was a useful label. This seemed outrageous to me that I should be labeled as that, especially since it carries such a stigma in America, yet no one could define it or describe anything about it! Stan and Christina Grof, in their Appendix III to *The Stormy Search for the Self,* explain my experience as mis-diagnosed by my psychiatrist:

> Careful analysis of the manifestations of the major types of spiritual emergency shows that they do not fit any of the official categories.... David Lukoff, a psychiatrist at the University of California... emphasized the need to clearly distinguish mystical states from psychotic reactions. He feels psychiatry should have, in addition, two categories for conditions in which the mystical and psychotic overlap: mystical states with psychotic features and psychotic states with mystical features.[30]

What I found out from studying *Huna* and the teachings of don Juan, the Mexican Sorcerer, gave me more of an explanation of what happened to me than I could find in my research of psychology at that time.

I knew that a *Kundalini* emergency like mine had been induced by too intense desire on my part to go through the subconscious mess, and this had overwhelmed me emotionally and physically. A terrifying memory from the age of four was coming back to my awareness to be healed. I also was not eating a proper diet for meditation. Meat is not something that was helping me as it gave me too much fire (*agni*); as a spiritual person, I feel the energy of the animal as I eat it, so that adds to the spiritual confusion. The brain gets burned out of trace minerals and *sattvic* (calming) nutrition is essential during long periods of meditation. I had been burning these up for five months without replacing them with a '*sattvic*' diet, a diet mainly of grains, legumes, dairy and nuts. All this I found out after the fact, but on some level I knew when that Ayatollah creature had come, that the right food was essential to endure the stress of it.

My teacher was an Ayurvedic doctor and knew what the body needed at such times. This I found out later is why, in ancient times, *chelas* or disciples spent twelve years preparing for such experiences and were kept in Ashrams where the food was designed for meditation. It is similar to people who prepare for a marathon by eating a special diet prior to the run and then a different diet afterwards. The wrong diet will affect the athlete's performance. In my case it took me a months to return to a feeling of being balanced again.

Return to Self:

So I had reached the edge of the abyss and even though I did not jump, a healing had come. Whatever that frightening rejected part of me had been, it had come 'home.' It was back with me, not moaning in misery in some far off region of my psyche. I was seeing God everywhere in rocks, in birds, in worms, in the grass. I seemed surrounded by manifestations of divine love. I heard my heart singing, "I am God" when

I looked into the mirror. My teacher had told stories of a famous Sufi Saint who had been killed for saying this. Yet it was coming out of my heart and erupting from the depths of my being. The whole energy of my meditation had mellowed and calmed down into a deep peaceful inner sanctuary of love. The crisis had passed.

Paul Rebillot writes in "The Hero's Journey: Ritualizing the Mystery" that "it is possible to find terror within the human psyche: monsters, ghouls,... But I have also learned that looking long enough and deeply enough into the eyes of the most frightening inner monster can transmute it into treasure."[31] The Grofs explain that an encounter with "these seemingly horrifying, wrathful deities is a very important part of the death-rebirth process.... they are carriers of a symbolic death of the ego, a step that is necessary for spiritual opening."[32] It is obvious now why I found the Grofs' book so enlightening when I read it in 1993 because from 1979 to 1993, I had felt ashamed and embarrassed about my "psychotic episode" thinking that I was somehow a pariah of society. Nothing could be further from the truth as it turns out from my research over thirty years. Counter to that of my culture, I was on a journey to cast off my disassociation with Nature, to escape the "tyranny of thinking,"[33] and to return to my true nature.

CHAPTER 17

Integration and Balance

Now is the time to recognize the core of peace
That exists within yourself. You are That!

Gangaji[1]

In the Hermetic alchemical tradition my crisis was alchemically at the stage of "Distillation" which is the death of the ego and rebirth of the transpersonal Self... "This can be an extremely painful process indeed."[2] The stage that follows is "Coagulation" the rise out of destruction, similar to "a soaring eagle, the winged Mercury, the balanced scales of justice" but the "primary symbol of Coagulation was the Phoenixa mythical bird that built its nest in a fire and then rose from the flames renewed." Dennis Hauck, author of *The Emerald Tablet* explains that this Phoenix bird is the "Morning Star" and an "archetypal symbol of the Sun and gold;" it is the "resurrected personality seen as a successful individuation resulting in peace of mind, heightened energy and a free-flowing adaptability to new situations."[3]

This parallel of the *Kundalini* process with chemical alchemy is unmistakable and well described in a small book I was given from India. This book *Alchemically Purified and Solidified Mercury* by Petri Murien, explains the parallels between the production of gold from mercury with the evolutionary process of the soul. For this reason mercury is called "the messenger of the Gods."[4] Mercury begins as a toxic poison, but through alchemy with sulfur and salt, it can be turned into a solid metal that has healing properties that "becomes a genuine elixir for whoever uses it."[5] I am fortunate to have a small nugget of this transcendent mercury which comes with a ribbon rather than a chain. It has healing properties and assists the wearer in many ways including blood purification. This much-transformed nugget is the parallel of the human being who comes out of the "dark night of the soul," through the abyss and the ghouls of the subconscious cleansing, and emerges into the day of healing and rejuvenation as I did. The process strips mercury to the essence and reconstitutes it as a new, healing element, like the human being who is burned to ashes in the crucible; the ego is destroyed and then a non-toxic being comes back integrated, whole and able to heal.

The metal mercury is considered a "hermaphrodite metal,"[6] just as I considered myself to be a hermaphrodite by being at one within myself through the merging of the *Kundalini* in the crown chakra. Mercury changes after it has been "killed" and can "communicate life only after having lost its own: after having been killed or fixed, it has changed its character, it takes on a nobler, more exalted form after having gone through death."[7] Petri Murien goes on to speculate that "Alchemy easily demonstrates us [sic] the divinity of the universe, this world which appears to us as divine in its essence, is in truth the body of God."[8] This is the *Kundalini* process transmuting the human being into a divine being, "as above, so below." This *Kundalini* is the power that transmutes the ego-mind into a unified, integrated intelligence that is fully connected to its source. This is what is required to become fully human.

One who goes through this annihilation, destruction of the ego, and merging with the dreaded parts of the lost psyche emerges "feeling healed, reborn, rejuvenated" having a greatly reduced "fear of death" and an enhanced ability to understand and enjoy life.[9] He or she comes back to "normalcy" with an inner knowledge of the "home" within themselves and the ability to heal others. I found this font of divine power within the center of my perineum that was the "Shiva Lingam," the phallus around which the *Kundalini* had been coiled. I had found it in my heart lotus with its undulating petals, and I found it in my third eye that could see inside bodies and see entities from other dimensions. I had found myself "Hermaphrodite" not dependent on any partner for utter orgasmic bliss. I had found the words, "I am God" reverberating from the core of my cells. I had found myself my own lover, my own mother, my own father, my own sibling, my own friend, my own wealth, and my own universe. I had found myself at one with my world.

Grounding:

After this crisis, my life returned to almost normal. I stopped meditating so much as I wanted to prove to myself and others that I was not crazy and unbalanced; I focused on my family and my university work. When I saw Bob on campus, I still felt love for him, but there was no more magnetic attraction either way. I focused on my studies and my duties to my family. I had weathered the storm. I still felt shame about what had happened with my Ayatollah episode, the psychiatrist visit and scaring everyone, but I had survived without further disruption.

I understood my "psychotic event" was like a fever in an illness that destroys the germs invading the body. It is very uncomfortable and distressing to have the fever, but it is the means to a cure. I was cured of the traumas of my past lives, cured of the mistaken belief programs of my subconscious, and cured of the influence of the predator Flyer's mind. The true beginning of this transformation had been April 28,[th] 1974, five years before from the "Tiger Dream." The direct experience of initiation had been July 13,[th] 1979. Now, with my heart opened, with my guru's chant and protection, I realized that I had come through the worst.

Guru Visit:

Unfortunately, all this drama had shaken my family to the core. My daughter, who is a very sensitive child, suffered a severe bout of pneumonia ending up in the hospital in early December. She had been bearing the weight of all this drama. These events put a pall over the usual Christmas celebrations. None of us looked forward to the Christmas Holiday, so my husband suggested we go to see my spiritual guru for Christmas in Miami. Could anything be more wonderful to me at this time than hearing these words? I wept in gratitude. It was about two weeks before Christmas. My husband went to the travel agency to arrange the tickets. This was before the Internet. We could only afford economy fares at that time for the three of us from Honolulu to Miami. The travel agent had laughed with disbelief that at such short notice we hoped to get economy fares for three people, but we just left her the details, and we waited to find out what she could arrange.

Within less than 24 hours she called back in amazement to tell us that she had arranged the trip. We would leave Honolulu on the afternoon of December 26th, spend the night of December 26th in Dallas and catch an afternoon flight out of Dallas to Miami on December 27th all at economy fare and all seated together. It was clearly the guru that made that miracle happen. We spent a quiet Christmas Day and without telling any of our relatives who lived in Texas, we caught the plane to Dallas the next day. Unbelievable as it may be, on our flight to Dallas, we were upgraded to first class by the stewards since the flight was not full. It was one more gift.

Releasing the Vows:

Thursday, December 27th, 1979 was our Tenth Wedding Anniversary and we were again in the city, Dallas, where we had been wed on December 27th, 1969, in a small chapel in Dallas near where my spouse had lived. The irony and coincidence was clear to both of us, so we did not have much discussion about it. We just knew this was what we had to do, so on this Tenth Anniversary, we took our four year-old daughter to the church and showed her where mommy and daddy had been married. The receptionist opened the chapel for us. We walked down the aisle to the altar with our child between us, remembering that special day in 1969 when we had made vows to each other. It was very moving. It was highly symbolic. The implications were gentle, full of compassion and love.

There was no mistaking the message that this trip had been organized by a cosmic miracle to have us meet again in this special place where we had made those sacred vows, so we could be released now. It was just one more sign of the magnitude of the guru's power and love. I was back there in that little chapel to now *take off* the ring as in the dream my dad had said, "A tiger will visit you tonight, when he does give him your ring." When the "Tiger" had come, I had removed my wedding band and put it on the dresser next to the bed in the dream. So here I was over five years later, and I almost felt my teacher standing in the chapel there with us, saying, "You see, it is over now. You can let go of your ring." This was the final fulfillment of that command. It took this dramatic return to the chapel to convince me that it was not impossible to admit my marriage was a failure. I was no longer the unconscious young woman who had made those vows. I was a transformed being. I had a new destiny. In a way I had reincarnated, been reborn as a new person, so the old contracts of the unconscious me no longer had control of my destiny.

Here I was back in the same chapel where I had put the ring on, and here I was ten years later being given permission to take it off just before I was going to meet the Tiger in person. Both my husband and I were silent and humbled by this incredible coincidence. It was the beginning of the miracles of reconciliation and healing.

The Ashram:

In Miami we arrived in the late afternoon at the Ashram of my guru. As we entered the front door, a voice came through my heart saying, "Welcome to my house." I was *home*. I could barely keep from weeping in relief. I knew I had found something I had been seeking for a thousand years. *Everything was going to be all right now.*

We had to sleep in separate quarters, the men in one part and my daughter and I in another. It was a huge hotel on the beach. It was exciting to be among other people who knew about meditation, who knew my teacher and experienced much of what I had gone through. I felt totally happy there. During the day, as a family we had to do our "*seva*" (work) together, but at night we slept apart in male and female dorms. In my dorm, I made friends with a lively lady called Margie, a psychologist from San Diego, who listened to the story of my spiritual crisis and took it on herself to make friends with my daughter.

Margie and my husband became instant friends and soon spent many hours laughing and chatting light heartedly together. Apart from the times when my husband and I were doing our "*seva*," Margie was with us for meals and the programs the entire visit to the Ashram. Margie would explain the protocols and give us advice about what to expect. Her interest in our family gave me freedom to meditate during the free times while the two of them babysat my daughter in the garden.

My spouse was not happy with the "*seva*" [work] as he considered it menial, mindless work, sorting grains of rice on large trays to get out dirt and twigs; but we were all relaxed and happily together near the beach in the sunshine of Miami. These were the kinds of jobs we were asked to do for several hours a day. Our daughter stayed with us during this time, and in the afternoon we were able to walk or swim on the beach and meet other people.

Seva Lessons:

After about the third day of such jobs as cleaning vegetables, sorting lentil grains for dirt and rocks and washing toilets, we were given the task of polishing green peppers. I was not sure what we were supposed to do, so I asked the supervisor to explain it again. She carefully demonstrated that these peppers had gotten slight mildew in transit from the fields, and that this mildew was something our guru, an Ayurvedic doctor, had said we should never ingest. So every trace of this blight had to be rubbed off the crevices of the peppers before these could be cooked and eaten.

With this knowledge and that understanding, I took a clean rag and began to rub on the shiny, green peppers wherever I saw the black mildew. I pushed my index finger into the stem area; I rubbed carefully in each crevice of the surface of each pepper with my thumb. Shortly, I lost track of time, and I reached a deep state of meditation and oneness. As I rubbed on the surface of the pepper with my thumb, so I felt this same movement on my solar plexus. I stopped for a moment, for my conscious mind did not understand how this could happen. Then I did it again. I pushed on the pepper in my hand in a certain direction, and the same sensation went across my solar plexus. I was feeling the same movement as I was pushing on the pepper! Which was the pepper, and which was me? There was no separation. The pepper was as much part of me as my own body. I got it! This was the purpose of *"seva"* to discover this oneness, this unity with all things. I was elated! This was one more gift from my guru.

The Song of my Soul:

On the Sunday of our visit, I was able to leave my daughter with Margie and my spouse and get up early to go to *The Guru Gita* chant. This was a treat that I anticipated eagerly, since I knew what it had done to heal me while I had been going through the 'Ayatollah' event. I arrived early to the main hall, got the book and found a place in the back; everyone was standing up. The Indian music with drum and harmonium began and the loud Sanskrit chanting followed.

I began to sway to the music of it. Other people were swaying wildly, arms swinging and almost dancing. For a while I watched and listened and then became aware that some part of me had begun to hum inside like a buzzing bee. I just listened with all my being to the sounds and realized that all I was aware of was the sound of this sonorous chanting. No other senses were registering. The people around me had disappeared. The large spacious ballroom had no boundaries but had turned luminous white. All that I knew was this music and sound flowing through me, enervating and familiar like a child's nursery rhyme almost forgotten in deep memory.

Then I understood; this was why I had spent hours in those dark, freezing churches of England singing in the choir in my little black gown each Sunday. This was the sound I had been searching for, yearning for, longing to hear through my whole life. What a great, great blessing. I had come home! I bought the chanting book at the bookstore and a tape to listen to it at home. I felt this was truly the best gift I could take home with me.

While we were in Miami we only saw my teacher once the first evening, as he had a heart attack the next day and went to the hospital. In my deepest feeling about this, I was afraid that I had brought so much karma with me, that I had nearly killed him. This was the little voice again "I am a very bad girl."

It is known that the teacher will take on the karma of his/her disciples, so this is what I felt I had done at that time. However, even though I did not get to meet him in person, the inner voice of my guru was strong and clear. During meditation I got clear messages: *I should take the Guru Gita home, chant it every day, do the practices my teacher had set out, do my work and take care of my family and he would take care of me.* It was something I knew I could do, and it was the same kind of feeling that I had had at 13 after I got the message from Jesus. Nothing could have been more simple or straight forward. Shortly after we returned to Hawaii, my guru returned to the Ashram and lived almost another three years. My life was transformed by this visit, and it was the end of the crazy entities, the end of confusion, the end of my escapism into the astral realms.

Grounding Practice:
I settled down with this wonderful chant that stabilized the *Kundalini* and it stopped the astral floating and demonic visions. I followed my guru's instructions and meditated less, did my duty or *dharma*, focused on my home and college work and kept up the practice of the *Guru Gita*. I studied for my exams, taking care of my family, and limiting my meditation time to an hour a day. My guru was taking care of me, so I had no need to take off into other worlds.

When I chanted the *Guru Gita* alone in my meditation area, I would feel the greatest love rising into my heart. This felt like the truest love between male and female that came from this chant which is the call and response of Shiva [God] and Parvati [Goddess]. It was exotic, beautiful, true bliss. This banished all the demonic energies that had been appearing in my meditations. This chant was the greatest blessing and balanced my final stages of awakening.

I was happy at last. I perceived my relationship to my husband improved tremendously. The irony was, that he was happier because he was secretly having a relationship with Margie by letter and phone; after he moved out of our house to a Waikiki apartment, in October of 1980, he went back to Miami to visit her. This separation came about as a surprise to me, for I had settled down to work very diligently, getting my Masters' exams completed with much dedication, clarity, success and hard work. I was not having any more episodes of floating away or meditating too much. The improvement in our relationship was my impression but not his.

Meeting my Guru:

In the winter of 1980, much calmed, balanced and confident by daily chanting of the *Guru Gita*, by completing my Masters and having a successful first term of teaching, I was able to visit my guru again in Santa Monica, California for a Christmas Program called *"So Ham."* At the Christmas Eve service, John Denver, draped with a shawl from my guru, was singing at the evening program. After the program of chanting, listening to a talk, we were able to go up and meet the guru face to face in *darshan*, or a meeting.

I had ordered a *maile lei* from the Christmas Islands to honor him; this was the Polynesian tradition of showing respect for a great chief, or *ali'i*. The *maile lei* is not circular, but it is a long string of sweet smelling vines that are woven into a scarf-like garment that hangs to the knees. At the program, when my turn came to walk up to the Guru, I held it in front of me with both hands palms up.

As I approached the Guru's chair to meet him, everyone in the program, probably two thousand people, stood up, applauded and cheered loudly. He nodded to me to put it around his neck and shoulders, which

I did. I was in a kind of daze. I did not know then that he almost never allowed anyone to put anything around his neck like that. Some time later I realized that this applause and cheering by the audience was perhaps his way of honoring *me!* I had not seen anything like this in other *darshans* then or since. This truly was a pinnacle of all I had been through. Somehow he knew everything I had been through, and that I had fought many of the battles of my subconscious programming to appear before him. At that moment, I truly knew what the hero feels as s/he returns home and is acknowledged. Even today I feel the beauty of this gesture.

At a two day intensive the next day, I sat next to the Hollywood actress, Jill Clayburgh, and by good fortune, I was just feet away from my guru's chair. During the program, he spent many minutes staring at me. He had us chant the *"Kundalini Stavaha"* as part of the program, and I immediately loved it. I could feel every syllable in my being. I still to this day chant it and I always remember this moment I first heard it.

My mind then was still in a state of confusion about what had happened to me, so during one of the small group sharing sessions, I told of some of the bizarre experiences I had gone through such as having been possessed by a being with four arms and three heads. As I sat down from saying all this in a rather hysterical way, I looked down and seemed to see the dead skin of a snake that had fallen off me. It felt as if, by blurting out all this fear and horror, I had shed the karma, the fear, and the terror of it all.

Later that day, a lady came up to me and said, "You are just like the hero in Joseph Campbell's book *The Hero of a Thousand Faces."* I had not read it then, but it comforted me when she said that because I realized that I was not alone in this journey. Someone else at a meal later informed me that my guru had been watching my sharing on a short circuit TV. This shocked and embarrassed me. I could not bear to think that I was a whining, pathetic creature before the Guru. However, I knew that in sharing my fear and horror, I had finally shed it like the snake skin. It was gone forever.

My Guru's Farewell:

My teacher passed away in that October 1982. I stayed numb about his passing for many years, but I also could not say his name for at least five years. After five years, I could only cry if I tried to say his name, and this is still true today, decades later. This is a love too deep to put into language. There is no relationship that can compare to this spiritual guide who gives one *everything.* There is no way to repay it, no way to recompense for what has been offered. The very idea renders one speechless. The relationship is a bond that is beyond anything one can describe or compare. People who met him concur that my guru lived on a level beyond anything most of us humans can understand. He was truly a prototype of what a full God-as-human is.

In the years since, the miracles have not stopped, but the flying and being possessed by entities did stop. Sometimes amazing things came to me that showed me the integration that was taking place in myself. Sometimes I could see into the future and forecast events which amazingly did occur. I could see evil when it was not obvious to others, and heal people of various issues. I could understand the world on another level, so I was able to live my life more easily. I found ways to cure issues in myself that I have used to help others, and to fathom deep metaphysical concepts, which today are fairly accepted, such as the idea of parallel universes, and the idea of zero point. All these concepts just came to me in meditation. This is the heritage of awakened humanity.

Heart Opening:

One day a year or two after the initial experience of awakening, I was driving along the H1 Freeway in Honolulu to have dinner with my English friends in Waikiki. It was a lovely, typical tropical evening with the sun setting to my right, sending the sky into wonderful pink and red billows. The indigo ocean touched with dashes of pink, set off the stark white sailboats sailing out for evening meditations from the Ilikai Marina.

I drove without thinking about anything in particular when suddenly I felt this pressure on my chest. It was as if someone were sitting on my heart; the pain went from heavy pressure to a sharp stab. Am I having a heart attack? The pain gripped my heart as if someone were squeezing it tightly. I grasped at my chest with one hand and just managed to steer the car with the other to the exit, so I could get off the freeway. The pains were like knots bursting from within the center of my upper chest—my heart area. I realized with astonishment, I was having a heart attack in my mid-30's.

As soon as possible, I got off the freeway and pulled over to get my breath. I had no car phone then, so I could not call for help. All I could do was sit and breathe into the pain and focus on my heart. The pains gradually subsided. Then a new feeling emerged. It felt as if a volcano of molten love had poured out of my heart. It was thick and viscous and infinitely warming. I had been parked only about 10 minutes, yet I had gone from fear and pain to a blissful fulfilling love pouring through every part of my heart. It was so divine. I looked at the cars streaming by and the sky again. Everything looked bathed in love; everything seemed to be infinitely dear. This was not a heart attack, but a heart chakra opening. I spent the rest of my evening with friends in a silent bliss which they remarked made them feel very peaceful. I had entered a universe of love.

This was the opening of my heart chakra. "The fourth chakra, the heart, can open on both physical and emotional levels... Many students report the heart opening feels as if they were having a heart attack and wonder if they need an ambulance."[10] How could I ever be the same again? This "heart attack" was another sign along the way of transformation by the *Kundalini*.

According to the Institute of Heart Math in Boulder Creek, California connected to Stanford University, "Heart intelligence is the intelligent flow of awareness that we experience once the mind and bodily emotions are brought into balance and coherence... the heart possesses its own independent nervous system, which they referred to as 'the brain of the heart,'" and "the heart's influence on the field is empowered by its own electromagnetic activity that is 5,000 times more powerful than the brain's electromagnetic field."[11]

It is noted in Drunvalo Melchizedek's book *Living in the Heart* that when the child is conceived, the heart "beats before the brain is formed." Heart Math scientists have found that about 40,000 cells in the heart are actually brain cells, and "the human heart generates the largest and most powerful energy field of any organ in the body, including the brain within the skull."[12]

A verse in the *Upanishads* in Chandogya says:

> Though old age comes to the body, the lotus of the heart does not grow old. At death of the body, it does not die. The lotus of the heart, where Brahman exists in all his glory—that, and not the body, is the true city of Brahman.... those who have realized the Self and its right desires find permanent happiness everywhere.... The Self resides within the lotus of the heart... The Self is the immortal, the fearless; the Self is Brahman. This Brahman is eternal Truth.[13]

1982–1991:

My husband and Margie began a long distance relationship and we got divorced; my daughter and I stayed in our house and he went back to work in Texas. I taught at the university part time and managed to also run a weekly Meditation Center for my guru's lineage. In 1984 I went with my daughter to India to celebrate my guru's *Samadhi* in the Ashram north of Mumbai. In spite of regular meditation practice, doing my *seva*, offering my home for others to meditate, and chanting, a part of me was still "seeking" something more. I was not "there."

The Direct Method:

Some spiritual friends started a discussion group to discuss the teachings of Ramana Maharshi's Direct Method. He says in repeating, "Who am I?" and being vigilant and honest about the answer, one can use the mind to penetrate the mind and come to a place beyond thought.

In 1991, I met one of Ramana Maharshi's disciples and teachers, Gangaji, in a home in Honolulu. With only a dozen people in the room, she answered personal questions about spiritual evolvement. One question I had asked was about visions I had had and what did they mean for my spiritual progress.

She shocked me by saying, "Forget all that. It has nothing to do with the truth of who you are." This came as a huge bomb to my spiritual ego which had thought my visions made me in some way more spiritually evolved than others who did not have this. In one stroke, she took all my spiritual pride and dashed it into smithereens! In Swami Narayananda's book he says, "Spiritual sounds, visions and light visions only show that one is making headway spiritually, and nothing else."[14] That same 'self-righteous me' from the age of 13 had resurrected itself out of the ashes like an unwelcome phoenix.

Once more, I had to face the fact that I had been given this gift of *Kundalini* awakening with all the amazing experiences that went with it, but still that ego had taken over this as something to be "proud" of and to feel self righteous about. Thus it was a great gift that Gangaji gave me at that moment, as the ground fell out from beneath my ego, and it was for a while, left suspended in mid-air! In that suspension was the real *me*! I had to find out more about this.

As a result of this revelation by Gangaji, I felt that "direct" method had something important to offer, and I loved reading about *Arunachala*, the mountain that Ramana so worshipped. So I studied Ramana Maharshi's teachings and allowed them to work away at my ego in the "direct experience approach" that he valiantly tried to convey to his followers. His concept was very clear. "Seeking the ego, i.e. its source, ego disappears. What is left over is the Self. This method is the direct one."[15] The mind is endless and powerful, so if we use the mind we can find the truth of who "observes" the mind; even in deep sleep someone is awake to observe that one is "sleeping." He says to discover the one who is observing. "Reality is simply the loss of the ego. Destroy the ego by seeking its identity... This is the Direct Method."[16]

I received a small brochure from the Advaita Vedanta Institute with some words of Shri Ramana Maharshi which comforted me enormously. It said:

> Place your burden at the feet of the Lord of the Universe who accomplishes everything. Remain all the time steadfast in the Heart, in the Transcendental Absolute... Don't worry. Abide in the Heart and surrender your acts to the Divine.

These were the concepts and practices that I was working with on a regular basis much as I had my spiritual verses when I was 13. As a result of Gangaji's kind advice, I had had a revelation in controlling anxiety about my teenage daughter going out on weekends with her friends. If she was late coming home, even though my heart said, *"All is well,"* I would begin to panic, adrenalin would kick in, and soon I would be racing around Honolulu, looking fruitlessly for her. I knew it was useless, but the animal instincts were overwhelming.

Gangaji told me to ask, "Who is afraid?" when this occurred again. Thus, the next event where I was worried about my daughter, I listened to my heart's voice. It said, *"She is fine, no need to worry."* Her entire life I could always know what was happening to her through my heart. Once she cut her finger at a neighbor's house, and I immediately ran over and arrived before my neighbor even knew what had happened to my daughter. So I knew she was not in harm's way. Yet the anxiety would begin like a sort of waking wolf in my belly, getting stronger and stronger over my emotions and muscles. I questioned within my mind, "Who is afraid?" several times. It seemed that something responded with a rather pathetic, "Me."

Again I asked, "Who is me?" With that question something seemed to evaporate inside me and tension released. I asked again, "Who is afraid?" This time there was no answering voice, but like air out of a balloon, there was a great exhale from deep within. I asked again, "Who is afraid?" and this time it was as if the wolf lay back down and went back to sleep. The fear-adrenalin-action sequence was foiled. It was one of the most empowering events of my life. I was free of this hungry animal that always seemed to force me into illogical, insane actions running after my daughter in the middle of the night.

The Final Gift:

One Saturday evening in early July of 1994, when I went to our meditation center for the evening program as usual, I entered the meditation hall, and on the etheric level, I saw Shree Ramana Maharshi standing next to my guru. I was pleased and surprised, but also confused. They welcomed me and ushered me together to a specific place on the carpet to sit for the program. I wondered what this was all about, for it was not any special religious holiday. My initiation at the meditation center in 1979 had been just 15 years before, and I had heard somewhere that odd years were opportunities for spiritual leaps. Could that be it?

As usual, the chant began and then the meditation time came. I went into my usual yoga posture and in a few seconds, it was if a curtain came down and I was in another reality. All the "noise" inside my head stopped. According to Ramana Maharshi this "noise" is called *nada*. He says, "The circulation of the blood, respiration of air, and other functions of the body are bound to produce sound. That sound is involuntary and continuous. That is *nada*." He also states that "*Isvara* is beyond *nada* (sound)."[17] There were no vibrating sensations in my ears, in my head, anywhere. It was as if I had stepped behind a curtain of "noise" and found a sanctuary where I was completely warm, safe, familiar and blessed. It only lasted a few seconds, perhaps 20 seconds in all, but this changed me radically then and ever since. Here is my account of it from my diary the next day:

Diary: *"July 3rd 1994 :*

Last night I knew for a few moments the knowledge I have sought so long. It was a moment of rest. It was a moment of no-mind. It was such peace. It was so simple, so easy, so natural. It was "home." I have no doubt it is THE state I seek. I knew then the reason yogis laugh about it. No words can convey it. No ideas can be there, yet it is all "I" and it is always known. The mind is an evaporated cloud. The 'Self' rises in wonderful normalcy. It is as if everything I struggle and weep over doesn't exist. It's as if all the efforts to be realized are as a man acting as if he is drowning, and there is no water. It is as if all the lifetimes have been a hysterical nightmare by comparison. No, that's not it. It is so "ME" yet so "ALL." It is the most basic natural state. There is no action. No action is required to be there. No action is required to remain. I have found the state the yogis can't speak of. This is my guru's house; after 15 years, I find it here."

I feel that this passage says it all. This was the goal of my life to know this state. It was almost exactly 15 years to the date of my *Shaktipat* in July of 1979. I suddenly understood Shri Ramana Maharshi's teaching as never before. When he speaks about the journey to find the Self, and when you get there, you realize that you did not need the cart ride, the bicycle ride, the bus ride, the train ride and then the long walk. None of it was required to find this, for it is right inside, closer than the breath. And yet... without the journey, the goal might never be found. It was another paradox of the human condition.

I stopped seeking after enlightenment after this experience, just like I stopped going to church and reading the useless verses when I was 13 after Jesus spoke to me. I did not need to seek any further once I had tasted this truth of my very nature. I know when I leave this body, it is this state to which I will return. I know that whatever happens to my body, I will always be in THAT place, unaffected, pure, clear and at one with All-that-Is.

It is like having a home you own always with you. You can travel all over the world and visit strange and exotic places, but you know there is always *home*. Mary Scott in her book *Kundalini in the Physical World* says that "unhappiness and homesickness end with the reunion of Shiva and Shakti."[18] It is safe and familiar and there is nothing that can harm that. With his shell on his back, the turtle never has to look for a shelter, for it is always with him.

The Jewel Inside:
The *Kundalini* brought me to a simple place, my own being. I went on a long journey through false ideas, mystic visions, possession, crazy demons, elevated planes, the edge of an abyss only to discover that everything was right here within my own heart, safe and sound the whole time. It was a jewel inside the cave of my own heart. I could not say that the journey was a waste of time or that I did not need to travel so far off into my mind, imagination and psyche because I had to go on that path within. Fortunately, the path has lead me back to the center of the maze. For some people it is possible that they can find the center without a Byzantine journey.

But I needed the Guru's grace, the Guru's gift in the form of *Kundalini* in order to get through this maze. I needed the help of the Goddess to transform who I had become in lifetimes and shrouds of ignorance. I needed Her help to become reborn as a much less neurotic and whole being into my own body. It was not easy, but it could have been much worse without my teacher's gift of love and care.

My friend Karin Hannigan from Australia is someone who has experienced this *Kundalini* journey also, and she concludes that the *Kundalini* awakening "is not an end point in itself, but the beginning of a transformation of consciousness which expands our capacity to KNOW the infinite."[19] This sums up my experience exactly. The *Kundalini* cleared out the illusions, the traumas and the blocks that a conditioned mind had created, and allowed me to find that silent ineffable SELF within.

The Goddess Shakti Kundalini:

I thank the Goddess *Kundalini*, the very essence of life itself, and my wonderful guru for their love and care. Every word here has come by virtue of both. I have spent years putting this down on paper and today, I can say it is completed. My debt to my guru cannot be repaid, but this account is one small token of my attempt.

The *Kundalini* is all powerful, unstoppable, erotic, terrifying yet most beautiful. Her love is "tough" love, without sentimentality or mercy. She is our fierce mother Goddess. I cannot say I love Her for that implies a duality, that I am separate from Her. The Goddess *is* me so closely that I do not even feel her as a being. She is the movement of my fingers on the keys of my computer and the thought that comes into my mind. I have no need to seek her. She is ever present. She loves truth and only responds to it. She melts my ego into a vapor which can be agony if I resist, yet if I surrender to Her, She always brings me great peace and joy. She dissolves the world. She is my creativity. She is the beauty in my eyes. She is the breath that breathes me. She is the presence of the cosmic One within me. She cannot be defined in words, for She is an experience of the divine ONE.

CHAPTER 18

Epilogue:
On Becoming Human

Throughout childhood, and since the *Kundalini* process that started in 1974 with my dream up to this day in 2012, I have felt the inner comfort of a guide or benevolent being watching over my evolution. Many people experience this and call this "angels" or "guides." Some call this "the Higher Self" which is a part of us that remains anchored in the truth before our birth to remain in a quantum state rather than get downloaded into flesh or third dimensional reality which is like a holographic time/space bubble. As a child I called my "Higher Self" "Jesus," and now I call it "my guru." A person who believes in angels would say it is a "Guardian Angel." It is in fact a part of ourselves that never leaves *reality* to fall into this bubble of illusions. This guide keeps us on track with our purpose when the "forgetfulness" or amnesia of being born human overcomes us.

I was always being guided on the perfect journey for me. My guide or higher self was with me at 13 when I was so upset about my lack of ability to change, and it was the being in the oval light which appeared before me. Since this was my Higher Self steering me through the intricate synchronicities and balances of time and place, I have to see how I have been guided as if through a maze to the right place to accomplish my spiritual goals that I had expressed fully at the age of 13, but which I truly believe I set up for myself before birth.

I also had to recognize that I created everything that I experienced on some level— all the good and the bad. This is a creative role that I now know is real, even though for much of my life I did not know this. Our human life is a play, a dance, a performance that we ourselves perform as all the characters, for in fact we imagine all of it on some level until we WAKE UP to know it is thus. We are both the earthly soul and the guide that steers us, but the veils between do not reveal this until there is an awakening which may not happen for most people for many lifetimes.

How does the guru as a person enter into this? To write about what a guru is would take a few libraries and there are many books that attempt to explain it. But simply put and cutting through a lot of words, the guru in his/her earthly shape or form is a surrogate for what is within us all, this same guide and "Higher Self." If the guru is a real one in a physical form, he or she will constantly send us to the inner guide or "Higher Self" and to our own hearts to find guidance. This is why a true guru, a being without any ego, is hard to find. Speaking to such a guru will be the same as speaking to the highest aspect of oneself, the "Higher Self."

The guru in physical form takes on a very serious responsibility with each disciple, and only those chosen for this job should be doing such powerful work. A being who operates from ego will not be aligned with our highest interests. Only a being who is situated in the highest detached state can bring us to our own being. These are advanced yogis without any ego. What you see in them is not "them" but your own Self. This is why we bow to the guru's feet because the guru is the representation that we can see and hear and know of our own hidden Higher Self. Until we can find that Higher Self within, the guru is the reminder or the surrogate of that state we are too blind to know. So this is why the guru is so precious, so rare and so valuable to all of us. It is not the man or woman that we bow to, but our very own being.

What did this *Kundalini* process really change? It certainly did not change my personality or alter my karmic destiny. I still had issues with past life karma that I had to work out and resolve, but I firmly believe the effects have been minimized since I became aware and could see my role in past lives. I understood my motives for doing what I had done, and knew that my "error" or "sin" was not in my actions, but in my identification as the "actor." There is only ONE actor in all that happens and the mysteries of this are well explained in the *Bhagavad Gita*.

How am I different? My character in many ways is the same, but thanks to serious intention and much inner work, I have delved into the subconscious to process and release much grief and anger. I find myself living on a more peaceful level. After the glimpse of pure consciousness, in 1994, I felt much like the Buddhist saying, *"Before realization, cut wood and haul water; after realization, cut wood and haul water."*

This was the reason I got born— to know this glimpse of the truth. How I got there was my journey, and once I experienced that moment, even for twenty seconds, I did not seek any more. It was as if all the answers had been revealed. There was nothing else to ask, to seek, to uncover. I still chant, I still meditate and I still feel my guide with me who has steered me through this book.

So what changed? After this awakening and my life settled down, everything was much the same except that I had a different attitude and point of view. I did have *siddhis* and powers to do things like fly or travel to distant planets while I was in the throes of the active *Kundalini*, but I do not have the desire or need to do it now; it has no practical value today. It is a *siddhi*, or power that is not consistent with daily life. It belongs with my subtle body. It will always be there as I have found out in subsequent experiences. It would be there if I needed it. It does not die with the body, but belongs to me as a spiritual entity. I believe it is true for every human being who has purified the *chi* in the body. We can actually take that with us from body to body. This is just part of the wonder of being humans.

My powers of intuitive insight are useful. I was able to see inside and heal the body of the man in the Pizza restaurant, but there are many people today with the skill of medical intuitive, so this is not remarkable. I often have an instant knowing about the levels of meaning in something and the meaning level is deeper and faster. It makes logic seem like a horse and cart compared to a super-train. Many of the new children coming to our planet do these things without any knowledge that this is not how we all experience reality.

Perhaps Ken Carey explains best what changes occur in this awakening:

> ... it is the human future to live:....instinctually. To simply be. To say the right words without thinking them out ahead of time. To experience the purity of a mind uncluttered by troublesome and misplaced responsibility. To know exactly the right gesture, the right behavior, the creative response for each and every situation. Such are the birthrights of each and every human being."[1]

It is a flow such as described in the Tao. There is less need to think. We become like children again, natural and free of inhibitions and shame. We act like the animals of the field, tuned in to the vibe of our own planet. And Mary Scott echoes this same concept:

> Those who develop through this partnership [of ego-self and greater self] are seldom aware of improvements in spiritual consciousness but are continually being surprised by the manner in which they are enabled to say, do or think the right thing.... We do not so much feel we are developing as discovering in ourselves the ability to do better."[2]

This is the gift which after all seems not so spectacular on paper, but in living it, it is an entirely better place to be than battered by ill-luck, relying on logic, having to think in limited ways before knowing what to do, feeling hesitant or uncertain of one's life path, feeling guilty or shameful for being entirely oneself, and not knowing what stroke of fate will strike one down. Certainly there are moments when I experience these again, but they seem to get resolved more easily.

I see the world afresh after the awakening. As Sri Yukteswar explains to his disciple, Yogananda, "Those who attain Self-realization on earth live a similar twofold existence. Conscientiously performing their work in the world, they are yet immersed in an inward beatitude."[4] And Yogananda replies, "I do realize now that I have found God, for whenever the joy of meditation has returned subconsciously during my active hours, I have been subtly directed to adopt the right course in everything, even in minor details."[5] He is attuned to the cosmic will.

Apart from the glimpse of absolute consciousness in 1994, not much changed in me after all the drama I went through. But Love as a power between people and a constant hum throughout the universe became more and more evident. I had nowhere to go, nothing to do to experience this love. It was a jewel inside me that never stopped sending me joy and warmth. I could experience this unconditional love with and for everything with the right open attitude and understanding. I could send it out like a beacon to warm others to make them remember that core heart connection. I could send it to babies and make them smile and visibly grow before my eyes. I could send it to students in an exam and find improved results. I could send it to enemies who wanted to harm me or injure me and change their attitude away from anger. It did not depend on any "other" being. It came from me like a constant fountain.

Love had been the key to the rising *Kundalini*. It would not have completed its path without that love for my guru, my family and my beloved ones. It was the juice or *rasa* that made my life such bliss, the force that seems to be a constant throughout the universe. This love survived death as I found when meeting loved ones from former lifetimes. Love is a force that grows and grows. It never dies; it is stronger than anything else *anywhere*. Khalil Gibran says: "When you love you should not say, 'God is in my heart,' but rather, 'I am the heart of God.'" For it truly is God's love that we are.

The End.

Notes

Chapter 1: The Opportunity

1   "Human Beings in Buddhism."
2   Powers and Eisendrath website.
3   Norman Shealy "Every Thought Is a Prayer," in *Audacious Aging*, p. 267
4   Eli Jaxon Bear, *Wake Up* p.74
5   Eli Jaxon Bear, *Wake Up* p.153
6   Christopher Isherwood, p.71
7   Jack Kornfield, p.50
8   Eckhart Tolle *A New Earth* p.140
9   Ibid. p. 5
10 Quoted in Grof, *Spiritual Emergency* p.140

Chapter 2: What is Kundalini

1   Joseph Campbell, *Transformations* p.134
2   David Gordon White p. 218
3   Bonnie Greenwell p. 22
4   Nathan Schwartz-Salant, p. 6
5   Lee Sannella, p.23.
6   Ibid. p. 8
7   Ibid. p.11
8   Ajit Mookerjee p. 9
9   Ibid p. 10
10 Elizabeth Gilbert, p. 195

11 Qtd. in Bragdon, *The Call* p. 94
12 Joseph Campbell, *Myths* p.391
13 T. N. Venkataraman, p. 130
14 Robert Powell, p. 24
15 Elizabeth Gilbert, p. 175
16 Joseph Campbell, *The Hero* p. 30.
17 R. Perala p.153

Chapter 3: The Time is Now: Earth Changes

1   John Major Jenkins p. 29.
2   Emma Bragdon, *The Call*. p.216
3   Barbara Marciniak, p.201
4   Prash Trivedi
5   El Collie and Kress.
6   Ken Carey, *The Third* p. 101.
7   Ken Carey, *Return of the Bird Tribes* p. 135
8   Eckhart Tolle, *A New Earth* p. 182
9   Barbara Hand Clow, *Catastrophobia* p. 18.
10 Barbara Hand Clow, *Alchemy* p.139.
11 David Wilcock, *The Source Field Investigations*, p.463
12 Hand Clow, *Alchemy* p.138.
13 Alice Bailey, p.111
14 Paul Ray, Ph.D.
15 David Wilcock, p. 210

16 Melchizedek, p.12

Chapter 4: The Gift of Kundalini

1   Ken Carey, *The Third* p.72.
2   Joseph Chilton Pearce, *The Magical Child Matures* p. 151
3   Speigelman and Vasavada p. 122
4   Max Freedom Long, *The Secret* p. 332

Chapter 5: Preparation

1   Sri Aurobindo, p. 5
2   Eckhart Tolle, *A New Earth* p.59
3   Ibid. p. 82.
4   Walsch *Book III* p. 9

Chapter 6: Mercurius: the Genie in the Bottle

1   Nathan Schwartz-Salant, p. 10
2   Arnold Mindell *Working* p.52
3   Ibid. p. 48-52
4   Ibid. p. 59.
5   Ibid. p. 52
6   Ibid. p. 59
7   Emma Bragdon, *Sourcebook* p. 45
8   Arnold Mindell, *Working* p. 57.
9   Ibid. p. 58.
10 Qtd. in Speigleman and Vasavada p.122
11 Wilber, *Atman* p. 181
12 Mindell, *Working* p.58
13 Ibid. *p.* 58

14 John Weir Perry, *Trials* p. 128 – 129.

15 Mindell, *Working* p. 59

Chapter 7: Shaktipat: Initiation

Chapter 8: The Kundalini Awakens

1 Harmon p.120

2 Darrel Irving, p. 179

3 Darrel Irving, p. 11

4 Jeremy Narby p. 95

5 Qtd. in Mookerjee, p. 10.

6 Sir Arthur Avalon, p. 110-112

7 Joseph Campbell, *Transformations, p.* 134

8 Sir Arthur Avalon, p. 48

9 Mookerjee p.10

10 Jeremy Narby, p. 186

11 Ibid.

12 Mookerjee, p.9 – 10

13 David Gordon White, p. 218 – 219.

14 Jeremy Narby, p.67-68

15 Ibid. p. 66.

16 Max Freedom Long, *Recovering* p. 265.

17 Alice Bailey, p. 409

18 Robert G. Chaney, p. 13

19 Bruce Lipton, *Biology* p. 111-112

20 Marconi, p. 15

21 Quoted in David Wilcock, p.51

22 Quoted in David Wilcock, p. 53

23 Rick Strassman, p. 60-61

24 Carlos Castaneda, *The Second Ring,* p.238

25 Ibid, p. 198

Chapter 9: The Journey Begins

1 Arnold Mindell, *Working* p. 59.

2 Swami Vishnu Tirtha p. 77

3 Ibid.

4 Ibid. p.79.

5 Joseph Campbell, *Transformations* p. 134.

6 Barbara Brennan, p.71

7 Bruce Lipton, *Biology* p. 111

8 Ibid. p.127

9 Ibid. p. 166

10 Ken Carey, *Return* p.172

11 Willis Harmon, p. 77

12 Gopi Krishna *Living with Kundalini,* p.162-163.

13 Sri Chinmoy, p. 74

14 Ibid.

15 Loren Mosher, qtd. in De Wyze p. 63.

16 Campbell, *The Hero with a Thousand Faces,* p. 101.

17 Perry, *Trials* p. xiii.

18 John Scudder Qtd. in John White, p. 196-197.

19 Stan Grof, *The Holotropic Mind* p.147

Chapter 10: The Ascending Goddess

1 Venkataraman, Shri Ramana Maharshi p. 363

2 Swami Vishnu Tirtha p. 102-103

3 Eli Jaxon-Bear, *Poonja* p. 109

4 Swami Vishnu Tirtha, p. 25

5 Ibid. p 23-25

6 Ibid. p. 26

7 Ibid.

8 Carlos Castaneda, *The Active,* p. 229

Chapter 11: Kundalini at Play

1 Arnold Mindell, *Working* p. 59

2 Eckhart Tolle, *Power of Now p.* 134

3 Swami Vishnu Tirtha p. 107

Chapter 12: No Boundaries

1 Ken Wilber, *No Boundaries,* p. 70

2 Bonnie Greenwell, p. 111-112.

3 Jill Bolte Taylor, *YouTube*

4 Bonnie Greenwell, p. 29 – 30.

5 Geoff Stray, p. 349

6 Castaneda, *The Second,* p.154

7 Ibid, p.213-214

8 Stan Grof, *Holotropic* p.135.

9 Dennis Gersten p. 102.

10 Itzhak Bentov *Stalking* p.77.

11 Ibid. *Stalking* p. 84
12 Carlos Castaneda, *The Power of Silence,* p.242
13 Ibid p. 243- 244
14 Qtd. in Lipton and Bhaerman. *Spontaneous* p.279-280
15 Swami Tirtha p.102
16 Venkataraman, p.134
17 Swami Vishnu Tirtha p. 96.
18 Carlos Castaneda, *The Art.* p.64
19 Dennis Gersten p. 193.
20 Robert G. Chaney, p. 47-48
21 Mookerjee, p. 78
22 Carlos Castaneda, *The Second* p.206
23 Ibid. p. 212
24 Castaneda, *The Fire* p. 120
25 Wilhelm, p. 51
26 Carl Johan Calleman, *The Purposeful Universe,* p. 163-165
27 "Eight Major Siddhis." Yoga-Age.com
28 Stan Grof, *Holotropic* p. 155
29 Carlos Castaneda, *The Eagle's Gift,* p. 87

Chapter 13: Dying While Living

1 John Weir Perry, *Trials of* p.46 - 47
2 Castaneda, *Art of* p. 193
3 Bentov, *Brief Tour* p. 61
4 Sogyal Rinpoche, p. 109.

5 Freemantle and Trungpa, p. 212-213
6 Joseph Chilton Pearce, *The Biology* p. 172
7 Sogyal Rinpoche, p. 249
8 Stan Grof, *The Holotropic Mind* p. 135.
9 Fremantle and Trungpa p.158- 159
10 Wm. Bodri p. 133
11 Fremantle and Trungpa. p.162.
12 Walsch *Book 3.* p. 150.
13 Castaneda, *The Art of Dreaming,* p. 48.
14 Jade Wahoo Grigori, "Spiritual Parasites"
15 Wm. Bodri p. 147
16 Dennis Gersten p.212.
17 B. S. Goel p.2.
18 Sogyal Rinpoche p.112

Chapter 14: Rising Kundalini: Rapture

1 Mihran K. Serailian artist
2 Robert Chaney, p. 37-38

Chapter 15: The Crucible

1 Qtd. in Wilhelm, p.88
2 Grof and Grof, *The Stormy* p.158.
3 Grof and Grof, *Spiritual Emergency* p. 16
4 Emma Bragdon, *The Call* p. 29
5 John Weir Perry *Trials* p.81
6 Ibid. p.xiii
7 Ibid. p.106

8 Ibid. p. xiii
9 Qtd. in Grof and Grof, *Spiritual Emergency* p.211
10 Rinpoche, p.117
11 Goel, p.140-141
12 Qtd. in Wilhelm p. 93
13 Chilton Pearce, p. 36
14 Qtd. in Pearce p. 36
15 Ibid. p. 36
16 Ibid. p.38
17 R.D. Laing, Qtd. in Grof and Grof, *Spiritual Emergency,* p.53
18 Qtd. in Wilhelm p. 95
19 Castaneda, *The Active,* p. 218 -219
20 Michael Harner, p. 4
21 Carlos Castaneda, *The Active* p.220
22 Ibid. p. 221
23 Qtd. in Lee Carroll, p.209.
24 Carlos Castaneda, *The Active.* p. 221
25 Marvin Meyer, *The Nag Hammadi Scriptures,* p. 194
26 Ibid p. 196
27 David Wilcock, p.422.
28 Carlos Castaneda, *The Active* p. 225
29 Goel, p. 141
30 Gopi Krishna, "The Phenomenon," p. 231
31 Dr. Bruce Lipton, *Biology* p.135
32 Ibid p.135
33 Rinpoche p.116
34 Eckhart Tolle p.30.
35 Tolle *A New Earth* p. 40
36 Tolle *A New Earth* p. 80

37 *A New Earth* p.144
38 Lipton and Bhaerman, p. 32- 33,
39 Tolle, *A New Earth*. p. 19

Chapter 16: The Abyss

1 John Weir Perry, *Trials of* p.47
2 Castaneda, *The Eagle's Gift*, p. 28 -29
3 Castaneda, *The Art of Dreaming*, p. 155
4 Singh, *Shiva Sutras* p. 245
5 Singh Khalsa, Qtd. in John White, p. 284
6 Ibid. p. 176
7 Singh, *Pratyabhijnahrdayam*, p.146.
8 Rick Strassman, Chapter 4.
9 Ibid. Chapter 4
10 Kunihiro Yamate, in Engler p. 235
11 Bentov, *A Brief*, 81-84.
12 Jaideva Singh, *Shiva Sutras p.* 78.
13 John Weir Perry, "Spiritual Emergence & Renewal," p.67
14 Perry, *Trials* p. 133.
15 Perry, *Trials* p. 131.
16 Joseph Campbell, *The Power of Myth*, p.184.
17 Castaneda, *The Art of Dreaming* p. 133
18 Castaneda, *The Eagle's Nest,* p. 301
19 Castaneda, *The Second Ring* p.324-325.
20 Freemantle and Trungpa, p. 104
21 Perry, *Trials* p. 130

22 R.D. Laing *The Politics* p.150
23 Max Freedom Long, *The Secret* p.288
24 Ibid. p. 168.
25 Ibid. p.258
26 Grof, *The Stormy Search* p. 150
27 Perry, "Spiritual Emergence" p. 73
28 Perry, *Trials* p.131
29 Grof and Grof, *The Stormy p.* 41
30 Ibid. p. 256
31 Rebillot p. 223
32 Grof, *The Holotropic Mind p.*160
33 Yamate in Engler, p. 186

Chapter 17: Integration & Balance

1 Gangaji, *You Are That!* p. 165
2 Dennis Hauck, p.253
3 Dennis Hauck, p. 274
4 Petri Murien, p.3
5 Ibid. p.5
6 Ibid. p.13
7 Ibid. p.15.
8 Ibid. p.15
9 Grof, *The Stormy, p.* 124
10 Kornfield, p. 127
11 Lipton and Bhaerman, *Spontaneous*, p. 280 – 281.
12 Qtd in Melchizedek, *Living* p. 62.
13 Prabhavananda, *The Upanishads,* p. 74- 75.
14 Swami Narayananda, p. 259
15 Venkataraman p. 145
16 Ibid. p. 130

17 Ibid p. 215
18 Mary Scott, p. 144
19 Karin Hannigan, Ph.D.

Chapter 18: On Becoming Human

1 Ken Carey, *The Third* p.72.
2 Mary Scott, p. 4
3 Yogananda, *Autobiography* p. 169
4 Ibid. p. 172-3

Helpful Books

Bentov, Itzhak. *Stalking the Wild Pendulum: On the Mechanics of Consciousness.* New York: Bantam, 1977. Print.

Bodri, William. *The Little Book of Hercules: The Physical Aspects of the Spiritual Path.* Reno, NV: Top Shape Publishing. 2011. Print.

Bragdon, Emma. Ph.D. *The Call of Spiritual Emergency: From Personal Crisis to Personal Transformation.* San Francisco: Harper & Row.1990. Print.

—-. *A Sourcebook for Helping People with Spiritual Problems.* Woodstock, VT 05091; Lightening Up Press, 2006. Print.

Brennan, Barbara. *Hands of Light: A Guide to Healing Through the Human Energy Field.* New York: Bantam Books, 1988. Print.

Ferrera, Dan Sifu. "QiGong Training." *developyourenergy.net/about-us/sifu-dan-ferrera/* n.d.Web.11 May 2013.

Gersten, Dennis, M. D. *Are You Getting Enlightened or Losing your Mind?* New York: Three Rivers Press, 1997. Print.

Grof, Stanislav, M.D. with Marjorie Livingston Valier, *Human Survival and Consciousness Evolution,* Albany, NY: State University of New York Press, 1988. Print.

—- and Christina Grof. Eds. *Spiritual Emergency: When Personal Transformation Becomes a Crisis.* Los Angeles: Jeremy P. Tarcher, Inc., 1989. Print.

—-.*The Stormy Search for the Self.* Los Angeles, CA: Jeremy P. Tarcher, Inc., 1990. Print.

Hannigan, Joan Shivarpita Ph.D. *Kundalini Vidya: The Science of Spiritual Trans-formation.* 6th *Ed.* Knoxville, TN: Patanjali Kundalini Yoga Care, 2005. Print.

Kason, Yvonne, M.D. *Farther Shores: Exploring How Near-Death, Kundalini and Mystical Experiences Can Transform Ordinary Lives.* New York: iUniverse, Inc. 2008. Print.

Kornfield, Jack. *A Path with Heart: A Guide through the Perils and Promises of Spiritual Life.* New York: Bantam, 1993. Print.

"Kundalini Stavaha." Chanting. *mysticrebels.com/kundalini/* n.d. Web. 11 May 2013.

Morris, Dr. Glenn. "The Institute for the Wholistic Arts." *wholisticarts.org/morris.html* n.d. Web. 11 May 2013.

Perry, John Weir. *The Far Side of Madness* Dallas, Tx: Spring Publications, Inc. 1974. Print.

—-. *Trials of the Visionary Mind: Spiritual Emergency and the Renewal Process.* Albany, New York: State University of New York Press, 1999. Print.

Rinpoche, Sogyal. *The Tibetan Book of Living and Dying* Eds. P. Gaffney and A. Harvey. San Francisco: Harper San Francisco, 1993. Print.

Sannella, Lee, M.D. *The Kundalini Experience: Psychosis or Transcendence* Lower Lake, CA.: Integral Publishing, 1976. Print.

Scott, Mary. *Kundalini in the Physical World*. Boston: Routledge & Kegan Paul, 1983. Print

SEE the Bibliography for more sources

Bibliography

The Guru's Gift: A Kundalini Awakening
By Ruth Angela © 2013

Arundale, G.S. *Kundalini: An Occult Experience*. Adyar, Madras: Theosophical Publishing House, 1974. Print.

Aurobindo Sri. *The Future Evolution of Man: The Divine Life upon Earth*. Twin Lakes, WI, Lotus Press, 1974. Print.

Avalon, Arthur. *The Serpent Power: The Secrets of Tantric and Shaktic Yoga*. NY: Dover Publ. 1974. Print.

Bailey, Alice. A. *Ponder on This: A Compilation*. New York: Lucis Publishing, 1996. Print.

Beattie, Paul. "Alchemy and the Great Work" *Kundalini: A Magazine Dedicated to the Evolution of Consciousness. Vol VII*. (1984): 27. Print.

Bentov, Itzhak. *Stalking the Wild Pendulum: On the Mechanics of Consciousness*. New York: Bantam, 1977. Print.

—-. *A Brief Tour of Higher Consciousness*. Destiny Books: Rochester, VT: 2000. Print.

Berney, Charlotte. *Fundamentals of Hawaiian Mysticism*. The Crossing Press: Freedom, CA. 2000. Print.

Bodri, William. *The Little Book of Hercules: The Physical Aspects of the Spiritual Path*. Reno, NV: Top Shape Publishing, LLC. 2011. Print.

Braden, Gregg. *The Divine Matrix: Bridging Time, Space, Miracles, and Belief*. Carlsbad, CA: Hay House, Inc. 2007. Print.

Bragdon, Emma. Ph.D. *The Call of Spiritual Emergency: From Personal Crisis to Personal Transformation*. San Francisco: Harper & Row.1990. Print.

—-. *A Sourcebook for Helping People with Spiritual Problems*. Woodstock, VT 05091; Lightening Up Press, 2006. Print.

Brennan, Barbara. *Hands of Light: A Guide to Healing Through the Human Energy Field*. New York: Bantam Books, 1988. Print.

Bynum, Edward Bruce. *The African Unconscious: Roots of Ancient Mysticism and Modern Psychology*. New York: Teachers College Press, 1999. Print.

Calleman, Carl Johan, Ph.D. *The Mayan Calendar and the Transformation of Consciousness*. Bear and Co.: Rochester, VT, 2004. Print.

—-. *The Purposeful Universe: How Quantum Theory and Mayan Cosmology Explain the Origin and Evolution of Life*. Rocherster, VT: Bear and Company, 2009. Print.

Campbell, Joseph. *Myths to Live by*. New York: Viking Press, 1972. Print.

—-. *The Hero with a Thousand Faces*. Princeton: Princeton University Press. 1968. Print.

—-. *Transformations of Myth through Time.* New York: Harper and Row. 1999. Print.

Capra, Fritjof. *Uncommon Wisdom: Conversations with Remarkable People.* New York; Bantam Books, 1988. Print.

Carey, Ken. *Return of the Bird Tribes.* San Francisco: HarperCollins, 1988. Print.

—-.*The Starseed Transmissions.* San Francisco: HarperCollins, 1982. Print.

—-. *The Third Millennium: Living in the Posthistoric World.* San Francisco: HarperCollins, 1991. Print.

Carroll, Lee. *The Twelve Layers of DNA: An Esoteric Study of the Mastery Within: Kryon Book 12.* PO Box 4357, Sedona, AZ: Platinum Publishing House, 2010. Print.

Castaneda, Carlos. *The Active Side of Infinity.* New York: Harper Collins, 1998. Print.

—- *The Art of Dreaming.* New York: Harper Collins, 1993. Print

—-. *The Eagle's Gift.* New York: Simon and Schuster, 1981. Print.

—-. *The Fire from Within.* New York: Simon and Schuster, Inc, 1984. Print.

—-. *The Power of Silence: Further Lessons of don Juan.* New York: Washington Square Press, 1987. Print.

—-. *The Second Ring of Power.* New York: Washington Square Press, 1977. Print.

—-. *The Teachings of Don Juan: A Yaqui Way of Knowledge.* New York: Ballantine Books, 1968. Print.

Chaney, Robert G. *Unfolding the Third Eye.* Upland, CA 91785: Astara Inc., 1970. Print.

Chatterji, Jagadish Chandra. *Kashmir Shaivism.* Albany, NY: State University of New York, 1986. Print.

Chinmoy, Shri. *Kundalini: The Mother-Power.* Jamaica, NY: Aum Publications, 1992. Print.

Clow, Barbara Hand with Gerry Clow. *Alchemy of Nine Dimensions: Decoding the Vertical Axis, Crop Circles, and the Mayan Calendar.* Charlottesville, VA: Hampton Roads Publishing, 2004. Print.

Clow, Barbara Hand. *Catastrophobia:The Truth Behind Earth Changes.* Rochester, VT: Bear & Co. 2001. Print.

—-. *The Mayan Code: Time Acceleration and Awakening the World Mind.* Rochester,VT: Bear and Company: 2007. Print.

Collie, El and C. Kress. *Shared Transformation.* Sun Chariot Press, PO Box, 5562, Oakland CA 94605. 2 Aug. 2004. Web.

Collie, El. "Kundalini Signs and Symptoms" *www.think-about-it.com* 2 Aug. 2004. Web. 11 May 2013.

Condron, Barbara, D.M, D.D. B.J. *Kundalini Rising: Mastering Creative Energies.* School of Metaphysics Publishing, Windyville, MI: 1997. Print.

Cousens, Gabriel, M.D. *Spiritual Nutrition: Six Foundations for Spiritual Life and the Awakening of Kundalini.* Berkeley, CA: North Atlantic Books, 1986. Print.

Dale, Cyndi. *Kundalini: Divine Energy, Divine Life.* Woodbury, MN: Llewellyn Worldwide,2011. Print.

DeWyze, Jeannette. "Still Crazy after all These Years." *The San Diego Weekly Reader* 9 Jan. 2003: 26+. Print.

"Eight Major Siddhis" *Yoga-Age.com:An Online Resource of Yoga Practice. Modern/ Misc. html* 2003-2007. Web. 30 Oct. 2011.

Engler, Robert and Yuriko Hayashi, Eds. *The Way of No Thinking: The Prophecies of Japan's Kunihiro Yamate.* Tulsa, OK: Council Oak Books, 1995.

Freemantle, Francesca, and Chogyam Trungpa. *The Tibetan Book of the Dead.* London, Shambhalla Pocket Classics, 1992. Print.

Gangaji. *You Are That! Vol 1.* Gangaji Org. Boulder, CO: Satsang Press. 1995. Print.

Gayatri, E., "Nada Yoga: Kundalini Stavaha: Jasmine Strings." *egayathri.blogspot.com* Web. 20 Oct. 2011.

Gersten, Dennis, M. D. *Are You Getting Enlightened or Losing your Mind?* New York: Three Rivers Press, 1997. Print.

Gilbert, Elizabeth. *Eat, Pray, Love.* London: Penguin Books, 2006. Print.

Goel, B.S. *Third Eye and Kundalini.* New Delhi: Paragon Enterprises, 1985. Print.

Goodbread, Joe. "Homage to R.D. Laing: a New Politics of Experience," *The Journal of Process Oriented Psychology (Vol. 6)* Sum. 1994: 11- 18. Print.

Greenwell, Bonnie, Ph.D. *Energies of Transformation: A Guide to the Kundalini Process.* Valencia, CA: Bonnie Greenwell, 1990. Print.

Grigori, Jade Wahoo. "Spiritual Parasite: A Shamanic Perspective Of Abuse, and Its Treatment." *Shamanic.net* 4 Jun. 2009. Web. 27 Feb. 2011.

Grof, Stanislav, M.D. with Hal Zina Bennett. *The Holotropic Mind: The Three Levels of Human Consciousness and How They Shape Our Lives.* New York: HarperCollins, 1990. Print.

—- with Marjorie Livingston Valier, *Human Survival and Consciousness Evolution,* Albany, NY: State University of New York Press, 1988. Print.

—- and Christina Grof. Eds. *Spiritual Emergency: When Personal Transformation Becomes a Crisis.* Los Angeles: Jeremy P. Tarcher, Inc., 1989. Print.

—-.*The Stormy Search for the Self.* Los Angeles, CA: Jeremy P. Tarcher, Inc., 1990. Print.

Hannigan, Karin Ph.D. "Kundalini and the Awakening of Spirit." Later published in *WellBeing Magazine.* March 1997. Web. 1996.

Hancock, Graham. *Supernatural: Meetings with the Ancient Teachers of Mankind.* Revised Edition. New York: The Disinformation Company Ltd., 2007. Print.

—. *Underworld: The Mysterious Origins of Civilization.* London: Three Rivers Press, 2002. Print

Harman, Willis. *Global Mind Change: The Promise of the 21ˢᵗ Century. 2ⁿᵈ Ed.* San Francisco: The Institute of Noetic Sciences, 1998. Print.

Harrigan, Joan Shivarpita, Ph.D. *Kundalini Vidya: The Science of Spiritual Transformation.* *6th Ed.* Knoxville, TN: Patanjali Kundalini Yoga Care, 2005. Print.

Harner, Michael. *The Way of the Shaman.* San Francisco: HarperSanFrancisco, 1990. Print.

Hauck, Dennis William. *The Emerald Tablet: Alchemy for Personal Transformation.* New York: Penguin Arkana, 1999. Print.

Hawkins, David R. M.D., Ph.D. *I: Reality and Subjectivity.* W. Sedona, AZ: Veritas, 2003. Print.

"Human Beings in Buddhism." in *en.Wikipedia.org* 17 Nov. 2013. Web. 23 Nov. 2013.

"An Interview with Arny Mindell on Extreme States." *Journal of Process Oriented Psychology.* (Vol.6) Sum. 1994: 7 -10. Print.

Irving, Darrel. *Serpent of Fire: A Modern View of Kundalini.* York Beach, Maine: Samuel Weiser, Inc., 1995. Print.

Isherwood, Christopher. *How to Know God: The Yoga Aphorisms of Patanjali.* Translated with commentary by Swami Prabhavananda and Christopher Isherwood. Hollywood, CA: Vedanta Press, 1953. Print.

Janis, Sharon. *Spirituality for Dummies.* Foster City, CA: IDG Books, 2000. Print.

Jaxon-Bear, Eli Ed. *Wake Up and Roar Vol 2: Satsang with H.W.L. Poonja.* Pacific Center Press: Kula, Maui, 1993. Print.

Jee, Swami Lakshaman. *Kashmir Shaivism: The Secret Supreme.* Albany, NY: State University of New York Press, 1988. Print.

Jenkins, John Major. *Galactic Alignment: The Transformation of Consciousness according to Mayan, Egyptian and Vedic Traditions.* Rochester, VT: Bear and Co., 2002. Print.

Johnson, Robert A. *Owning Your Own Shadow: Understanding the Dark Side of the Psyche.* San Francisco: HarperCollins, 1991. Print.

Jung, Carl G. et al. *Man and His Symbols.* New York: Dell Publishing Co. Inc., 1964. Print.

Kaku, Michio and Jennifer Thompson. *Beyond Einstein: The Cosmic Quest for the Theory of the Universe.* New York: Anchor Books. 1995. Print

Kason, Yvonne, M.D. *Farther Shores: Exploring How Near-Death, Kundalini and Mystical Experiences Can Transform Ordinary Lives.* Bloomington, IN: Author's Choice Press, iUniverse, Inc. 2008. Print.

King, Serge. *Kahuna Healing.* Wheaton, IL: The Theosophical Publishing House, 1983. Print.

Kornfield, Jack. *A Path with Heart: A Guide through the Perils and Promises of Spiritual Life.* New York: Bantam, 1993. Print.

Krishna, Gopi. *Kundalini: The Evolutionary Energy in Man.* Boston: Shambhala, 1967. Print.

—-. *Living with Kundalini: The Autobiography of Gopi Krishna.* Boston: Shambhala, 1993. Print.

—-."The Phenomenon of Kundalini." In *Kundalini: Evolution and Enlightenment* Ed. John White. St. Paul, Minnesota: Paragon House, 1990. 221- 253. Print.

Kryon, Book 12. *The Twelve Layers of DNA: (An Esoteric Study of the Mastery Within)*. P.O. Box 4357, Sedona, AZ 86340: Platinum Publishing House, 2010. Print.

Laing, R.D. *The Politics of Experience*. NY: Pantheon Books, 1967. Print.

—-. "Transcendental Experience in Relation to Religion and Psychosis" in *Spiritual Emergency: When Personal Transformation Becomes a Crisis*. Eds. Stanislav Grof, M.D. and Christina Grof. Los Angeles: Jeremy P. Tarcher, Inc., 1989. 53 – 60. Print.

Lipton, Bruce, Ph.D. *The Biology of Belief: Unleashing the Power of Consciousness, Matter and Miracles*. Santa Rosa, CA 95404: Mountain of Love/Elite Books, 2005. Print.

Lipton, Bruce, Ph.D. and Steve Bhaerman, *Spontaneous Evolution: Our Positive Future (and a Way to Get There from Here)*. Carlsbad, CA: Hay House Inc., 2009. Print.

Long, Max Freedom, *Growing into Light: A Personal Guide to Practicing the Huna Method*. Marina Del Rey, CA: DeVorss & Co., 1955. Print.

—-. *Recovering the Ancient Magic*. Cape Girardeau, MO: Huna Press, 1978. Print.

—-.*The Secret Science Behind Miracles*. Marina del Rey, CA 90291: DeVorss & Co. 1954. Print.

Marciniak, Barbara. *Earth: Pleiadian Keys to the Living Library*. Santa Fe, NM: Bear and Co, 1995. Print.

Marconi, Dr. Lana. *Dr. Lana's Mind Body Approach to Stress Relief and Mental Clarity*. Toronto, Canada: Celestial Sun Communications, 2006. Print.

Marohn, Stephanie, Ed. *Audacious Aging*. Santa Rosa, CA; Elite Books, 2008. Print.

McFadden, Steven. Director Chiron Communications, 7 Avenida Vista Grande #195, Santa Fe, NM 87508, USA. 2009. Web. 13 Dec. 2008.

McGraw, Philip C. Ph.D. *Self Matters: Creating Your Life from the Inside Out*. New York: Simon & Schuster, 2001. Print.

McTaggart, Lynne. *The Field: The Quest for the Secret Force of the Universe*. New York: Harper, 2008. Print.

Melchizedek, Drunvalo. *The Serpent of Light: Beyond 2012*. San Francisco: RedWheel/Weiser, 2008. Print.

—-. *Living in the Heart*. Flagstaff, AZ 86003: Light Technology Publishing. 2003. Print.

Menken, Dawn. "Madness as Feminism." *The Journal of Process Oriented Psychology*. (Vol. 6) Sum. 1994: 19 -26. Print.

Meyer, Marvin Ed. *The Nag Hammadi Scriptures: The Revised and Updated Translation of Sacred Gnostic Texts*. International Edition. New York: HarperCollins, 2007. Print.

Mindell, Arnold. *City Shadows: Psychological Interventions in Psychiatry*. New York: Routledge, 1988. Print.

—-. *Working with the Dreaming Body*. London, Arkana Penguin Group, 1985. Print.

—-. *The Shaman's Body: A New Shamanism for Transforming Health, Relationships and the Community*. San Francisco: HarperSan Francisco, 1993. Print.

—-. and Amy Mindell *Riding the Horse Backwards: Process Work in Theory and Practice*. New York: Penguin Books USA Inc.,1992. Print.

Mookerjee, Ajit. *Kundalini: The Arousal of the Inner Energy*. New York: Destiny Books, 1982. Print.

Murdock, Maureen. *The Heroine's Journey*. Boston: Shambhala, 1990. Print.

Murien, Petri. *Alchemically Purified and Solidified Mercury*. Pune Rasa Vidya Marg, 1992. Print.

Narayananda, Swami. *The Primal Power in Man or the Kundalini Shakti*. 3rd Revised ed. Rishikesh UP: Narayananda Universal Yoga Trust, 1950. Print.

Narby, Jeremy. *The Cosmic Serpent: DNA and the Origins of Knowledge*. NY: Jeremy P. Tarcher/Putnam, 1998. Print.

Ohio State University. "Global Warming Natural, May End Within 20 Years, Says Ohio State University Researcher." *ScienceDaily*. 15 June 2001. Web. 27 Jan. 2011

Pagels, Elaine. *Beyond Belief: The Secret Gospel of Thomas*. New York: First Vintage Books/Random House. 2003. Print.

Pearce, Joseph Chilton. *The Biology of Transcendence: A Blueprint of the Human Spirit*. Park St. Press, Rochester VT, 2002. Print.

Pearson, Carol S. *The Hero Within*. San Francisco: Harper & Row, 1989. Print.

Perala, Robert with Tony Stubbs. *The Divine Blueprint*. Campbell, CA: United Light Publishing, 1998. Print.

Perlmutter, David Ph.D. and Alberto Villoldo, *Power Up Your Brain*. Carlsbad, CA: Hay House, 2011. Kindle

Perera, Sylvia Brinton, *Descent to the Goddess: A Way of Initiation for Women*. Toronto, Canada: Inner City Books, 1981. Print.

Perry, John Weir. *The Far Side of Madness*. Dallas, Tx: Spring Publications, Inc. 1974. Print.

—-. *Trials of the Visionary Mind: Spiritual Emergency and the Renewal Process*. Albany, New York: State University of New York Press, 1999. Print.

—-. "Spiritual Emergence and Renewal." In *Spiritual Emergency: When Personal Transformation Becomes a Crisis Eds*. Stanislav Grof, M.D. and Christina Grof. Los Angeles: Jeremy P. Tarcher, Inc. 1989. p. 63 – 75. Print.

Phaigh, Bethal. *Gestalt and the Wisdom of the Kahunas*. Marina Del Rey, CA: Vorss & Co., 1983. Print.

Pinchbeck, Daniel. *2012 The Return of Quetzalcoatl*. New York: Jeremy P. Tarcher/Penguin, 2006. Print.

Powell, Robert. Ed. *The Ultimate Medicine: As Prescribed by Sri Nisargadatta Maharaj: Dialogues with a Realized Master*. Berkeley, CA: North Atlantic Books, 2006. Print.

Powers, James and Stuart J. Eisendrath. The Gale Group Inc., *Macmillan Reference* USA, New York, *Gale Encyclopedia of Public Health*, 2002. Print.

Prabhavananda, Swami and Frederick Manchester. *The Upanishads: Breath of the Eternal.* New York: NAL Penguin Inc., 1948. Print.

—. and Christopher Isherwood. *How to Know God: The Yoga Aphorisms of Patanjali.* Vedanta Press: Hollywood, CA, 1953. Print.

—. *Shankara's Crest-Jewel of Discrimination (Viveka Chudamani).* Vedanta Press: Hollywood, CA. 1947.

"Rare is Birth as a Human Being." *www.Buddhas.net/when.html* C and TWU. 2002. Web. 13 Oct. 2013.

Ray, Paul, Ph.D. "Institute for the Emerging Wisdom Culture." Wisdom University.Org. 2002. Web. 10 Oct. 2009.

Ray, Sondra. *Pele's Wish: Secrets of the Hawaiian Masters and Eternal Life.* Makawao, Maui, Hi: Inner Ocean Publishing, 2005. Print.

Rebillot, Paul. "The Hero's Journey: Ritualizing the Mystery" in *Spiritual Emergency: When Personal Transformation Becomes a Crisis* Eds. Stanislav Grof M.D. and Christina Grof. Los Angeles: Jeremy Tarcher Inc. 1989. p.211-224. Print.

Reich, Wilhelm. *The Function of the Orgasm: Vol. 1 of the Discovery of the Orgone.* Translated by Vincent R. Carfagno New York: The Noonday Press,1973. Print.

Rinpoche, Sogyal. *The Tibetan Book of Living and Dying* Eds. P. Gaffney and A. Harvey. San Francisco: Harper San Francisco, 1993. Print.

Sannella, Lee, M.D. *The Kundalini Experience: Psychosis or Transcendence* Lower Lake, CA.: Integral Publishing, 1976. Print.

Scott, Mary. *Kundalini in the Physical World.* Boston: Routledge & Kegan Paul, 1983. Print

Serailian, Mihran K. "The Opening of the Third Eye." copyright to Manly P. Hall. 1962. Philosophical Research Society. Reproduction.

Shealy, Norman. "Every Thought Is a Prayer." *Audacious Aging.* Ed. Stephanie Marohn. Santa Rosa, CA; Elite Books, 2008. 267-272. Print.

Silburn, Lilian. *Kundalini: Energy of the Depths.* Albany, NY: State University of New York, 1988. Print.

Singh, Jaideva. *Pratyabhijnahrdayam: The Secret of Self-recognition.* Delhi, India: Motilal Barnasidass,1963. Print.

—. *Siva Sutras: The Yoga of Supreme Identity.* Delhi: Motilal Banarsidass, 1979. Print.

—. *Spanda-Karikas: The Divine Creative Pulsation* Delhi, India: Motilal Barnasidass, 1980. Print.

—. *Vijnanabhairava or Divine Consciousness.* Delhi: Motilal Banarsidass, 1979. Print.

Singh Khalsa, M.S.S. Gurucharan and Sadhu Singh Khalsa, "Kundalini Energy." in *Kundalini: Evolution and Enlightenment.* Ed. John White. St. Paul, Minnesota: Paragon House, 1990. 254-290. Print.

Sitchin, Zecharia. *The Cosmic Code.* New York: Avon, 1998. Print.

Spiegelman, Dr. J. Marvin and Dr. Arwind U. Vasavada. *Hinduism and Jungian Psychology.* Phoenix, AZ: Falcon Press, 1987. Print.

Steiner, Rudolf. *Occult Signs and Symbols.* Dornach, Switzerland: Anthroposophic Press, Inc. 1972. Print.

—-. *The Meaning of Life: And Other Lectures on Fundamental Issues.* Trans. By Johanna Collis. London: Rudolph Steiner Press, 1999. Print.

Strassman, Rick, Dr. *DMT: The Spirit Molecule: A Doctor's Revolutionary Research into the Biology of Near Death Experiences.* Rochester, VT: Park Street Press, 2001. EPUB. (Kindle Version.)

Stray, Geoff. *Beyond 2012: Catastrophe or Awakening? A Complete Guide to End-of-Time Predictions.* Rochester, VT: Bear and Co., 2009. Print.

Svoboda, Robert E. *Aghora II:Kundalini.* Albuquerque: NM, 1993. Print.

Tart, Charles. M.D. *Altered States of Consciousness: A Book of Readings.* New York:John Wiley & Sons Inc., 1969. Print.

—-. *Waking Up: Overcoming the Obstacles to Human Potential* Boston: Shambala, 1986. Print.

Taylor, Jill Bolte. Ph.D. *My Stroke of Insight: A Brain Scientist's Personal Journey.* New York:Penguin Books. Ltd. 2006. Print.

—-."Jill Bolte Taylor: The Singin' Scientist." *YouTube.com* P.O. Box 1181 • Bloomington, IN 47402 • drjill@drjilltaylor.com • © 2006 Jill Bolte Taylor. 17 May 2008. Web. 2 May 2011.

Temple, Robert K. G. *The Sirius Mystery.* Rochester, VT: Destiny Books, 1987. Print.

Tirtha, Swami Vishnu. *Devatma Shakti (Kundalini): Divine Power* Rishikesh, UP: Murari Fine Art Works, 1962. Print.

Toben, Bob and Fred Alan Wolf. *Space-Time and Beyond: The New Edition* NY: Bantam Books, 1975. Print.

Tolle, Eckhart. *The Power of Now: A Guide to Spiritual Enlightenment.* Novato, CA: New World Library, 1999. Print.

—-. *A New Earth: Awakening to your Life's Purpose.* Penguin Books: London, 2005. Print.

Trivedi, Prash. Radio Interview with Laura Lee, "Moving Out of the Age of Darkness" Aired: 3 Apr 2002. Copyright 2000. Radio. 5 Jan.2004.

Venkataraman, T. N. *Talks with Sri Ramana Maharshi; Three Volumes in One.* 8th edition. Tiruvannamalai: Kartik Offset Printers, Madras. 1989. Print.

Walsch, Neale, Donald *Conversations with God: An Uncommon Life. Dialogue Book 1* New York: Putnam and Sons, 1995. Print.

—-. *Conversations with God: An Uncommon Dialogue Book 3* Charlottesville, VA: Hampton Roads, 1998. Print.

Walsh, Roger, M.D., Ph.D. and Frances Vaughan, Ph.D. *Paths Beyond Ego: The Transpersonal Vision:* Los Angeles, CA: Jeremy P. Tarcher, 1993. Print.

White, David, Gordon. *The Alchemical Body*: *Siddha Traditions in Medieval India*. Chicago: Univ. of Chicago Press, 1996. Print.

White, John. Ed. *Kundalini: Evolution and Enlightenment*. St. Paul, MN: Paragon House, 1990. Print.

Wilber, Ken. *The Atman Project: A Transpersonal View of Human Development* London: Theosophical Publishing House, 1980. Print.

—-. *A Brief History of Everything*. Boston: Shambhala, 1996. Print.

—-. *No Boundary: Eastern and Western Approaches to Personal Growth*. Boston: Shambhala, 1985. Print.

—-. *The Spectrum of Consciousness*. Wheaton IL: Quest Books, 1977. Print.

Wilcock, David. *The Source Field Investigations: The Hidden Science and Lost Civilizations Behind the 2012 Prophecies*. New York: Dutton, 2011. Print

Wilhelm, Richard. translated & explained by. *The Secret of the Golden Flower: A Chinese Book of Life* with a Commentary by C. G. Jung. San Diego, CA: Harvest, Harcourt Brace & Co. 1962. Print.

Williamson, Marianne. *A Woman's Worth* New York: Random House, 1993. Print.

Yogananda, Paramahansa. *Autobiography of a Yogi*. Los Angeles: Self Realization Fellowship. 1972. Print.

—-. *Why God Permits Evil and How to Rise above It*. Los Angeles: Self Realization Fellowship, 2002. Print.

Yukteshwar Giri, Jnanavatar Swami Sri. *The Holy Science*. 8th Edition. Los Angeles: Self-Realization Fellowship. 1990. Print.

Index

A

absence of true knowledge
ego 165
abyss 163
Abyss 174
acceptance 188
Adam and Eve 161
addiction 151
adept meditator 67
adolescence 29
adultery 95
Advaita 18. *See* Direct
Method
Advaita Vedanta Institute
205
advanced meditators 180
aerial feat
flying 118
aeronautical dance
spinning xix
afraid of death 188
agape 32
Ajna
Third eye 67
ajna chakra 57, 59
Akashic records 61, 62
alchemical cleansing process
Kundalini process 55
alchemical process
kundalini 58
alchemy 192
Alchemy 192
Alchemy of Nine Dimensions
24. *See* Clow, Barbara
Hand
Alice in Wonderland 153
allies 103. *See* ka, beloved,
aumakua;
All-that-Is 207
alteration of time 106

amnesia of being born
human 210
analysis by the mind 9
ancient memory 136
ancient rock art 134
annihilated 181
another reality 206
antenna 62. *See* Rising
Kundalini
anti-gravity 120
anti-gravity episodes. *See*
flying
anxiety-based thinking 86
apparitions 140
archetypal images 152
archetypal realm 17
archetypical characteristics
153
Archon 160, 162
ascent of consciousness 49
Ashram 117, 195, 203
astral floating 198
attachments 39
attachment to creatures 139
aumakua. 101
auric structure
sushumna 58
Aurobindo, Sri 36
Avalon, Arthur 59
awakening 29
ayahuasca 158
Ayatollah 182
Ayurvedic doctor 189

B

Bailey, Alice 24, 61
balanced person 29
barbaric spirit 47

bardo 130, 135
gap between lives 130
bardos. 133
bardos of my mind 142
battle for my soul 181
beaten down slave 87
belief paradigms 163
belief system 72
Bentov, Itzhak 106, 174
Bhaerman, Steve 166
Bhagavad Gita 212
Bible 116
bifurcated mind 9
big earthquake 153
biological and spiritual
evolution 24
biological cells 68
biological inheritance 148
biological store
subconscious 69
Blake, William 156
bleeding left brain 98
blissful spinning 20
bliss in meditation 93, 110
blue electricity 53, 66
Bodri, William 99, 136,
140
bone chi 140
bones were vibrating
skeleton 140
boomerang 94
born again 79
bottled up 48
bottomless hole 180
boundaries 108
boundaries disappearing 99
Bragdon, Emma Ph.D. 22,
48, 152
Brahman 203

Brahmananda 51
the brain of the heart 202
brainwashing of society 36
breathing ceased 113
Brennan, Barbara 68
bridge of thin micro strings 103
bright lights 173
bubbles of tension 53
buoyancy 118
bursting feeling 48
butterfly 167

C

caduceus 57, 119
Calleman, Carl Johan Ph.D, 120
Campbell, Joseph 13, 20, 67, 74, 153, 200
Carey, Ken 23, 29, 69, 213
Castaneda, Carlos 63, 118
cat analogy 8
Catechism 131
caverns of time 109
celibate 146
cellular development 80
cellular disintegration 104
chaitanya. See living mantra
chakras 67
Chaney, Robert 145
chanting 52, 91, 129
chaos 175
chattering left-brain 155
Chi 58
Chia, Mantak 147
Chicchan number 9 55
childhood trauma 182
Chinmoy, Shri 56, 73
Christian redeemer concept 35
chronic fatigue syndrome 139
clairvoyance 150

Clayburgh, Jill 200
cleansing light 71
cleansing system. See Kundalini Shakti
cleansing toxic relationships 96
clear yellow light, 179
close to dying 74, 180
Clow, Barbara Hand 24
Coagulation 191
cobra 59, 61, 63
cobra out of a basket 146
cobra rising from a basket 13
cobras 61
cobweb 28
co-creators 123
Collie, El 23
companion being 102. See Beloved, aumakua
conch shell 79
conditioned mind 165
conscious co-creation 81
conscious inner space 125
conscious mind 181
consciousness 104
Consciousness-Force 36
conscious Samadhi 169
consensual reality 16, 104, 138, 171, 172. See third dimensional awareness
conserve the sexual energy 146
constant rebirth 70
Continent of Polynesia Hawaii 41
controlling mind 163
controlling time 183
a cosmic combat 152
cosmic guide 10. See Goddess Kundalini
cosmic miracle 195
The Cosmic Serpent 60

counterbalance. See Parallel Universe
courage 20, 153
crash-landed 96
creativity. 87
Crouching Tiger, Hidden Dragon xx
crucible 43
cunning animal 165
cycle of misery 134
cycles of hells 133

D

Dallas 194
Dark Ages 25
dark night of the soul 6, 9, 70, 192
a dark veil 182
darshan or vision 137
dead snake skin 200
death energy 96
death-like inner spiral 125
death-like sleeping state 103
death myths 177
death of Osiris 153
death of the ego 190
death of the old self 167
the death-rebirth process 190
death spiral 153
deep emotional appeals 31. See higher self
defy gravity 118
demonic entities 142. See spiritual parasites
demonic visions 198
demons 135
demons appear 134
denied in the darkness 183
Denver, John 199
departmentalized awareness 127
depressed 4

depression 4, 38, 40, 70, 91, 151
dervish 91
descends into hell 153
desire for sex 146
Destroy the ego 204
devil 137, 182
Devonshire 85
dharma 198
dictator of time
    ego 155
diet for meditation 189
diminished logical abilities 172
Direct Method 18, 204
direct realization 133
disappearance of time 156
discomforts of Kundalini kriyas 82
disintegration 103
dissolution of the ego 38
dissolution of the world 175
dissolves the world
    Goddess Kundalini 209
distant thunder
    noises 113
Distillation 191
divine intoxication 90
DMT (Dimethyltryptamine) 172
DNA spiral 60
dogs were everywhere 178
dominant dictator 155. See left brain
don Juan 63, 82. See Castaneda, Carlos
Don Juan 160
double helix DNA 61
dragon 178
drained and exhausted 129
dreaming 170
dreaming emissary 114
the dying process 143

dying while living 124, 133, 135
dysfunctional family 88

E
ecstasies of breath 123
ecstatic flying 120
Ego 8
The Ego 7, 36
ego death 181, 184
egoic mind 36, 86
egoic sense of self 153
Einstein-Podolsky-Rosen Paradox 57
electric current 66
electromagnetic frequencies 62
elemental energies 127
elementals 128. See spirits, entities
elixir 192
emancipation 80, 81
embrace of compassion 180
emergence 167
Emotional Freedom Techniques 70
empty tree skeletons 178
empty yellowed skeletons. 178
end of the world 184
End of Time 162
energetic debts 128
energetic probes 82
England 83
English 84
English picnic 85
enlightened insight 15, 78, 101
enlightened my awareness 110
enlightened person 90
enlightened sage
    awakened being 57

enthusiasm 97
entities 87, 136, 139
epic 177
Episcopal Church 38
Equal and Opposite 122
Eros principle 152
essence of all life. See Kundalini
establish self-hood 89
eternity
    of time 156
etheric form 116
evolution 80
expands the second 106
experiment
    of death 124
explosions 179
eye of the pineal gland. See Third Eye

F
face one's own death 142
fake being
    the ego 156
false beliefs 164
false life 37
falsely programmed 166
Faustian bargain 87
fearful animal
    ego 166
fear of death 40
fear of ghosts 140
feathered serpent 119
female consort 149
female victim
    social role 36
feminine holy spirit 15
feminine power of God 157
fetal position 79
fierce goddess of the universe
    Kundalini 166
fierce mother Goddess 209

fierce thunderbolt 86
Fifth dimension healing
    energy
    Scalar wave 63
Find the opposite 122
The Fire from Within 119
    Castaneda, Carlos 119
Fish Pose 114
flashlight beam. *See* lingam
fleeting shadows 158
floating above the ground
    54
floats upward. *See* flying
fluidity of time 106
Flyer 166
Flyers 158
Flyer's mind 193
flying 40, 118
flying in the air xix
flying lessons 39
fly like a bird 91
font of divine power 193
foreign element 157
foreign mind 167
form of exorcism 88
fourth state of conscious-
    ness 170. *See* Turiya
frazzled nerves 109
free spirit 49
Friday, 13th of July. *See*
    Shaktipat
frozen façade 38
full heart 167
full human being 21
fully human 192

G
Galactic Center 22. *See*
    source of spiritual fuel
Gangaji 188
Garden of Eden 134, 164
genie 47
genius 57

Gersten, Dr. Dennis 106,
    115
ghost
    in my bedroom 138
ghost-like form 136
giant reptilian creatures 158
Gibran, Khalil 214
Gilbert, Elizabeth 19
giving birth 79
giving birth to myself 79
glottal 'hung' 86
glowing coat of awareness
    160
goal of all spiritual practices
    132
Goddess Kundalini 157,
    165
    Shakti 165
god-realization 57
Golden Age 162
golden opportunity 22. *See*
    Golden Age
The Great Invisible Serpent
    61
great ocean of healing 187
greed 93
Greenwell, Bonnie 13, 98
Grigori, Jade Wahoo 139
Grimm's Fairy Tales 46
Grim Reaper 140
Grof, Christina 17, 74
Grof, Dr. Stanislav 17, 106,
    121
grounding 144
Guardian Angel 210
guilt
    as a control device 35
guru 57, 211. *See* Higher
    Self
    Higher Self 210
Guru Gita, The 187, 197,
    198
Guru's gift 208
Guru's grace 208

H
Halloween 96
Hannigan, Karin 208
happiness 3
Harmon,Willis 70
Harner, Michael 158
hatchets inside 115
Hatha Yoga 115
Hauck, Dennis 191
Hawaii xx, 40, 41, 45, 57, 61,
    76, 83, 88, 89, 90, 198
Hawaiian huna 61
Hawaiian royalty 62
Hawaii,University of 111
healing crisis 186
heal others 117
heart
    Sacred City 110
the heart 110
    Center of Wisdom 110
heart attack 202
heart center 73
heart chakra 202
heart lotus 193
HeartMath Institute 110
Heart Math scientists 203
heart opening 202
heaven 111
hell-focused conscience 132
hell realms 131
heresy
    concept of sin 132
herm-aphrodite 148
hermaphrodite metal 192
Hermes 57
hero 18, 20
heroic journey. *See* Joseph
    Campbell
hero returns 200
hero's journey 18
hero-warrior 20
hidden serpent, dragon or
    flying snake 120

higher octave 59
Higher Self 210
higher vibration 182
High Self, 31
Himalayan Mountains 115
Hinduism and Jungian
    Psychology 29
Hindus 80
holographic time/space
    bubble 210
Holotropic Mind
    Grof, Dr. Stanislav 106
Holy Grail 20
Holy Spirit 12, 28, 161
home 109
home within 193
Honolulu 41, 176, 204
human alchemy 72
human birth 3, 5
human condition 207
human evolution 25
human predator 158
hum inside 197
Huna 94, 183, 189
hyper-awareness 109

I

I am God 193
ida 58, 72. *See* pingala
idyllic life 42
Ilikai Marina 201
impending catastrophe 184
impulse 175
impure illusory body
    Bodri, William 136
Indian Guru 76
individuate 49
ineffable inner bliss 148
infinity 107, 156
initiation 50
inner adversary 8

inner beloved 102. *See*
    Companion, Ka,
    aumakua
inner guide 46
inner lingam/phallus 149
inner maturation 65
inner monster 190
inner natural self
    the Self 28
inner spirit 14. *See*
    Kundalini
inner voice 185
inorganic beings 139
Institute of Heart Math
    202
integrate
    psyche 152
integrated 181
integration 50, 91, 186. *See*
    left and right brain
intellectually-dominated
    dualistic thinking 98
intelligent flow of awareness
    202
intense fear 71
intention 117
interminable time for sor-
    cerer 109
International Transpersonal
    Association 134
intoxication of the saints
    149
intuitive insight 116, 212
invisible beloved compan-
    ion xix
involution 80
Irving, Darrel 57
island magic 41

J

Jabba the Hut 158
    Entity 136
Jenkins, John Major 22
Jesus 30, 131

Jnaneshwar, Prince 105
journey of inner discovery
    14
jumping into an abyss 167
Jung, Carl 49

K

Kaballah origin 137
kahuna 61
Kailash 117
Kailua Bay 41
Kaku, Michio 106
ka or double 102. *See*
    Companion, aumakua
karma 69
karma was discharged 105
Kashmir Shaivism 118
Kason, Yvonne 182
Khomeini, Ayatolla 178
Khul, Djwhal 24
kicks the ghouls out
    Kundalini 182
knot of fear 39
knots bursting 202
Kornfield, Jack 6
Krishna 111
Krishna, Gopi 17, 57, 72,
    74, 163
kriyas 77, 112
Kukulcan
    Quetzalcoatl 119
kumbhak 113. *See* Filling
    lungs with air; *See*
    Retention of breath
Kundalini 10, 14, 15, 54, 73
Kundalini awakening xx,
    154
Kundalini emergency 189
Kundalini energy 13
Kundalini flying
    astral travel 117
Kundalini process 15, 151,
    155, 210
Kundalini rising 48

Kundalini Shakti 28, 59. *See* Kundalini
  feminine aspect of God 60
Kundalini transmutes fear and grief 72

L

lack of boundaries 98
lack of judgment 180
lack of life force 129
Laing, R.D. 157, 181
large snake 78
lasting joy 5
law of karma 128
leap in human consciousness 23
Lee, Ang
  Crouching Tiger, Hidden Dragon xix
left brain 158
  Middle Self 156
legumes 189
  Sattvic diet 189
let go 39
levels of awareness 104
levels of the mind 134, 135
levitation 120
life loved itself 125
lifting off the ground 150
lightning
  Mercury 58
lingam 13, 149
  phallus 13
Lipton, Bruce, Ph.D. 62, 164, 166
The Little Book of Hercules
  Bodri, William 136
little child's voice 185
Little Ego 8, 9, 11, 16, 19, 28, 36, 60, 69, 70, 98, 102, 107, 108, 109, 121, 155, 157, 160, 163
living nightmare 151
Loevinger 49

lokas 104. *See* Levels of awareness
Long, Max Freedom 31, 61, 183
Lord Indra 141. *See* Lord of Heaven
Lord Yama. *See* The Lord of Death
loss of ego 181
lost boundaries 98
lost self 182
lost track of time 197
lotus 110
lotus of the heart 5, 203
love
  force 214
loving being 101
loving sympathy 181
lowering the veils between dimensions
  Kundalini process 73
low self [self without mind] 183
luminosity 104
luminous white. 197

M

magical alchemical spirit 167
magic wand 126, 149. *See* lingam
magnetic influence 65
Maharaj, Sri Nisargadatta 18
Maharshi, Ramana 5, 18, 76, 80, 113, 188, 203, 204, 205, 206, 207
maile lei 199
makeshift image 165
manipulation of human consciousness. 159
mantra 52, 53. *See* *Om Namah Shivaya* 52
Maslow 49

mass Kundalini awakenings 120
The Matrix 159
Mayan 22
Mayan Calendar 55
medical intuitive 116
meditation 7, 10, 52, 70, 87, 93, 105, 173, 201
  process 127
meditation center 48, 50, 187
meditation revolution 56
Meditation Revolution 133
meditator 7
meditators 73
medulla oblongata 145
melatonin 172
Melchizedek, Drunvalo 25, 203
mental derangement
  effect of entities 139
mentally imbalanced
  misfortune in USA 73
mental straight jackets 132
Mercurius 44, 47, 58, 72
Mercury 46, 48, 49, 58, 192
merged 101
message from Jesus 198
messianic visions 152
Mexico City 96
Miami 195, 196
middle self 183
  left brain 156
middle self [logical mind] 183
Midlothian, Texas 34
mind 204
Mindell, Arnold 46, 47, 49
mind-stopping 28
Minerva 145
mini-births 104
miniscule mosaic 104
modern psychotherapists 49
Moksha 81

moments of terror 108
Mookerjee, Ajit 16, 59
mosaics of meaningful
    pieces 177
Mosher, Loren 73
mother 85
Mount Kailash 115
Mud Shadows 158
    Archon 158
multi-dimensional 78, 123
multidimensional human
    being 91
multiple births 104. See of
    consciousness
multiplicity of meanings
    177
Mumbai, India 27, 203
Murien, Petri 191, 192
muscles twitch 164
mystical state 188
My Stroke of Insight 98
my teacher 97
mythical challenge
    to be human 50
myth-styled reality
    inner world 74

N
nada 206
Nag Hammadi 160
    Scriptures 161
nagual 63
Narayananda, Swami 204
Narby, Jeremy 60, 61
Natha 118
natural sexual urges 146
nectarean pleasure 148
negative critic 87
negative forces 162
nervous breakdown 154,
    163
nervous wreck 54
neutralize the pain 122

new being
    transformed 54
newborn baby 79
A New Earth 8, 36, 165
next phase of human evolu-
    tion 21
next step in human evolu-
    tion 24
No action
    state 207
no logical mind 178
non-logical dream state 177
noosphere 17
normal reality 173
no shell 107
no-time 163. See infinity
not reacting 142
nourishing food. 180
nuclear bomb 178
numinous experiences 28
numinous realms 142
nutritious food 171

O
observing mind 106.
old emotional pain 7
Om Namah Shivaya 52,
    77, 123
omnipotent 82
omnipresent 82
on-going orgasm 148
Opening of the Third Eye
    145
oppressive religious dogma
    132
ordinary life 31
orgasmic bliss 193
orgasmic ecstasy 123
other dimensions 138
oval shaped light 30

P
pain body 7
pains around my heart 122
Pali Highway 179
Pandora's box 86, 136
paradigm of false beliefs
    154
paradox 3, 207
parallel universe 121, 143
paralytic depression 129
paralyzed
    hands and arms 53
parasite 136, 139
pastel lotus 110
past life 105
past life companions 45
past lives 127
Patanjali 5
peaceful balm 187
peaceful inner sanctuary
    190
Pearce, Joseph Chilton 13,
    29, 132, 154
penetrate the veil 181
Perala, Richard 20
perceivers 109
perpetual ecstasy 150
Perry, John Weir 50, 74,
    124, 152, 169, 175, 181,
    185, 186
persecutors 181
personal struggle 151
phallus 149
Pharaohs 61
phases of death 131
Phoenix 191
physical death 181
physio-nuclear energy 16
pilot 40
Pineal DMT 173
pineal gland 61, 63, 112,
    144, 145. See Third Eye
pineal gland extracts 173

pingala 72. *See* ida
pinnacle
    experience 200
pioneer 10
pituitary 116
the pituitary 144
Plato 63
play of your mind 136
Polynesian tradition
    maile lei 199
Poonja, H.L. 5, 80
portal 125. *See* death
portals 67
possession 140
possible worlds 103
potential as humans 167
powerful inner urge 176
prana 66
pranic system
    cosmic energy 13
prayer verses 30
praying mantis 144
predator 163
    human 158
predatory entities 151, 159
predatory mind 172. *See*
    Ruler, Archon
pressure on my chest 201
primal 90
primal rhythms of creation
    23
primitive animal world 183
primitive will 178
projections 135
psychedelic amounts of
    DMT. *See* Pineal Gland
psychedelic experiences 172
psychedelic meandering
    108
psychedelics 172
psychiatrist 185, 188
psychophysiological trans-
    mutation 15

psychosis 73, 172
psychospiritual energy 15
psychotic 49, 175, 179
    states 186
psychotic episode 186, 188
psychotic pathology 186
psychotic reaction 188
psychotic vision 115
pterodactyl-like wings 158
puberty 13
pure consciousness and
    bliss 171
pure spirit 172
purification of the bones
    bone chi 140
purpose of man's life 3
python
    serpent 120

Q

quantum physics 57
quantum state 210
Quetzalcoatl 119, 120. *See*
    Flying Serpent
Queztalcoatl. *See* Flying
    Serpent
quickening 12. *See* Kund-
    alini awakening
quicksilver. *See* Mercury

R

Radha 111
radiant insight 135
radical cleansing 186
rainbow spiral of color 125
rainbow vortex 125
rapid vibrations. *See* Pineal
    Gland
rapture 149
rare birth 14
rare human birth 82
rare human life 10
ravages of great suffering 94

reacting to my ego 180
real battle of sorcerers 163
Reality 204
realization 19
realm of myth 176
reassemble 104
rebirth 79
reconciliation 195
reconstructing physical
    reality 104
Redbird Airport 39
reenact a scene 105
re-feel death and birth 126
reincarnation 44, 126
rejuvenated 192
relief from misery 4
renewal
    psychic healing 152
replenishing food 172
replenish the brain 171
reptilian greenish skin 136
resisting the flow 48
resurrected personality
    the phoenix 191
revengeful energies 127
reverse gravity xx
reverse of normal awareness
    98
Right Brain dominance 98
right hemisphere 155
    right brain 155
Rinpoche, Sogyal 133, 134,
    142, 153, 165
ripples of blisses 148
roaring noises 113
root of the mind 6
root of truth 161
roto-rooter
    Kundalini 136
*The Hero with a Thousand
    Faces*
    Campbell, Joseph 17
The Rulers 160

S

sacred union 46
sahasrara 59, 150
same karmic scenario 105
samskaras 67
Samskaras
    past life karma 69
sanctuary 206
Sannella, Lee 15
San people of Botswana 120
Sanskrit 52, 150
Sanskrit chanting 197
Santa Monica 199
sattvic (calming) nutrition
    189
scalar energy 63
scalar wave 62, 63
schizophrenia 73, 173
Schwartz-Salant, Nathan
    46
Scott, Mary 208
sea change 37, 83
*The Secret Science Behind
    Miracles* 183
Self 13, 44, 101, 207
Self is Brahman 203
self-luminous
    light 116
self-realization 19
self–reflection 160
serpent 120
serpent/life principle 61
seva 196
sexual feelings 136
sexual fluid 148
sexuality 146
sexually abused 137
sexual prime 42
Shakti 148
Shakti Kundalini 59, 71
Shaktipat 27, 32, 34, 51, 64,
    66, 76, 83, 95, 124, 207
shaktipat dream 60

shamanic teachers 70
shamans 62
Shatchakra-nirupana 58
Shealy, Norman, M.D.
    Ph.D. 4
Shipibo-Conibo Indians 58
Shiva 117, 147, 148, 199
Shiva Lingam 193
Shiva Sutras 170
short cut through the dying
    process 135
Siberian Shamans 62
sickly light 179
siddhi 117
    spiritual power 212
siddhis. *See* mystic powers
siddhis or powers 116
silent self 208
silent self within 9
silent witness 121
silver light 48
silvery streak 72
simultaneously processing
    108
Singh, Jaideva 171
Singh Khalsas 171
singing in the choir 197
single engine pilot's license
    40
single point of consciousness
    125
skanda 179
skeleton 140
Sky Serpent
    Kundalini 55
sleepless sleep 170
    turiya state 170
snake-like movement 12
snakes and cobras 61
snake skin 126
social convention
    as control device 35
social obligation 35

software 69
So Ham 199
solar plexus
    effect 197
solid nutritional food 180
Space Consciousness 174
special chant
    Guru Gita, The 184
spin and twirl 91
spine stiffened 53
spinning xix, 144
spinning into this abyss 180
spinning wheels of energy
    chakras 67
spiral of fear 156
spiral snakes 61
The Spirit in the Glass Bottle
    46
The Spirit Molecule 172
spirit possession 141
spirit rising within 14. *See*
    Kundalini
Spirit sports with time
    107. *See* Ralph Waldo
    Emerson
spiritual attainment 64
spiritual awakening xx
spiritual development 14
spiritual emergency 22, 152,
    188
spiritual evolution 28
spiritual illumination 146.
spiritual journey 60
spiritual labyrinth 74
spiritual parasites 139. *See*
    entities
spiritual pride 204
spiritual quest
    search for God 31
spiritual teacher xx
Spontaneous Evolution. See
    Bruce Lipton and Steve
    Bhaerman
spontaneous mudras 115

spread fingers
   receiving electricity 53
Stalking the Wild Pendulum 106. *See* Itzhak Bentov
Stanford University 202
state of meditation 197
Stormy Search for the Self 188
Strassman, Dr. Rick 172
structure of the cells 98
St. Theresa of Avila
   flying nun 133
subconscious 7, 17, 68, 70, 71, 73, 90, 102, 127, 129, 135, 138, 164, 166, 171, 181, 182, 188
subconscious programming 200
subtle body 17
subtle nervous system 59
Sufi
   dervish dancing 14
sulfuric yellow 178
sulfur yellow 179
   realm boundary 179
supercharged Xray 116
superimposed 183
suppressed feelings 7
Supreme I-consciousness 174
surrender 153, 209
surrender control 154
sushumna 58
   subtle spinal column 58
suspended in the air. *See* flying
Swami 141
Swartz-Salant, Nathan 14
sweet smelling vines. *See* maile lei
symbol of healing 61

T

tangerine tree 125
Tantalus 176
Taylor, Dr. Jill Bolte 98
teacher 206
tears pouring down 38
Tenth Anniversary 194
terrifying memory 189
Texas 83
thanatology 134
third eye 57
Third Eye 62. *See* pineal gland
   Pineal Gland 116
The Third Millennium 29
thousand impressions 107, 108
throat chakra 116
The Tibetan Book of Living and Dying 133
Tibetan Book of the Dead 132, 136
Tibetan Buddhism 15
Tibetan lamas 62
Tibetan Master 24
ticket to immortality 143
tidal wave 176. *See* tsunami
Tiger 195
Tiger Dream 41, 60
tiger-man 33
Time and mind
   inseparable 165
time and space 106
timelessness 173
timeless realm 107
time-space coordinates 107
time traveling 106
time warp 178
tip of the tongue 112
Tirtha, Swami Vishnu 65, 77, 81, 90

toad-like creature 158
   human predator 158
Tolle, Eckhart 7, 8, 24, 36, 37, 86, 90, 165
Toltec 22, 157
tongue 112
trace minerals 171, 189
traditional path 10
trance 177
transcendence 31, 131, 151
transcendental Self 170
transcendent mercury 192
transcend physical death 143
transcend the mind 146
transformation in human consciousness 24
transformation of consciousness 208
transforms ignorance. *See* Kundalini
transition point of dying
   bardo 130
transmigration of souls 81
transmutation 66
transmute 105
transmuting the human being
   Kundalini process 192
Tree of Life 120
Trials of the Visionary Mind 74
true humans 159
true masters of humanity 158
true nature xx, 10, 18, 20, 22, 26, 123, 166
true Self 11
truth of human existence 133
truth of my heart 88
truth of oneself 10
tsunami 176

Turiya 169
    4th State of awareness
        170
twelve years preparing 189
twirling in space xix
two kites against the
    sky 118. See Carlos
    Castaneda

U

ultimate terror 167
unconscious society 37
uncontrollable laughter 71
underworld 153
United Kingdom 132
unity with all things 197
unity with one Self 150
universal phenomena 14
universe of love 202
University of Hawaii 41,
    44, 96
unknown etiology
    psychotic episode 188
unrelenting tension 54
    before awakening 54
upwardly directed sexual
    energy 149
upwardly-mobile 36
Uranus 23
Urdhvareta 150

V

vampire energy 87
Venus 111
vibrating finger
    Pineal gland 145
vision of a demon 185
visions 115, 204
void 167, 174.
    abyss 121
void of nonbeing. See R.D.
    Laing

volcano of molten love 202
voyeur 137

W

Walsch, Neale Donald 37,
    138
wander in samsara 135
warrior of truth 89
war within 46
waves of joy 20
wedding vows 42
weeping 38
weeping catharsis 54
whale-like bodies 158
wheel-less chariot 117
Where is Kundalini located?
    13
White, David Gordon 13,
    60
white serpent 72
White Tara 130
Who is afraid? 205
Wilber, Ken 49, 97
Wilcock, David 25, 162
Wilhelm, Richard 119, 157
will 89
wily predator 159
wings at the third eye 119
wisdom of the heart 121
witch-like spirit 87
Within the Heart 147
witnessing consciousness
    170
witnessing of the mind 161
wolf lay back down
    adrenalin 205
woman is worthless
    social programming 35
Woodroffe, Sir John 59
world dissolve 175
worry mind 86
wrathful deities 190

Y

Yamate, Kunihiro 174
yellow sulfur world 179
Yemaya 109
YIN/YANG logo 60
yoga 114
Yoga 6, 12, 70, 104
Yogananda 214
Yukteswar, Sri 214
Yuppie 31

Z

Zoroastrian scripture 162

www.ingramcontent.com/pod-product-compliance
Lightning Source LLC
Chambersburg PA
CBHW031151270326
41931CB00006B/228